From votes to seats

MANCHESTER
UNIVERSITY PRESS

From votes to seats

The operation
of the UK electoral system
since 1945

Ron Johnston, Charles Pattie,
Danny Dorling and David Rossiter

Manchester University Press
Manchester and New York

distributed exclusively in the USA by Palgrave

Copyright © Ron Johnston, Charles Pattie, Danny Dorling and David Rossiter 2001

The rights of Ron Johnston, Charles Pattie, Danny Dorling and David Rossiter to be identified as the authors of this work has been asserted by them in accordance with the Copyright, Designs and Patents Act 1988.

Published by Manchester University Press
Oxford Road, Manchester M13 9NR, UK
and Room 400, 175 Fifth Avenue, New York, NY 10010, USA
http://www.manchesteruniversitypress.co.uk

Distributed exclusively in the USA by
Palgrave, 175 Fifth Avenue, New York
NY 10010, USA

Distributed exclusively in Canada by
UBC Press, University of British Columbia, 2029 West Mall,
Vancouver, BC, Canada V6T 1Z2

British Library Cataloguing-in-Publication Data
A catalogue record for this book is available from the British Library

Library of Congress Cataloging-in-Publication Data applied for

ISBN 0 7190 5851 1   *hardback*
      0 7190 5852 X   *paperback*

First published 2001

10 09 08 07 06 05 04 03 02 01   10 9 8 7 6 5 4 3 2 1

Typeset in Sabon
by Northern Phototypesetting Co. Ltd, Bolton
Printed in Great Britain
by Biddles Ltd, Guildford and King's Lynn

Contents

List of figures

List of tables

List of boxes

Preface

Electoral reform frequently makes an appearance on the UK's political agenda, though it rarely gets sustained attention from other than a small sector of the population – supporters of the Liberal Democrat party who feel (understandably) aggrieved by the results of general elections when their share of the seats allocated in no way matches their share of the votes; a small number of members of the Labour and (to a much lesser extent) the Conservative parties; and a section of the 'chattering classes', including some academic political scientists. Only rarely does the issue capture wider attention for more than a short period, involving both politicians and the media (many of which seem to want to denigrate any of the alternative voting systems on offer because they are 'too complicated' – which means that they would have to explain them to their readers!).

The 1990s was one of those periods. In the years immediately preceding the 1997 general election, there was clear evidence that senior members of the Labour party were giving electoral reform serious consideration. This was not the first occasion on which they had done so in recent history. At the end of the 1980s, when it seemed that Labour might never win another general election, the party commissioned a study of the subject from a committee chaired by Professor (later Lord) Raymond Plant.[1] Its analyses and recommendations were the basis for the system implemented for the Scottish Parliament and Welsh Assembly in 1999. But there was too much opposition within the party for there to be any serious contemplation of reform for elections to the House of Commons. Indeed, because of that, Lord Plant was asked not to report on the issue of those elections until after the 1992 general election, and a hint by Neil Kinnock during the 1992 campaign that the party might consider electoral reform was deemed not to have stood the party in good stead. But reform remained on the agenda, even if low down, and a number of Labour MPs and activists continued to campaign for it, if relatively *sotto voce*.[2]

In the immediate run-up to the 1997 general election, however, Labour apparently embraced electoral reform with much greater fervour than at any time in the previous half-century.[3] Having failed to win four general elections in a row – including one that they were expected to in 1992 – the Labour party leadership was very unsure of its prospects for the 1997 election, despite an overwhelming lead according to all public opinion polls. They feared they would get neither an overall majority nor one substantial enough to see them through a full Parliament and so entered negotiations with the Liberal Democrats on a range of constitutional reform issues over which it was hoped the two could agree and then work together, if necessary, as a left-of-centre majority in the next Parliament. This included a commitment, which appeared in the Labour party's manifesto for the 1997 election, to appoint a Commission to investigate more proportional systems, whose recommendation would be put to the electorate in a referendum during the next Parliament. The Liberal Democrats' manifesto included a statement reiterating the party's continued commitment to a proportional representation electoral system.

Labour won the 1997 general election handsomely. Nevertheless, it continued to have close links with the Liberal Democrats on a range of constitutional issues, and to meet some of the obligations set out in their pre-election compact. These included new electoral systems, which were quasi-proportional in the case of elections to the Scottish Parliament, the Welsh Assembly and the Greater London Assembly and almost pure proportional in the case of elections to the European Parliament.

The commitment to establish a Commission to investigate alternative electoral systems for the House of Commons elections was also kept. The five-member Independent Commission on the Voting System, chaired by Lord Jenkins (a former Labour Cabinet Minister, President of the European Commission and then leader of the Social Democratic Party) was appointed in December 1997 with the following terms of reference:

- The Commission shall be free to consider and recommend any appropriate system or combination of systems in recommending an alternative to the present system for Parliamentary elections to be put before the people in the Government's referendum.
- The Commission shall observe the requirement for broad proportionality, the need for stable Government, an extension of voter choice and the maintenance of a link between MPs and geographical constituencies.

It reported in October 1998.[4]

The Jenkins report showed that the UK's electoral system – used throughout the twentieth century – not only produces disproportional results, but also can produce results that are biased as to their impact on different parties. The first is well appreciated; that parties do not get the same percentage of seats in the House of Commons as the percentage of the votes cast to elect those MPs was obvious at most election results over the twentieth century; according to Jenkins it 'distorts the desires of the voters' (p.2). But what was not widely appreciated, or analysed by political scientists and other commentators, was that this disproportionality tendency does not necessarily operate equitably; one party may get a different percentage of the seats from the same percentage of the votes as its opponent. In other words the system is biased as well as disproportional, as Jenkins expressed it (using a graph from our research, see Figure 1.4) 'a given number of votes translates into significantly more seats for one party than for the other' (p.11). But which party is favoured by the operation of that bias – at which elections and in what situations?

Answering these questions is the focus of this book. We accept that the system produces disproportional results and instead concentrate our attention on differences between parties – specifically between the Conservative and Labour parties, by far the largest in British politics throughout the second half of the twentieth century; over the 14 general elections between 1950 and 1997 inclusive, some 405 million votes were cast in the United Kingdom, of which the Conservatives won nearly 43 per cent and Labour 41 per cent. Yet the Conservatives were in power for almost three-quarters of the 47 years between the first and last of those elections (excluding the 1997 election; the Conservatives won 45 per cent of the votes cast but 50 per cent of the 8227 seats contested: Labour's percentages were 41 and 45, respectively).

Our goal is to show why bias is almost certain to occur in electoral systems that use 'first-past-the-post', and then to illustrate the processes by analysing the 14 general elections that occurred after implementation of the *House of Commons (Redistribution of Seats) Act 1944*, which introduced a new way for defining the constituencies employed in the election process (i.e. the 1950–97 general elections).

At the core of our argument is the importance of geography – not the academic discipline, although all four of us have doctoral degrees in geography and we have all either worked in or been associated with university geography departments. Our concern is with geography as it is more generally interpreted – with answering the question 'what is where?'. Two features of that geography are at the core of the case we develop here. The first is the distribution of different types of people across the United Kingdom, as reflected in their electoral proclivities – which party they support, whether they are likely to abstain, etc. The second is the set of geographical containers (divisions of the national territory) within which they are placed for electoral purposes – the Parliamentary constituencies, of which there were 625 at the beginning of the period and 659 at the end, each returning one MP to the House of Commons. Neither geography is fixed. Population distributions change, new constituency maps are drawn and parties campaign with different intensities in different places.

Appreciating the nature of those geographies, and trying to influence how they change, is an important task for political parties, who want the best outcome from the operation of the electoral system – how it translates votes into seats. Not surprisingly, therefore, they have developed sophisticated strategies and tactics – some, as we shall see, more sophisticated than others, and also more successful than others.

Manipulation of the electoral system for partisan gain is common, whatever the system, and so manipulating geographies is an important political tactic. This has been amply demonstrated in many parts of the world by two sets of strategies which have been given American names – malapportionment and gerrymandering.[5]

The UK's electoral system introduced by the 1944 Act was designed both to limit malapportionment, by having regular and frequent reviews of constituency electorates, and to prevent gerrymandering, by giving the task of redrawing the constituency map to independent Commissions. Has the system succeeded? There can be no absolute answer to such a question, of course, because we cannot readily pose a counter-factual – what would have happened if either no system had been created to replace the ad hoc situation that existed before 1944 or some other system had been introduced – even one that was based on first-past-the-post.[6] All we can do is explore the extent of the bias that has characterised the current system, how that has changed over time, and how the political parties have learned to work within and on it. Our findings show that the system incorporates a number of separate components (all geographically related) which generate bias, that together these have produced biases which were the equivalent at some elections of more than 25 per cent of the total number of seats then contested, and that the weight of those biases has come to favour the Labour party – in significant part because of its greater geographical sophistication at working within and on the system.

Those conclusions, and a significant number of others associated with them, are based on a substantial volume of research that we have been involved with, separately and together, over the last three decades. This book brings that work together, synthesising what we have already done but, much more importantly, introducing a great deal of new material. Although the core of our argument has been presented in other media – to specialist audiences – it has not previously been developed fully, either theoretically or empirically. This book is thus a major original contribution to understanding how the UK's electoral system works. It also offers a methodology with which electoral systems in other countries (and at other levels of government) that are based on single-member constituencies and the first-past-the-post (or plurality) method of determining the winner in those constituencies can be studied.

The research on which this book draws is, necessarily, based on mathematics and statistics. We are dealing with a system involving millions of voters in hundreds of places (some 44 million registered electors at the 1997 general election, living in 659 constituencies returning MPs to the House of Commons). The analysis of such large data sets necessarily involves mathematical procedures to identify their salient features. We have eschewed filling this book with technical material, however. The procedures that we use and report have been widely published and publicised, and are readily available to those who want to follow them up in detail. (They are referenced in numbered notes at the appropriate places in the text.) Our goal here is to explain what happens in the operation of the UK's electoral system, and why geography is so important to that, and we have chosen to do so by words and 'pictures'. The latter are crucial to our task. This book is replete with simple diagrams which depict the processes and trends simply and accurately, and allow us to convey our argument without recourse to formulae and great tables of data, let alone results of statistical analyses. The latter are fundamental to our work, but only as means of teasing out the processes and underpinning our conclusions.

We have also eschewed another feature of much academic writing on electoral systems – filling our sentences with references to the work of others (and ourselves!). This does not mean that we present others' work as our own – wherever necessary, we indicate our sources in the notes, and direct readers to them. But we have decided not to impede the flow of the book and its message with long lists of references in the Harvard style.

All analytical work is based on, and grows out of, the ideas and publications of other scholars, and ours is no exception. There have been several important contributions to the analysis of electoral systems in the mould that we follow – not least the seminal book by Graham Gudgin and Peter Taylor (with whom two of us have been pleased to work), which has unfortunately not received the attention its contributions merit.[7] But neither other books on the disproportionality of electoral systems,[8] nor general treatments of the UK's system,[9] consider the related issue of bias – whether that disproportionality is experienced equally by the separate political parties. And analyses of electoral behaviour – of which there is a growing volume in the UK, mostly linked to specific elections – largely ignore the process by which votes are translated into seats, focusing instead on who votes for which party, and why. We therefore move beyond the norm in British election studies.

Our particular debt is to an English-born New Zealand political scientist, Ralph Brookes, who none of us ever met but who published two papers some forty years ago, which both raised the issue of bias as a major element of the operation of a first-past-the-post electoral system and presented a way of measuring it. Ron Johnston was attracted to this when working in New Zealand in the 1960s and 1970s, and one of his first papers when he returned to England in 1974 applied Brookes' measure to the two UK general elections held that year.[10] He revisited the issue occasionally over the next two decades, during which he was involved in a range of other studies of aspects of electoral geography, most involving one or both of Dave Rossiter and Charles Pattie, with Danny Dorling joining them in the 1990s. But it was only in the mid-1990s, during a major study of the UK Boundary

Commissions, that we returned to bias and its measurement in a major way,[11] when Dave Rossiter convinced us of its value in looking at the electoral impact of their work and their attempts to eliminate malapportionment and prevent gerrymandering.[12] In doing that, we drew on the only other piece of work, to our knowledge, that has employed Brookes' methodology, Roger Mortimore's Oxford DPhil thesis.[13] We realised the importance of some of the modifications that he suggested and incorporated them into our work. Along the way others have been involved in various aspects of the work that underpins what we have brought together here, notably Dave Cutts, Ed Fieldhouse, Iain MacAllister, Andrew Russell, Andrew Schuman and Helena Tunstall. We are grateful to them for their contributions and collaboration, as we are to the Economic and Social Research Council (and its predecessor, the Social Science Research Council), the Leverhulme Trust, the Nuffield Foundation and the University of Sheffield who have at various times funded aspects of our work. We are also very grateful to David Denver for reading the full manuscript and making valuable constructive comments.

If you want to change something, you need to know in detail what is wrong with that you wish to replace, and why. Discussions of electoral reform in the United Kingdom have focused almost exclusively on the issue of the disproportionality of the results of elections held under the current system, largely ignoring a range of other aspects of that system, such as the bias, the differential treatment of parties within the overall pattern of disproportionality. Our basic goal here, therefore, has been to explore and to explain the bias, to introduce it (since its presence appears not to be widely appreciated), to show how it can be measured, to indicate how it is produced and to map its importance. Thus we have several audiences in mind, including our academic peers who specialise in the study of elections in the United Kingdom and elsewhere, who tend to give this issue less attention than we believe it deserves (perhaps because we are geographers and they are not!); to students of elections more generally, interested in how electoral systems work; and to a wider audience interested in a range of constitutional reform issues, in order to inform their debate and also, we hope, the conclusions which the UK Parliament and, ultimately, its electorate if a referendum is ever held on the issue of changing the voting system for the House of Commons, may reach. The book has been written and presented in ways that we hope make it accessible to all of those groups.

Notes

1 See Plant (1999).
2 The Labour campaign for Electoral Reform was the main forum: two of its members produced a book on the issue soon after the 1997 election (Linton and Southcott, 1998).

3 It had previously been in favour, and had proposed electoral reform soon before it was defeated in the House of Commons in 1931 (Marquand, 1997; see also Hart, 1992).

4 Jenkins (1998).

5 The original gerrymander was produced in 1810 by Governor Elbridge Gerry of Massachusetts. He created an odd-shaped constituency in Essex county which contained a majority of his supporters. A journalist likened its shape to that of a salamander – and coined the term 'gerrymander'. (For a reproduction of this map, see Taylor and Johnston, 1979, 373.)

6 The first constituencies produced under the 1944 Act were not ready for use until 1949, so the 1945 election was held in the constituencies defined in 1918 and is therefore excluded from the analyses in this book.

7 Graham Gudgin and Peter Taylor (1979).

8 For example, Rae (1971), Taagepera and Shugart (1989) and Lijphart (1994).

9 Notably Butler (1963) and Blackburn (1995).

10 Johnston (1976).

11 The only substantial study using the Brookes methodology that we published was as part of an evaluation after the 1992 general election of whether Labour was doomed always to lose: Johnston, Pattie and Fieldhouse (1994).

12 Rossiter, Johnston and Pattie (1999).

13 Mortimore (1992).

A note on the figures

As we indicate above, much of the evidence on which our arguments are based is presented in diagrammatic form. A considerable number of the diagrams show trends across the 14 general elections studied, from 1950 to 1997 inclusive. For clarity, these elections are evenly spaced along the horizontal axis of those diagrams rather than being shown in 'real time' (and hence compressing the 1950–51, 1964–66 and, especially, February 1974–October 1974 inter-election periods). Since none of our arguments are based on changes per unit of time (e.g. rates of change per year), the chosen method provides a much better way of appreciating what happened over the sequence of elections.

Many of the diagrams were generated by us with SPSS for Windows. The six maps in Chapter 6 were prepared for us by Simon Godden of the School of Geographical Sciences, University of Bristol, and many of the diagrams in Chapters 2 and 3 by Lois Wright of the School of Geography, University of Leeds. We are very grateful to them both.

1

From votes to seats: disproportionality and bias

The Conservative party won 43.9 per cent of the votes cast at the 1979 UK general election, and 339 of the 635 seats – 53.4 per cent of the total. Four years later, at the 1983 election, it won a slightly smaller percentage of the votes cast (42.4), but this time it obtained 397 (61.1 per cent) of the seats. In 1987, it again won almost the same shares of both votes and seats (43.4 and 57.8 per cent respectively), but in 1992, although its vote share stayed about the same (42.3 per cent), it won only 336 seats, 51.6 per cent of the total. Five years later, the Labour party won its first general election victory since October 1974. With 43.3 per cent of the total number of votes cast in the United Kingdom, its share was very similar to those obtained by the Conservatives at each of the previous four contests, but it won 419 (63.6 per cent) of the 659 seats.

Over five consecutive elections, therefore, the percentage of the votes cast won by the largest party only ranged between 42.3 and 43.9. The percentage of the seats won by the winning party ranged much more widely – from 51.6 to 63.6 per cent. The same result in terms of votes produced very different outcomes in terms of seats won – in every case the largest party getting a substantially larger percentage of the seats than of the votes.

Three immediate conclusions can be drawn from these data. First, the British electoral system produces disproportional results; parties do not get the same share of the seats as they do of the votes. Secondly, the same share of the votes cast can result in substantially different shares of the seats. And thirdly, the system seems to favour Labour over the Conservatives. With approximately the same share of the votes cast in 1997 as its opponent obtained at the previous four elections, Labour got a much larger share of the seats.

Disproportionality

Such conclusions are based on only a small amount of information, however. Before proceeding to analyse them in greater detail – to try to discover why such varying disproportionality occurred – we need to look at these figures in broader perspective.

Table 1.1 Votes and seats at the 1997 UK general election

	Votes	Seats		Difference	
	(%V)	No.	%S	|%S – %V|	S:V Ratio
Conservative	30.7	165	25.0	5.7	0.81
Labour	43.3	419	63.6	20.3	1.47
Liberal Democrat	16.8	46	7.0	9.8	0.42
Scottish Nationalist	2.0	6	0.9	1.1	0.45
Plaid Cymru	0.5	4	0.6	0.1	1.20
Ulster Unionist	0.9	10	1.5	0.6	1.67
Democratic Unionist	0.4	2	0.3	0.1	0.75
UK Unionist	0.1	1	0.2	0.1	2.00
SDLP	0.7	3	0.5	0.2	0.71
Sinn Féin	0.5	2	0.3	0.3	0.60
Other	4.1	1	0.2	3.9	0.05
Sum of Differences				42.2	
Index of Disproportionality				21.1	

Key to columns: %V – percentage of the votes cast; %S – percentage of the seats won; |%S - %V| difference between %S and %V, irrespective of sign; S:V ratio – the ratio of %S/%V.

First, is disproportionality the norm with British election results? A number of different ways have been devised to measure disproportionality;[1] we use a very simple index here, illustrated by Table 1.1. This shows the percentage of the votes and seats won at the 1997 general election (%V and %S, respectively) by each of the three main parties which contested all seats in Great Britain, plus the Scottish National Party and Plaid Cymru, the five parties which won seats in Northern Ireland and a catch-all 'other' category (which includes the Referendum party and a range of minor party and independent candidates who obtained only one seat between them – the victory by the independent candidate Martin Bell over the Conservative Neil Hamilton at Tatton). The next column shows the difference between these two percentages for each party, irrespective of sign. The largest difference is for Labour, whose percentage of the seats was 20.3 points greater than its percentage of the votes. Both Labour and Plaid Cymru got a larger share of the seats than their share of the votes apparently entitled them to. If there were proportional representation (i.e. if %V = %S), they were 'over-represented', whereas the others were 'under-represented'.

Our index of disproportionality is derived by summing those differences, as shown at the foot of the last but one column in Table 1.1, and dividing it by two. It can be interpreted as the minimum percentage of the seats that would have to be redistributed across the parties in order to achieve proportional representation. Thus 21.1 per cent of the seats would have to be redistributed to achieve proportional representation, almost all of them from Labour and with nearly half of them (9.8 per cent) being reallocated to the Liberal Democrats.

So was the result in 1997 out of line with previous elections? Figure 1.1 shows the trend in our disproportionality measure since the 1950 general election. (We focus on the period 1950–97 in all of our analyses in this book, because the current method of defining constituencies has been in use throughout that period. We will be arguing that the disproportionality displayed here and the other aspects of election results discussed later are very much a product of that system.[2]) The 1997 election was clearly not out of line on this measure; its level of disproportionality was little different from that of the three previous elections. There was a general trend to greater disproportionality over the half century, but rather than a continuous sequence there was really just one major 'step-change' in the amount – between the 1970 and February 1974 general elections. The reason for this is given in Table 1.2, which shows the percentages of the votes cast and seats won by the Conservatives and Labour together. Before the two 1974 elections, their joint share of the votes cast fell below 90 per cent on only one occasion and their share of the seats was always above 97 per cent. After 1970 however

Figure 1.1 The index of disproportionality for UK general election results, 1950–97

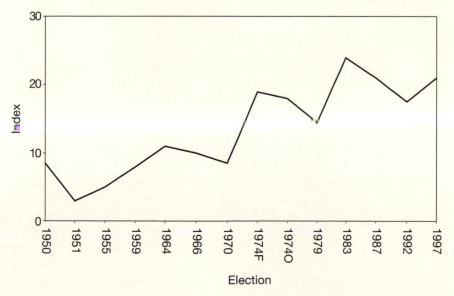

their vote share was over 80 per cent at only one election, because of substantial increases in voter support for the Liberals (later to become the Liberal Democrats after the Liberal–SDP Alliance of 1983–87) and the two nationalist parties (SNP and Plaid Cymru). There was no commensurate fall in the percentage of seats won by the Conservatives and Labour, however, which remained above 90 per cent until the 1997 election. Disproportionality was higher in the last quarter of the twentieth century because the two largest parties retained a predominant share of the seats, while losing a substantial proportion of voter support.

Table 1.2   Percentage of the UK votes and seats won by the Conservative and Labour parties combined, 1950–97

	Votes	Seats
1950	89.6	98.1
1951	96.0	98.6
1955	97.5	98.6
1959	94.1	98.9
1964	87.5	98.6
1966	90.5	97.8
1970	90.0	97.9
1974(F)	76.8	94.2
1974(O)	76.9	93.9
1979	82.7	95.7
1983	71.8	93.2
1987	73.1	93.1
1992	76.3	93.2
1997	74.0	88.6

Secondly, is Labour better treated than the Conservatives by this disproportionality? To answer this, we look at the trends in seats:votes ratios (S:V ratios) over the period. Calculation of these ratios is shown in the final column of Table 1.1; they are derived as the %S value for each party divided by its %V value – with a ratio of 1.0 indicating 'proportional representation', less than 1.0 'under-representation' and over 1.0 'over-representation'. Thus Labour was over-represented by 47 per cent (a ratio of 1.47) in 1997, for example, whereas the Conservatives were under-represented by 19 per cent.

Figure 1.2 shows the seats:votes ratios for the Conservatives, Labour and the Liberals over the full set of 14 elections from 1950 to 1997. (Throughout this book, we use the term Liberal party to apply to that party at elections prior to 1983, the Alliance at the 1983 and 1987 general elections and the Liberal Democrats thereafter.) The clearest feature is that the Liberals were always very substantially under-represented, with seats:votes ratios of

Figure 1.2 Seats:votes ratios for the three main parties at UK general elections, 1950–97

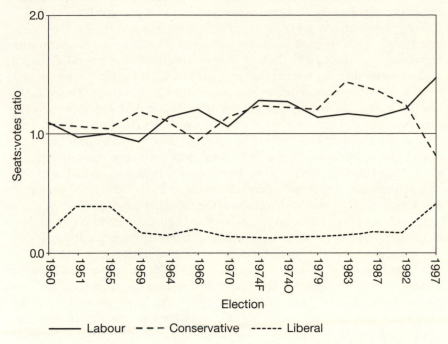

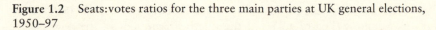

0.40 or below at every election except one – 1997 – and even then, as Table 1.1 shows, it was only just over 0.40. The electoral system has clearly delivered very disproportional outcomes for the Liberals, and although they improved their situation somewhat between 1992 and 1997 (their ratio doubled), nevertheless they remained very much under-represented according to our proportional representation norm.

Over-representation has been the norm for the Conservatives and Labour, however. On only two occasions – the 1966 and 1997 general elections, which were Labour's best victories during the period – did the Conservative ratio fall below 1.0, and just marginally on the first of those occasions. In general, the Conservatives have obtained a larger share of the seats than of the votes – between 10 and 20 per cent more in the period up to and including 1970 and from 20 to just over 40 per cent in the next two decades. But 1997 was very different, with a ratio of just 0.81. For Labour, over-representation became the norm after the 1959 general election, and even when it performed relatively badly at the polls in 1983 and 1987 (when it obtained 27.6 and 30.8 per cent of the votes cast in the UK respectively), it still managed to get nearly 20 per cent more of the seats than it would have been 'entitled to' under proportional representation. And then, as with the Conservatives, 1997 produced something very different, with by far its highest seats:votes ratio.

The overall level of disproportionality was much the same in 1997 as at previous elections (Figure 1.1), but the relative treatment of the parties differed very substantially then from what had occurred previously.

The first two graphs in Figure 1.3 confirm these interpretations. They relate each party's percentage of the votes cast to its percentage of the seats won across the 14 elections, with the best-fit regression line indicating the direction of that relationship: the greater the votes percentage, the greater the seats percentage. Two things stand out with regard to the Conservatives (Figure 1.3a). The first is the wide spread of percentage of seats won with approximately the same percentage of the votes obtained (just over 40) at six of the elections; the process of translating votes into seats operated differently in apparently very similar situations. Secondly, the 1997 result (shown by the separate symbol) was substantially less than predicted by the best-fit regression from the party's vote percentage[3] – but it had never performed so badly before, so whether it was just a one-off cannot be determined. On the other hand, 1997 was clearly very much out of line from the general trend of Labour's results (Figure 1.3b); its percentage of the seats then was very different from when it previously obtained the same percentage of the votes – or even more.

The final graph in Figure 1.3 shows how the operation of the electoral system has disadvantaged the third party in British politics, the Liberals, and how different the 1997 result was for that party too. With one exception, the party never achieved more than 4 per cent of the seats, even with well over one-quarter of the votes (Figure 1.3c). The exception was in 1997, when it obtained 7.0 per cent of the seats with 16.8 per cent of the votes; indeed, between 1992

Figure 1.3a   The relationship between votes and seats for the Conservative party, 1950–97

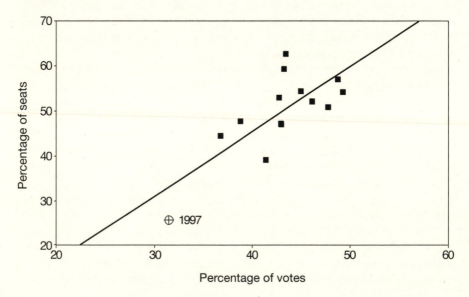

Figure 1.3b The relationship between votes and seats for the Labour party, 1950–97

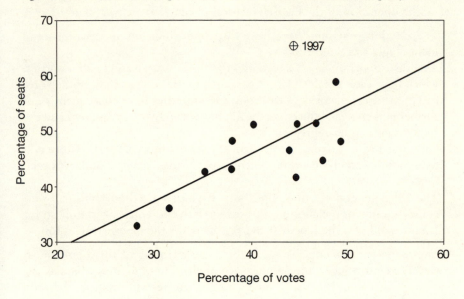

Figure 1.3c The relationship between votes and seats for the Liberal party, 1950–97

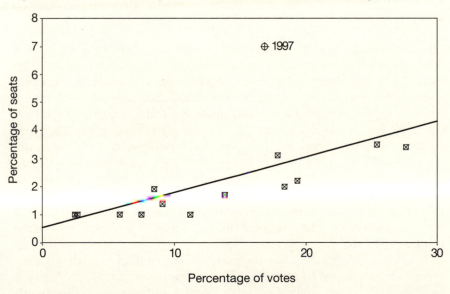

and 1997 its share of the votes fell by one percentage point, whereas its share of the seats more than doubled. More than anything else, this exemplifies both the inequity and the unpredictability of the British electoral system.

Four clear conclusions can be drawn from these initial descriptive analyses of the operation of the British electoral system between 1950 and 1997:

1 The election outcomes have been disproportional on all occasions and increasingly so since 1970.
2 That disproportionality has favoured the Conservative and Labour parties, which have each obtained larger percentages of the seats than of the votes cast at the great majority of elections. Other parties have consequently got smaller percentages – the larger parties have been over-represented and the smaller ones under-represented.
3 Since the 1950s, Labour has probably benefited more than the Conservatives, notably so in the 1980s, when its performance at the polls was relatively weak.
4 The 1997 general election appears to have produced an abnormal outcome in terms of the allocation of seats relative to votes – certainly so for Labour (and also the Liberals) and probably for the Conservatives too.

Accounting for these conclusions is the focus of most of this book. First, however, we introduce a further measure of election outcomes which assists our later analyses, because it gives us far more information than do seats:votes ratios.

Bias

The simple measure of disproportionality used above gives a good general impression of how the British electoral system produces results which are far from equitable in their treatment of all parties – on the assumption that proportional representation, or something close to it, is a desirable goal. It does not indicate which parties are treated more and which are treated less than equitably, but this is readily obtained by the seats:votes ratios. There are problems with these measures, however. The seats:votes ratios for the Conservative and Labour parties in 1997 suggest that the electoral system treated the former much less favourably (or equitably) than the latter. However, the Conservatives got 12.6 percentage points less of the votes cast than did Labour. What would have been the situation if, say, they had both obtained the same number of votes – or if Labour had obtained 30.7 per cent and the Conservatives 43.3?

Answering this question is made possible by a method of analysing election results developed by a New Zealand political scientist, Ralph Brookes, modified by a British political scientist, Roger Mortimore and subsequently extended and adapted by us. The algebra for the full method is lengthy – and the proof can be consulted elsewhere for those interested.[4] The method is readily appreciated without the algebra (which is relevant to the decomposition of our measure into several constituent contributory parts, discussed in

Chapter 4, and is included in an Appendix for those interested in applying it); it is introduced here using a short example.

At the first elections to the Welsh Assembly in 1999, voters had two ballot papers, one for electing a Member to represent their constituency and one for a party list to elect top-up Members to represent their region. We are interested in the first only, which used the same 40 constituencies as employed for the 1997 general election in Wales. The results are in Table 1.3. Labour was the largest party, in terms of the votes cast, with 37.64 per cent of the total, followed by Plaid Cymru (28.43), the Conservatives (15.87) and the Liberal Democrats (13.37). In addition, 47,992 votes (not shown in the table) were won by candidates of other parties and independents. Labour won 27 of the 40 seats (67.5 per cent of the total), giving it a seats:votes ratio of 1.79; second-placed Plaid Cymru won nine seats (22.5 per cent), giving a seats:votes ratio of only 0.79 and the other two parties won one and three seats, respectively.

What if the first two parties had won the same percentages of the votes, but the performance of the others remained the same? Together, Labour and Plaid Cymru won 66.07 per cent of the votes. If they had equal shares, this would have been 33.035 per cent each, which would mean reducing Labour's share by 4.605 percentage points of the total number of votes cast and increasing Plaid Cymru's by the same percentage. This would involve taking 47,050 votes from Labour – reducing its total to 337,616 – and adding that number to Plaid Cymru. That procedure was undertaken constituency by constituency, producing the vote totals for Labour and Plaid Cymru shown in the sixth and seventh columns of Table 1.3. (LABE is the number of votes Labour would have if it and Plaid Cymru had equal shares across all 40 constituencies, and PCE is the similar number for Plaid Cymru.) In other words, we shift votes uniformly from one party to another across all constituencies, much as the pundits do on election night when talking about 'uniform swing'. Swing is never entirely uniform of course with variations in its extent (though rarely its direction) across constituencies, but this procedure provides us with a very useful benchmark. It says that if the geography of support for the two parties remained the same, i.e. they remained relatively strong in the same places, etc., but the overall level of support changed somewhat, being increased for one and decreased for the other by the same relative amount in every constituency, this is what the result would be.[5] Any shift can be used – you could, for example, ask what the result in each constituency would have been if Plaid Cymru obtained 37.64 per cent of the votes and Labour 28.43; we prefer the equal shares position as a clear indicator of the parties' relative seat-winning capacities.

With 33.035 per cent of the votes each, the two parties would not have the same number of seats, however; as the final columns of Table 1.3 indicate, Labour would have won 21 to Plaid Cymru's 14. (Note that with the transfer of votes between the two parties, in one constituency – Vale of Glamorgan –

Table 1.3 The constituency results at the 1999 Welsh Assembly election

	LAB	PC	CON	LD	TOTAL	LABE	PCE
Aberavon	11,941	5,198	1,624	3,165	23,294	10,868	6,270
Alyn & Deeside	9,772	2,304	3,413	1,879	19,030	8,895	3,180
Blaenau Gwent	16,069	5,501	1,444	2,918	25,932	14,875	6,694
Brecon & Radnorshire	5,165	2,356	7,170	13,022	29,215	3,819	3,701
Bridgend	9,321	4,919	5,063	3,910	25,032	8,168	6,071
Caernarfon	6,475	18,748	2,464	791	28,478	5,163	20,059
Caerphilly	12,602	9,741	2,213	3,543	28,511	11,289	11,053
Cardiff Central	7,769	3,795	3,034	10,937	25,873	6,577	4,986
Cardiff North	12,198	4,337	9,894	5,088	31,517	10,746	5,788
Cardiff South	11,057	3,931	4,254	2,890	23,036	9,996	4,991
Cardiff West	14,305	3,402	3,446	2,063	23,216	13,236	4,470
Carmarthen East	10,348	17,328	2,776	2,202	32,654	8,844	18,831
Carmarthen West	9,891	8,399	5,079	1,875	28,149	8,595	9,694
Ceredigion	5,009	15,258	2,944	3,571	31,898	3,540	16,726
Clwyd South	9,196	5,511	4,167	2,432	21,814	8,191	6,515
Clwyd West	7,824	6,886	7,064	3,462	25,236	6,662	8,047
Conwy	8,171	8,285	5,006	4,480	27,102	6,923	9,532
Cynon Valley	9,883	9,206	1,046	1,531	21,666	8,885	10,203
Delyn	10,672	4,837	5,255	3,089	23,853	9,573	5,935
Gower	9,813	6,653	3,912	3,260	27,700	8,537	7,928
Islwyn	9,438	10,042	1,621	2,351	23,927	8,336	11,143
Llanelli	11,285	11,973	1,864	2,920	28,387	9,978	13,279
Meirionnydd Nant Conwy	3,292	12,034	2,170	1,378	18,874	2,423	12,902
Merthyr Tydfil	11,024	6,810	1,246	1,682	25,088	9,868	7,965
Monmouth	10,238	1,964	12,950	4,639	31,702	8,778	3,423
Montgomeryshire	2,638	3,554	4,870	10,374	21,436	1,651	4,540
Neath	12,234	9,616	1,895	2,631	26,895	10,995	10,854
Newport East	9,497	2,647	4,386	2,684	19,214	8,612	3,531

Constituency	LAB	PC	CON	LD	TOTAL	LABE	PCE
Newport West	*11,538*	3,053	6,828	2,820	24,239	10,422	4,168
Ogmore	*10,402*	5,842	1,415	496	20,594	9,453	6,790
Pontypridd	*11,330*	9,755	2,485	5,040	29,326	9,979	**11,105**
Preseli Pembrokeshire	*9,977*	7,239	6,585	3,338	29,083	8,638	8,577
Rhondda	11,273	*13,558*	774	1,303	27,821	9,992	**14,838**
Swansea East	*9,495*	5,714	1,663	3,963	20,835	8,535	6,673
Swansea West	*8,217*	6,291	3,643	3,543	23,727	7,124	**7,383**
Torfaen	*9,080*	2,614	2,152	2,614	23,922	7,978	3,715
Vale of Clwyd	*8,359*	4,295	5,018	1,376	22,203	7,336	5,317
Vale of Glamorgan	*11,448*	7,848	**10,522**	2,938	32,756	9,939	9,356
Wrexham	*9,239*	2,659	2,747	2,767	17,412	8,437	3,460
Ynys Mon	7,181	*16,462*	6,031	1,630	31,304	5,739	**17,903**
Total	384,666	290,565	162,133	136,595	1,021,951		
% of total	37.64	28.43	15.87	13.37			
Redistributed totals						337616	337616
%						33.04	33.04
Wins	27	9	1	3			
%	67.50	22.50	2.50	7.50			
Redistributed wins			2	3		21	14
%			5.00	7.50		52.50	35.00
Seats:votes ratios original	1.79	0.79	0.16	0.56			
Redistributed			0.32	0.56		1.59	1.06

Key to columns: LAB – Labour votes; PC – Plaid Cymru votes; CON – Conservative votes; LD – Liberal Democrat votes; TOTAL – total votes cast; LABE, PCE – Labour and Plaid Cymru votes when they have equal shares nationally. A total in bold (highlighted) indicates the winning party in the constituency. A total in bold (highlighted) indicates a seat won by a different party in the equal shares allocation compared to the original result.

An italic vote total (highlighted) indicates the winning party in the constituency. A total in bold (highlighted) indicates a seat won by a different party in the equal shares allocation compared to the original result.

victory was switched from Labour to the Conservatives, who were in second place in the original poll.) This difference of seven seats between Labour and Plaid Cymru is our measure of the bias in the system, given those two geographies of support; there was a bias of seven seats favouring Labour.

This measure of bias is both straightforward to calculate and readily appreciated; it is the difference in number of seats between the two parties when they have equal vote shares and the same relative geographies of support across the constituencies.[6] If the two geographies had been the same, then Labour would have lost nine seats with the redistribution of votes and Plaid Cymru gained them all, to give them 18 each. But Labour lost only six, one of them to the Conservatives, and the switch of votes was insufficient for Plaid Cymru to gain others – notably Gower and Neath, which Labour retained with very small majorities. As a result, Labour had a much larger seats:votes ratio than Plaid Cymru with an equal share of the votes, although the latter's was slightly larger than 1.0. Why this bias was produced, we leave to the next chapter.

Bias in the UK, 1950–97

The bias measure has been applied to the 14 election results between 1950 and 1997 to see whether one of the two main parties – Conservative and Labour – has consistently been favoured over the other. In this, and in all of our discussions of the bias measure and its components that follow, a positive bias means that Labour would have been advantaged by the system (i.e. would have had more seats than the Conservatives when they had the same percentage share of the votes), whereas a negative figure indicates a Conservative advantage over Labour.[7]

Figure 1.4 indicates that there was a major shift over the period of study. For the first five elections in the sequence (1950–64), the bias in the system strongly favoured the Conservatives. If they and Labour had achieved equal shares of the votes cast at those elections, the Conservatives would have had at least 20 more seats than Labour (the 1964 outcome) and almost 60 in 1951. Over the next seven elections (1966–87) there was relatively little bias. In five cases it was almost zero, indicating that equal shares of the votes were matched by virtually equal shares in the allocation of seats; in the other two elections (February 1974 and 1979), the advantage went to Labour, by around 20 seats. Finally, in the 1990s the system very clearly favoured Labour, to the extent of 38 seats in 1992 and 82 in 1997. If the Conservatives and Labour had achieved the same percentage of the votes cast in 1997 (37.7 per cent) and with the same geographies, then Labour would have won 82 more seats than its opponent – a seats:votes ratio of 1.42 for Labour compared to 1.08 for the Conservatives.

Clearly, the operation of the British electoral system very strongly favoured the Labour party in the 1990s, especially so at the 1997 general election which it won by what many pundits referred to as a landslide.[8] Its

Figure 1.4   Bias at the UK general elections, 1950–97. A positive bias indicates that Labour obtained more seats than the Conservatives with an equal vote share; a negative bias indicates that the Conservatives obtained more seats

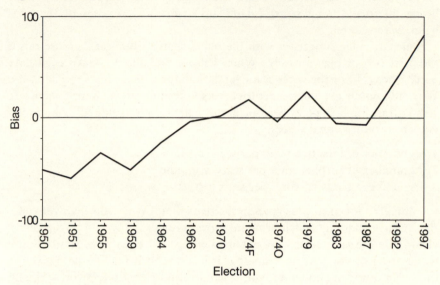

Parliamentary majority then was very much larger than it would have achieved with the same vote share at earlier elections. Accounting for this, and the apparent major shift over the period 1950–97 from a pro-Conservative to a pro-Labour bias in the system, is the focus of the remainder of this book. First however, we need to introduce one final set of descriptive data.

Wasted, surplus and effective votes

The seats:votes ratio provides us with a useful measure of the effectiveness with which a party's votes are translated into seats; the larger the ratio, the greater the return that the party gets for its votes. This is because of differences between the parties in the degree to which their votes 'work' for them.

To illustrate this, we define three types of vote – wasted, surplus and effective. *Wasted votes* are those that bring no return, because they are cast in constituencies where the party's candidate loses. *Surplus votes* also bring no return, but for another reason; they are cast in constituencies where the party's candidate wins, but by more votes than are needed to defeat the second-placed candidate. *Effective votes* are those needed to win in the constituency – the total number of votes obtained by the second-placed party, plus one.[9] This can be illustrated by the first constituency in Table 1.3 – Aberavon. Labour won 11,941 votes there, 6743 more than the second-placed Plaid Cymru candidate: 5199 votes would have been sufficient to give

Labour victory, so of its 11,941 votes, 5199 were effective (they delivered the seat to Labour) and the other 6742 were surplus (i.e. of its votes there, only 43.53 per cent were effective, and the majority were surplus in that they brought it no additional seats). All of Plaid Cymru's 5198 votes, on the other hand, were wasted.

Our particular concern is with the equal shares situation, because this is the basis of our bias measure. When Labour and Plaid Cymru each have 33.035 per cent of the votes cast overall, Labour gets 21 seats to Plaid's 14. Why did Labour get a better return for its votes than its main opponent? To answer this, for each party we look at three figures after the redistribution of votes to produce equal shares:

1 its number of effective votes per seats won;
2 its number of surplus votes per seats won; and
3 its number of wasted votes per seats lost.

If it obtains a lot of surplus votes in the seats that it wins, this involves victories by large margins which bring no more return than would be the case if victories in the same seats were obtained with smaller margins. Similarly, if it wastes a lot of votes in the seats that it loses, then it may be doing well in them, but not well enough to win; it would still lose with less votes. Finally, if its number of effective votes per seat won is less than its opponent's, then it is winning where the second-placed party is relatively weak, and victory is relatively easily obtained.

Table 1.4   Classification of votes for Labour and Plaid Cymru at the 1999 Welsh Assembly election, with equal vote shares

	Labour	Plaid Cymru
Effective votes per seat won	6,552	7,352
Surplus votes per seat won	3,194	5,623
Wasted votes per seat lost	6,998	5,999

The numbers of effective, surplus and wasted votes for our Welsh example, when Labour and Plaid Cymru have equal shares, can be derived from Table 1.3. In Aberavon, for example, of Labour's 10,868 votes after the redistribution, 6271 are effective (the number needed to defeat the second-placed party's candidate, who received 6270) and the other 4597 are surplus. On average, as shown in Table 1.4, Labour needed 6552 votes to win a seat, 800 less than was the case for Plaid Cymru. Plaid Cymru also had more surplus votes per seat won than Labour – a difference of some 2500 votes, indicating that Plaid Cymru tended to win by much larger majorities (as in Carnarfon, Carmarthen East, Ceredigion, Meirionnydd Nant Conwy and Ynys Mon, in each of which its majority was over 10,000; Labour's largest majority was 8181 in Blaenau Gwent, and there were only four other cases of majorities of 5000 or more). Plaid was disadvantaged, therefore, both by the relative weakness of the second-placed party in the seats that it won and by the large majorities that it built up there, especially in its west Wales heartlands. This was partly countered by its smaller average number of wasted votes than Labour in the seats that it lost (a difference of almost exactly 1000 votes), but overall it got a much poorer return for its equal share of the votes than did Labour (seats:votes ratios of 1.06 and 1.59, respectively, see Table 1.3).

The major difference between the two parties is in the number of surplus votes per seat won: Labour amassed 3194 votes on average to win its 21 seats, whereas Plaid Cymru obtained 5623 (some 2400 more) to win its 14. The differences between the parties were less on the other two measures: Labour won seats with an average effective vote total of some 6600, 800 less than did Plaid Cymru, for example, but Labour wasted on average 1000 more than Plaid Cymru in the seats lost. In other words, the seats where Labour was victorious were relatively easy to win compared to those won by its main opponent: fewer votes were needed for those victories, and it got a better return overall despite wasting a few more votes where it lost.

Wasted, surplus and effective votes at British general elections, 1950–97

Figures 1.5–1.7 show the trends in wasted, surplus and effective votes (with equal vote shares) for the Conservative and Labour parties over the 14 elections between 1950 and 1997, indicating not only major differences between the two, but also significant changes over the five decades.

With regard to *effective votes*, for example, the two parties diverged after the 1959 election (Figure 1.5). Until then (when, as Table 1.2 shows, the Conservatives and Labour won almost all of the votes and seats) there was little difference between the two; each needed on average around 17,000 votes to win a seat. That remained the situation for the Conservatives over the remaining ten elections, though with substantial variation around the average. For Labour, on the other hand, there was a general downward trend, with on average a smaller number of votes needed to win a seat at each successive election. By 1997, whereas the number of effective votes was some 13,500 in a Labour-won seat (when the parties had the same share of the vote), for Conservative-held seats it was approximately 3000 votes more. Over the 50-year period, it required progressively fewer votes to elect a Labour than a Conservative MP.

The pattern for *surplus votes* also shows a divergence, mainly in the 1980s when Labour averaged 2500–3000 more surplus votes per seat won than did the Conservatives at the two elections held in that decade (Figure 1.6). Until the 1979 election, Labour's surplus votes per seat won were larger than those

Figure 1.5 Effective votes per seat won for the Conservative and Labour parties at UK general elections 1950–97, when they have equal shares of the votes cast

of the Conservatives' at every election save 1970. In general, over that period Labour-held seats had slightly larger majorities (never more than about 1000 votes) than was the case in those held by its opponent. The gap between the two widened at the 1974 elections, narrowed again in 1979, and then was very wide in 1983, 1987 and (to a lesser extent) 1992 before returning to the position at the beginning of the 1950s in 1997 – a gap of a little over 1000 votes.

Finally, Figure 1.7 shows that, save for the gap between the two parties at the 1966 and 1970 elections, the main change with regard to the number of *wasted votes* per seat lost came in 1997. Until then, there was either virtually no difference between the two parties (the situation prior to 1966 and at the two 1974 elections) or Labour wasted slightly more votes per seat lost than did the Conservatives: Labour tended to come a slightly better second than did its opponent. But then in 1997, the situation was reversed quite substantially. Not only did the Conservatives waste more votes per seat lost than Labour, but the gap between them was almost 2000 votes. Whereas Labour's number of wasted votes fell to almost its lowest level, the Conservatives' ratio had increased in 1992 and stayed about the same five years later.

Figure 1.6 Surplus votes per seat won for the Conservative and Labour parties at UK general elections 1950–97, when they have equal shares of the votes cast

Conclusions

We began this chapter by observing that similar shares of the votes cast at the 1979, 1983, 1987, 1992 and 1997 general elections in Great Britain were not matched by similar percentages of the seats won. The electoral system was not only producing disproportional results, favouring the largest two parties, but the extent of that disproportionality varied both between elections and between parties. The process by which votes are translated into seats appears to be somewhat fickle as well as unfair – if proportional representation (the same percentage of the seats as of the votes won) is taken as the fairness criterion.

Further analysis of the relationship between votes and seats won showed that it was a consistent feature of British election results over the second half of the twentieth century, though with a major shift in the extent of that disproportionality after 1970, when the Conservative and Labour shares of the votes cast fell substantially, but their allocations of seats fell much less. This disproportionality in outcomes has not affected the two parties equally, however. For the first two decades in the period, the bias in outcomes substantially

Figure 1.7   Wasted votes per seat lost for the Conservative and Labour parties at UK general elections 1950–97, when they have equal shares of the votes cast

favoured the Conservatives; over the last two elections in the sequence, it favoured Labour, very substantially in 1997.

There appears to have been a major shift in how the electoral system treated the two main British political parties over the half century, with Labour the beneficiary. A classification of votes into three types – surplus, wasted and effective – further exemplified that trend and focused attention on changes in the efficiency of each party's vote-winning. Explaining those changes is the focus of attention in the remainder of this book. As the next chapter illustrates, the main reason for them lies in the geography of vote-winning and the associated process of seat allocation.

Notes

1   On which see Loosemore and Hanby (1971) and Dunleavy and Margetts (1997)
2   Full details of the system are in Rossiter, Johnston and Pattie (1999).
3   Regression is a widely used technique for fitting a straight line to a scatter of points, which minimises the average (squared) distance between each of those points and the line; for an introduction, see Johnston (1978).
4   The full algebra is set out in Brookes (1959, 1960; see also Brookes 1958), Johnston (1977) and Rossiter, Johnston and Pattie (1998). Mortimore's DPhil thesis (1992) details his modifications.

5   There is plenty of evidence that this assumption is a reasonable first approxima-
    tion. There does tend to be a uniformity of shift in support for each of the two
    main British parties between elections.
6   The bias need not be calculated between the top two performing parties. It can
    be calculated for any pair – between Labour and the Liberal Democrats, for exam-
    ple – in the same way and for the same purpose.
7   In our Welsh example, Labour had a positive bias of +7.
8   See Worcester and Mortimore (1999).
9   The effective number of votes in a constituency may be much smaller than half of
    the total number cast, plus one, depending on the number of parties and the dis-
    tribution of votes. In a constituency with 100 votes cast and three parties, there-
    fore, the effective number of votes may be as large as 50 (if the winning party got
    50 votes, the second-placed party 49 and the third 1), but it may be as small as
    34, if two of the parties obtained 33 votes each. The larger the number of parties
    with a fixed number of voters, the smaller the minimum feasible number of effec-
    tive votes, whereas the maximum remains at 50. (With six parties, for example,
    if three got 16 and two got 17, then the effective number of votes for the sixth
    party would be just 18.)

2

Geography, malapportionment and gerrymandering

Having identified and determined the amount of disproportionality and bias in UK general election results since 1950, the next chapters set out to appreciate why these have occurred. The basic argument is that disproportionality and bias are necessary outcomes of the electoral system used to elect the UK's House of Commons (often termed first-past-the-post), although the extent of the disproportionality and the size and direction of the bias cannot be determined in advance.[1] This is because both are influenced by the specific features of the geography of aspects of the electoral arrangements.

Constituency building

Members of the House of Commons are elected to represent constituencies, divisions of the national territory. Each constituency returns a single MP, the candidate who gets most votes there, which may not be a majority of the votes cast; the larger the number of candidates, the smaller the vote tally which in certain circumstances might lead to a candidate winning with minority support. With 100 votes to be cast, and only two candidates, for example, 51 votes are necessary for victory. With three candidates, however, one could win with just 34 votes if the other two got 33 each; with four, 26 votes would be sufficient for victory in certain circumstances; with five, 21 votes, and so on.

How is a constituency defined? There are no absolute rules derived from first principles and applicable in all circumstances. The method of defining constituencies is very much a political decision and, as we illustrate later in this book, the nature of the decision can have very significant electoral and political consequences. Indeed, it is not absolutely necessary that the constituencies are geographically defined; until 1949, for example, the House of Commons included a small number of MPs who represented 'non-geographical' constituencies – the graduates of various British Universities.[2] But geographically defined constituencies have been the norm throughout

British Parliamentary history. The earliest MPs represented the Shire Counties; each was invited in 1254 to select two by election in the County Court. The incorporated towns (Boroughs with Royal Charters) were similarly invited to send two members; as the number of incorporated Boroughs increased, so did the size of the elected Parliament. This system was substantially modified by each of the three nineteenth-century Reform Acts (1832, 1867, 1885), whose main purpose was extension of the franchise, but which also dealt with constituency definition. The third of these Acts established single-member constituencies as the 'British system'. Of the 670 MPs elected after its enactment, 613 represented single-member constituencies – 48 were returned from Boroughs with two MPs each and the remainder represented the Universities.[3]

The great majority of those single-member constituencies were geographically defined, contiguous blocks of territory. The small number of exceptions involved groups of non-contiguous small towns – termed Districts of Boroughs (Burghs in Scotland), of which seven remained before they were abolished in 1949. Increasingly, it was necessary to define constituencies for the specific purpose of electing MPs, rather than use areas defined for other purposes. Until the first of the Reform Acts in 1832, the constituencies were the same as the country's major administrative divisions – the Counties and the Boroughs, each of which returned two MPs. But as more single-member constituencies were employed, many of these had to be defined as subdivisions of the Counties and Boroughs.

For any area such as a County or Borough, there is a finite but extremely large number of ways in which it could be subdivided into constituencies. From the outset, the range was restricted (though it was still very large) by adopting the policy of building constituencies as amalgams of small administrative units – such as Hundreds and Petty Sessional Divisions within Counties and wards within Boroughs. This method, which remains at the core of British constituency definition, is thus explicitly geographical; it involves combining small areas to create larger ones.

Constituency-building and election outcomes

The process of constituency building could be presented as an entirely neutral procedure, for which explicit rules are produced and followed. That ideal is rarely followed, however, because how constituencies are defined can have very significant political impacts – and hence politicians want to be involved in order to promote their own electoral interests and constrain their opponents'.

A first example
This geographical problem of how to produce a set of constituencies from a larger set of small areas is illustrated by the very simple example in Figure 2.1. There are four small areas to be used as the building blocks, each

Figure 2.1   The constituency-definition problem: a simple example

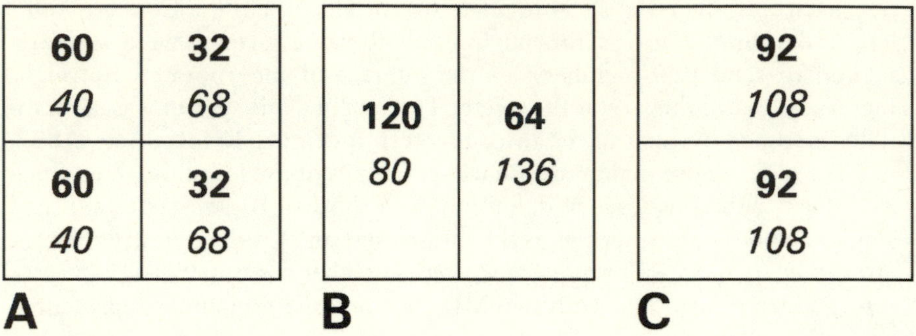

60	32
40	*68*
60	32
40	*68*

A

120	64
80	*136*

B

92
108
92
108

C

containing 100 voters split between those who vote for party X (the top figure in each cell in Figure 2.1a) and those who support party Y (the bottom figure). These four areas have to be used to create two constituencies, each containing half of the voters. Two configurations meet that criterion. In the first case (Figure 2.1b), adjacent areas are grouped on a north–south basis, and each of the parties wins one constituency. In the second case (Figure 2.1c), the grouping is organised east–west and party Y wins in both constituencies. In the latter case, therefore, party Y would have a seats:votes ratio of 1.85 (it gets 100 per cent of the seats with 54 per cent (216/400) of the votes) and party X a ratio of 0.0. In the latter case, party X would have a ratio of 1.09 (50 per cent of the seats and 46 per cent of the votes) and party Y a ratio of 0.93.

Three important conclusions can be drawn from this simple example:

1 It is possible to produce more than one set of constituencies which meet the relevant criteria.[4]
2 Without other criteria – such as north–south constituencies are preferable to east–west ones! – it is not possible to say that one set is superior to the other.
3 Which solution is chosen can have important political consequences in terms of the number of representatives each party gains and the efficiency of their vote-winning, as measured by the seats:votes ratio.[5]

The clear implication from the first two conclusions is that more criteria are needed, but this may not remove the third conclusion. Whatever the number of criteria, it is very likely that different solutions to a constituency-building problem, where the number of small areas and votes for each party are fixed, will nevertheless produce different electoral outcomes, especially where the number of small areas and constituencies is large. Indeed, all constituency-building exercises have political consequences, with different configurations of the small areas potentially producing different results – which suggests that the exercise should be carried out by a non-political body, although this will only ensure that the outcome is not the product of self-interest, since it may favour one party over others.

What if we relax the criterion requiring equal-sized constituencies? This gives four more possibilities, shown in Figure 2.2. In the first four, three of the small areas are grouped into one constituency containing 300 voters, whereas the fourth comprises the remaining area, having only 100 voters. In all four cases (A–D), the seats are divided between the two parties. Finally, if we relax the other criterion, contiguity and allow two constituencies to be created by diagonal amalgamation, as in Figure 2.2E (the definition of contiguity could be stretched to allow this, with the two sections of each constituency touching!), then party Y would win both seats.

In total, therefore, there are seven ways in which two constituencies can be created from these four building blocks, depending on the criteria employed. In two cases, party Y would win both seats, which would be disproportional; in all others, the seats would be divided equally between the two parties, which involves a slight discrimination in favour of party X. Even though neutral criteria are being applied in the constituency-building

Figure 2.2 Further solutions to the simple constituency-definition problem

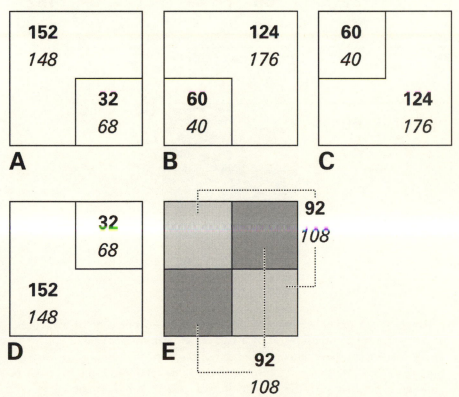

Figure 2.3   The simple constituency-definition problem with a different pattern of support for the two parties

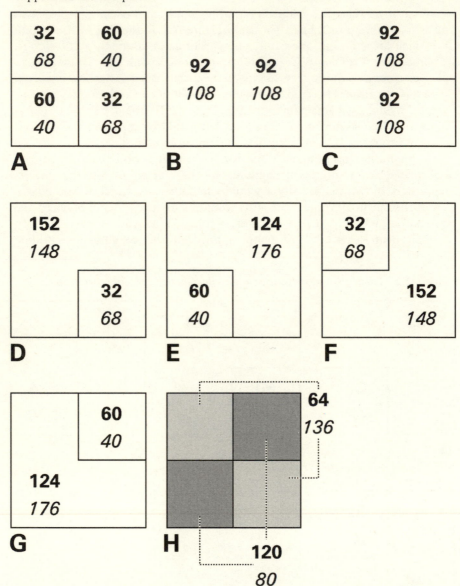

process, X can never win two of the seats with 46 per cent of the votes, whereas in several situations party Y can do so with 54 per cent.

The reason for these outcomes lies in the geography of support for each of the two parties. Another geography, with the same total for each party in each building block, but with the two small areas where Y has a majority of the votes being diagonally opposite rather than adjacent to each other (Figure 2.3A), produces a different set of outcomes. The two solutions to the constituency-building problem involving both the equal-size and contiguity constraints (Figure 2.3B and C) each give both seats to Y. The four involving unequal-sized constituencies each have both parties winning one seat each (Figure 2.3D–G), and that with equal-sized but non-contiguous constituencies also has an even split (Figure 2.3H). Thus party X is advantaged when one of the criteria is relaxed, but substantially disadvantaged when both are applied.

So, geography matters – both the geography of where each party wins votes and the geography of constituency-building. Of course, the situation is never as simple as the examples in Figures 2.1–2.3 – there are almost invariably more building blocks (the smaller areas) and usually more constituencies. (In addition, it is virtually impossible in 'real world' situations to achieve total equality of electorates.) Even so, the problem remains. Indeed it becomes more complex, because the number of possible combinations increases exponentially.

A larger problem

Take the situation in Figure 2.4A, which shows 25 small area building blocks to be combined into five constituencies: there are 100 voters in each building

Figure 2.4   A larger constituency-definition problem

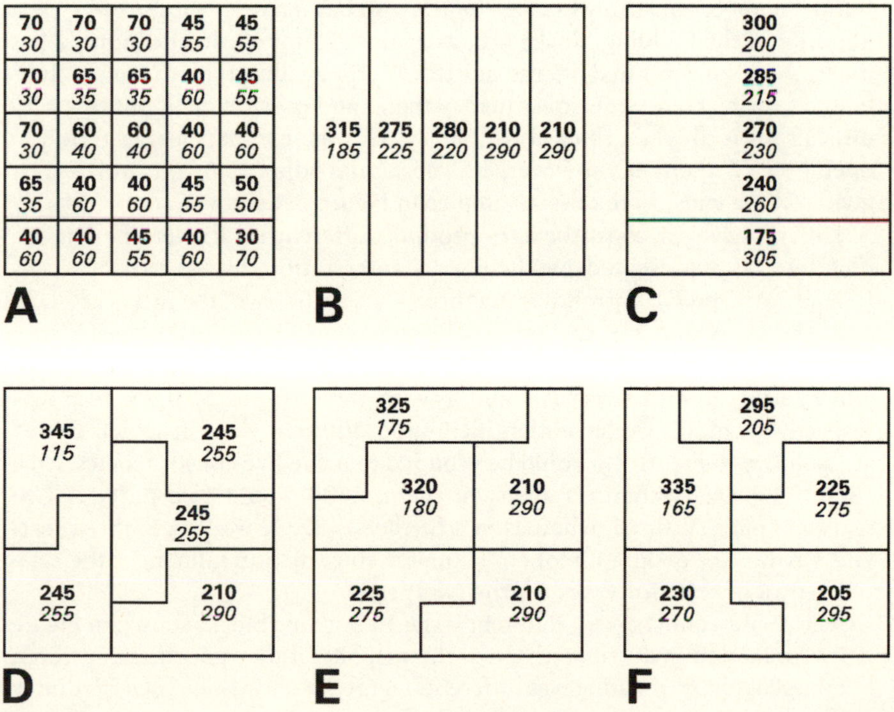

block, party X (the top one in each square) has 1290 (51.6 per cent) of the 2500 votes and party Y has the remaining 48.4 per cent (1210). Party X is strongest in the northwest of the area, and party Y in the southeast.

How might the five constituencies be created, with all constituencies having the same number of voters (500) and comprising contiguous areas? Two simple ways would be to have either five north–south trending or five east–west trending seats, as shown in Figure 2.4B and C. In each case, party X would win three seats and party Y two, which is the least disproportional outcome (X would be somewhat over-represented, with a seats:votes ratio of 1.16, and Y under-represented, with a ratio of 0.83). But such long constituencies are not very compact and might be difficult for their MPs to service. Why not produce more compact sets? Figure 2.4D–F shows three possibilities, in each of which the minority party – Y – obtains a majority of the seats, by 4:1 in one case (Figure 2.4D). In all three, however, applying two exact criteria – each constituency should have 500 voters and each should comprise a single block of contiguous territory – and one which lacks a precise definition – that each constituency should be relatively compact – produces results that are far from proportional and favour the minority party, Y.

Again, the answer to why this should be so can be found in the geography of each party's support. Party X is the slightly larger of the two, but has its support spatially more concentrated than its opponent. X has a substantial lead (70:30) in more building blocks (5) than Y (1) – where it amasses substantial numbers of surplus votes – but X also has majority support in only a minority of the building blocks (10, as against 15 for Y). In addition, X has its support concentrated in the northwestern quadrant of the map. It is bound to win at least one constituency there, and possibly two, but it is very difficult for it to win a third constituency with the compactness criterion in operation. Without it, however, its substantial support in the north-west gives it three wins, as the first examples in Figure 2.4 show.

Different sets of constituencies produce different returns to the parties, therefore, as represented by their seats:votes ratios. In the first two sets (Figure 2.4B and C), with X getting three seats and Y, two, the ratios are 1.29 and 0.83 for X and Y, respectively. The third set (Figure 2.4D) gives Y four seats to X's one, with ratios of 0.39 and 1.65, and the other two (Figure 2.4E and F) have X with two seats and Y with three, ratios of 0.78 and 1.24 respectively. In all, we have identified 4006 different ways in which the 25 areas shown in Figure 2.4 could be grouped to make five constituencies, each comprising five contiguous areas; of them, 2100 would give party X two seats and party Y, three, whereas in a further 1487, X would get three seats and Y two.[6] The geography of constituency construction influences the relative return of seats for votes for the two parties.

The results could be very different if the 15 building blocks shown in Figure 2.4 were randomly distributed across the map, i.e. if they got the same votes, but the geography of voting was different. Figure 2.5 shows one such randomly

Figure 2.5   The larger constituency-definition problem with a different pattern of support for the two parties

40	**65**	**65**	**40**	**70**
60	*35*	*35*	*60*	*30*
45	**70**	**60**	**40**	**45**
55	*30*	*40*	*60*	*55*
70	**45**	**40**	**65**	**45**
30	*55*	*60*	*35*	*55*
45	**40**	**50**	**40**	**40**
55	*60*	*50*	*60*	*60*
60	**40**	**70**	**70**	**30**
40	*60*	*30*	*30*	*70*

generated distribution, with each party getting the same number of votes as in Figure 2.4, but in different places. If the blocks are combined into the five sets of five constituencies shown in Figure 2.4B–F, party X would win four seats and party Y only one in each of the first two (i.e. the 'long thin' constituencies). In the other three, the results would be: D – party X, 3; party Y, 1 and one tied; E – party X, 2; party Y, 2 and one tied and F – party X, 3 and party Y, 2. Overall, party X does better from this geography than it does with the geography of Figure 2.4, because its support is not concentrated in one corner of the map.

Wasted and surplus votes
The importance of the geography of constituency building to election outcomes is further illustrated by data on each party's ratios of surplus votes per seat won and wasted votes per seat lost in each of the five constituency configurations of Figure 2.4 (see Table 2.1). In the first two – the 'long thin' constituencies extending either north–south or east–west (B and C) – the figures are virtually identical. But in the other three they are very different, with party X having a much less efficient 'vote geography' than party Y; X has much larger surpluses in the seats that it wins and much larger numbers of wasted votes in the seats that it loses.

The two parties do not have equal vote shares of course, so in the bottom part of Table 2.1 we report on the situation if they did, using the procedure described in Chapter 1 to redistribute votes between the two parties; it involves party X losing 1.6 per cent of the votes in each of the building blocks, with those votes being reallocated to party Y. None of the seats changes hands in any of the sets of constituencies shown in Figure 2.4 (see Table 2.1), so in the first two configurations the bias favours party X (shown by a +ve sign in the relevant row), whereas in the other three it favours party Y (shown by a –ve sign). The largest bias is in configuration D, in which X wins a single seat by a very large majority – hence its large average number of surplus votes per seats won – relative to Y's four victories by an average margin only one-fifth as large. As a consequence, X also wastes many more votes on average than Y in the seats that it loses.

Table 2.1 Surplus and wasted votes in the constituency configurations of Figure 2.4

	Configuration				
	B	C	D	E	F
Original result					
Votes					
Party A	1,290	1,290	1,290	1,290	1,290
Party B	1,210	1,210	1,210	1,210	1,210
Seats					
Party A	3	3	1	2	2
Party B	2	2	4	3	3
Surplus votes per seat won					
Party A	79	69	229	145	129
Party B	79	69	27	69	57
Wasted votes per seat lost					
Party A	210	218	264	215	220
Party B	210	215	115	178	185
Effective votes per seat won					
Party A	211	216	116	179	186
Party B	211	219	237	216	221
With equal vote shares					
Votes					
Party A	1,250	1,250	1,250	1,250	1,250
Party B	1,250	1,250	1,250	1,250	1,250
Seats					
Party A	3	3	1	2	2
Party B	2	2	4	3	3
Bias	+1	+1	−3	−1	−1
Surplus votes per seat won					
Party A	63	53	213	113	153
Party B	95	90	43	75	85
Wasted votes per seat lost					
Party A	202	210	228	212	207
Party B	218	223	163	193	186
Effective votes per seat won					
Party A	219	224	164	194	187
Party B	203	211	229	213	208

The equal shares solution for the constituency configurations produced from the geography of votes in Figure 2.5 does result in some seats changing hands as well as a winner being identified for the ties (in each case favouring party Y). In every case, as Table 2.2 shows, the party favoured by the biases in the system (party X in the first three configurations and party Y in the other two) has the smallest average number of surplus votes per seat won.

Table 2.2 Surplus and wasted votes in the constituency configurations of Figure 2.5

	Configuration				
	B	C	D	E	F
Original Result					
Votes					
Party A	1,290	1,290	1,290	1,290	1,290
Party B	1,210	1,210	1,210	1,210	1,210
Seats					
Party A	4	4	3	2	3
Party B	1	1	1	2	2
Surplus votes per seat won					
Party A	39	37	39	49	49
Party B	39	69	39	29	34
Wasted votes per seat lost					
Party A	230	215	230	275	233
Party B	235	225	230	235	233
Effective votes per seat won					
Party A	236	226	231	236	234
Party B	231	216	231	276	234
With equal vote shares					
Votes					
Party A	1,250	1,250	1,250	1,250	1,250
Party B	1,250	1,250	1,250	1,250	1,250
Seats					
Party A	3	4	3	2	2
Party B	2	1	2	3	3
Bias	+1	+3	+1	−1	−1
Surplus votes per seat won					
Party A	20	19	23	35	53
Party B	30	85	35	31	35
Wasted votes per seat lost					
Party A	235	207	232	232	232
Party B	240	239	238	233	223
Effective votes per seat won					
Party A	241	240	239	234	224
Party B	236	208	233	233	233

The victors were advantaged because they won by smaller majorities than their opponents.

Shifting voter preferences

People do not always vote for the same party at every election of course and

Figure 2.6   The larger constituency-definition problem with a further pattern of support for the two parties

56 44	56 44	56 44	36 64	36 64
56 44	52 48	52 48	32 68	36 64
56 44	48 52	48 52	32 68	32 68
52 48	32 68	32 68	36 64	40 60
32 68	32 68	36 64	32 68	24 76

the population is always changing – some voters die and are replaced by new members of the electorate, who may prefer a different party. Thus the parties' relative strengths might vary over time. Will a shift in the electorate's support be reflected in the allocation of seats or will it be either accentuated or ameliorated by the process of translating votes into seats? To answer this, we look again at the five sets of five constituencies in Figure 2.4. What happens if party X loses 20 per cent of its support in each building block (so that, for example, the 70:30 split in the northwestern block is reduced to 56:44: Figure 2.6)? Overall, party X now has 41.28 per cent of the 2500 votes and party Y has 58.72 per cent, so that a 2:3 split of the seats would be the most proportional outcome. But in four of the five possible sets of constituencies shown in Figure 2.4, party X would get only one seat to Y's four; only in one case (configuration E) would it get two seats (Table 2.3). The geography is against X.

The bottom block of data in Table 2.3 explores whether this is so at the equal shares allocation, which involved switching 6.72 per cent of the votes cast from Y to X. In the first configuration (B), the north–south trending constituencies, X would win more seats than Y because of its much smaller average surpluses in the constituencies where it is victorious. In the remaining four configurations, the bias favours party Y, however, substantially so in configurations C and D, but for different reasons. In configuration C, its main advantage over X is that it wastes fewer votes per seat lost and in configuration D it needs many fewer effective votes in order to win a seat. Different aspects of the distributions of wasted and surplus votes are crucial in different geographies.

If the same loss of support were applied to the geography of support for the two parties in Figure 2.5 (shown in Figure 2.7), an even more extreme outcome would emerge; party Y would win all five seats in each of the five constituency configurations. The reason for this can be seen by a quick inspection of that geography. Party X is the larger of the two in eight of the 25 building blocks, but these are widely scattered across the map. Basically, it needs three of these building blocks in a constituency if it is going to win

Table 2.3 Surplus and wasted votes in the constituency configurations of Figure 2.6

	Configuration				
	B	C	D	E	F
Original result					
Votes					
Party A	1,032	1,032	1,032	1,032	1,032
Party B	1,418	1,418	1,418	1,418	1,418
Seats					
Party A	1	1	2	1	1
Party B	4	4	3	4	4
Surplus votes per seat won					
Party A	3	39	51	15	35
Party B	90	103	121	155	117
Wasted votes per seat lost					
Party A	195	198	189	172	191
Party B	248	210	224	242	232
Effective votes per seat won					
Party A	249	211	225	243	233
Party B	196	199	190	173	192
With equal vote shares					
Votes					
Party A	1,250	1,250	1,250	1,250	1,250
Party B	1,250	1,250	1,250	1,250	1,250
Seats					
Party A	3	1	1	2	2
Party B	2	4	4	3	3
Bias	+1	−3	−3	−1	−1
Surplus votes per seat won					
Party A	27	63	17	49	24
Party B	129	69	62	121	113
Wasted votes per seat lost					
Party A	185	215	206	189	193
Party B	221	193	241	225	231
Effective votes per seat won					
Party A	222	194	242	226	232
Party B	186	216	207	190	194

there. This only occurs in the northwest, but the two blocks in the far northwest strongly favour party Y, which counter X's smaller victories nearby; any northwestern constituency is bound to include those pro-Y blocks. The geography of voting for party X makes it very difficult for it to win many seats. Indeed, it produces a very large bias against the party. With equal vote shares, in one of the five configurations Y would still win all five

Figure 2.7   A further example for the larger constituency-definition problem

32	52	52	32	56
68	*48*	*48*	*68*	*44*
36	56	48	32	36
64	*44*	*52*	*68*	*64*
56	36	32	52	36
44	*64*	*68*	*48*	*64*
36	32	40	32	32
64	*68*	*60*	*68*	*68*
48	32	56	56	24
52	*68*	*44*	*44*	*76*

seats (configuration E in Figure 2.4) and in the other four it would achieve victory in four of the five.

These simple examples have illustrated the geographical nature of constituency building and the problems involved in that process. The geography involves the superimposition of one map – of constituencies – upon another – of voters. Problems are raised by the difficulties in deciding which of the many ways available for doing that should be used – what criteria to employ when determining how to build the constituencies from small areas – and the political implications (disproportionality and bias) that can result. Those features of recent British elections discussed in Chapter 1 are consequences of the interaction of the two geographies there. Other factors are involved too, as examined in the remainder of this chapter.

The geography of support by constituency

Once the constituencies have been created, we can see the impact of the geography of support for the two parties in terms of the seats:votes ratio. We illustrate this by returning to the diagram in Figure 2.4, only this time we treat each of the squares as a constituency. Of the 25 constituencies, party X has a majority in just 10, or 40 per cent, despite having 51.9 per cent of the votes overall. This gives it a seats:votes ratio of 0.78. The largest party not only fails to get a majority of the seats, it gets only about three-quarters of its 'entitlement' if the seats were allocated proportionately.

Standard deviations and disproportional election results

Why is this? To answer that, we need an excursion into simple statistics. To begin with, we produce simple examples making one basic statistical assumption – the percentage of votes that a party gets is normally distributed around its average (or mean). The normal distribution is bell-shaped and symmetrical around the mean, but the nature of that shape varies according to the

Figure 2.8a The frequency distribution of votes for party A across 2000 constituencies, with a mean of 50% and a standard deviation of 6.09

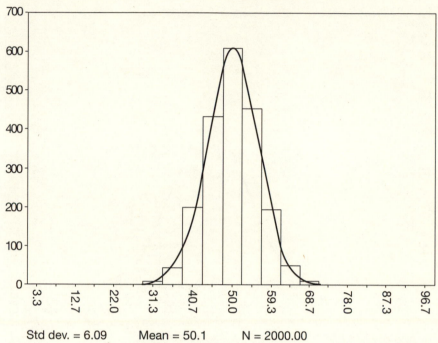

Std dev. = 6.09   Mean = 50.1   N = 2000.00

value of a further statistical parameter – the standard deviation. The larger the standard deviation,[7] the greater the scatter of values, while still retaining the basic symmetrical bell-shape to the distribution. This is illustrated in Figure 2.8. We have randomly generated three normal distributions involving 2000 separate observations, each with a mean of 50 per cent, but with standard deviations of approximately 6, 9 and 12, respectively. The symmetrical shape occurs in all three, but as the standard deviation increases, so does the spread of values.[8]

The size of the standard deviation is crucial to the allocation of seats. We illustrate this again with the 25 constituency configuration of Figure 2.1. We have randomly generated a number of frequency distributions for party X's percentage of the votes in each of the 25 constituencies, with a mean of 53 per cent but a varying standard deviation.[9] If the standard deviation is extremely small (i.e. close to 0.0), then X gets 53 per cent of the votes in every seat and wins all 25. As the standard deviation increases, then the number of constituencies where X's vote falls below 50 also increases. This is shown in Table 2.4, which includes the results of eight simulations with varying standard deviations. (None of these has an exact mean of 53.00, but all are very close to it.) In general, the larger the standard deviation, the smaller the number of seats won by party X though its smallest number

Figure 2.8b   The frequency distribution of votes for party A across 2000
constituencies, with a mean of 50% and a standard deviation of 8.87

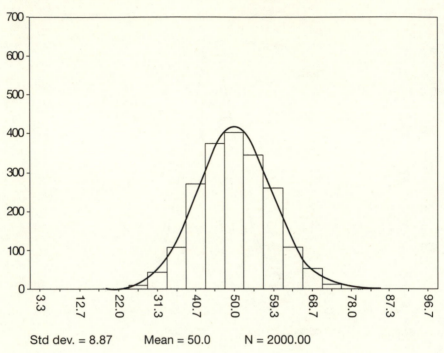

Std dev. = 8.87   Mean = 50.0   N = 2000.00

Table 2.4   The number of seats won by a party averaging *c.*53% of the votes across
25 constituencies, with varying standard deviations

Simulation	Mean	Min	Max	SD	Seats
	53.00	53.00	53.00	0.00	25
1	52.74	51.14	54.63	1.00	25
2	53.07	50.23	55.73	1.55	25
3	52.77	43.50	59.08	3.53	21
4	53.44	44.78	60.19	3.74	21
5	52.88	44.83	62.68	5.19	18
6	53.55	42.50	64.53	5.62	16
7	54.34	39.92	69.03	8.50	14
8	53.78	37.23	71.46	9.33	16

Figure 2.8c The frequency distribution of votes for party A across 2000 constituencies, with a mean of 50% and a standard deviation of 11.83

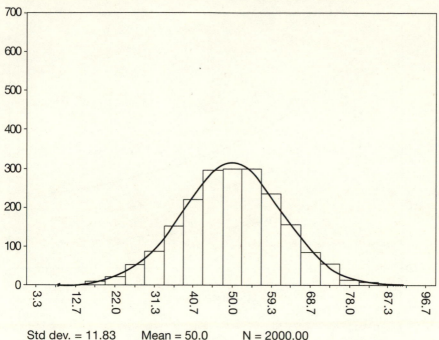

Std dev. = 11.83   Mean = 50.0   N = 2000.00

(14, or 56 per cent) is larger than its proportional share, given that it has 53 per cent of the votes. The relationship is not a smooth one, because there are many different ways of producing a normal distribution of 25 numbers with a given mean and standard deviation. Nevertheless, the principle is clear. The larger the standard deviation, the wider the range between the minimum and maximum percentages won by the party and, as a consequence, the larger the number of constituencies in which that percentage falls below 50. With a small standard deviation, the party is likely to win virtually all of the seats with just a small majority of the votes; the larger the standard deviation, the smaller its number of victories and the less the disproportionality.

Large-scale simulations

With a large number of constituencies, and continuing to assume a normal distribution in the percentage of the votes won by party X (and thus of the percentage won by Y), it is possible to predict the allocation of seats extremely accurately. Two geographers – Graham Gudgin and Peter Taylor[10] – have derived the relevant tables, and Figure 2.9 is based on them. It shows the average percentage of the seats which a party would get for a given mean percentage of the votes and standard deviation around that mean, for a small

Figure 2.9   The mean percentage of the seats that a party will get with a given mean standard deviation percentage of the votes

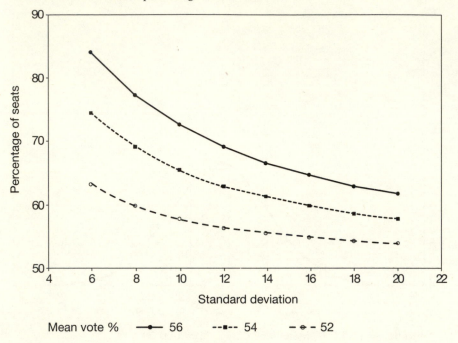

Source: Based on data in Gudgin and Taylor, 1979, 23.

number of possible values only. (The averages are derived over a very large number of simulations.)

Several conclusions can be drawn from this diagram, which apply to all situations where party X's mean vote percentage exceeds 50 and the distribution of its percentage over all constituencies is normal.

1 The larger the mean percentage, the larger the average percentage of the seats won.
2 The smaller the standard deviation, with any given mean, the larger the average percentage of the seats won.
3 The smaller the standard deviation, the greater the difference between means in the percentage of the seats won.
4 Whatever the mean and standard deviation, the average percentage of seats won never falls below 50 – although, as shown in our earlier examples, it is possible, if rare save in special circumstances, to get *both* more than 50 per cent of the votes, but less than 50 per cent of the seats *and* less than 50 per cent of the votes, but more than 50 per cent of the seats in any particular configuration of constituencies.

Thus 56 per cent of the votes and a standard deviation of 6, for example, led to the party getting 84 per cent of the seats on average, and even with just 52 per cent of the votes but the same standard deviation, it would get 63 per cent of the seats. With a standard deviation twice that value, however, the respective average seats percentages would be 69 and 56, and with a standard deviation of 18 percentage points, the respective allocations would be 63 and 65.

These formal statistical analyses show why, given certain statistical assumptions, a party with more than 50 per cent of the votes in a two-party set of contests across a system of constituencies very probably wins more than 50 per cent of the seats.[11] Furthermore, they suggest that the best situation for a winning party, whatever its mean percentage of the votes, is to perform to the same level in every constituency, i.e. to achieve a small standard deviation. That could create problems over time, however. A party with 52 per cent of the votes virtually everywhere is in danger of losing the great majority of its seats if there is even a small overall swing away from it to its opponent; with 52 per cent of the votes and a standard deviation of 6, it wins 63 per cent of the seats. If its support slipped to 49 per cent and its opponent got 51 per cent with a standard deviation of 6, then the former would get only 44 per cent of the seats – a drop in its share of the votes of 3 points (from 52 to 49) would produce a drop in its share of the seats of 19 points (from 63 to 44). The way in which the electoral system translates votes into seats exaggerates the impact of X's declining vote share. A larger standard deviation would reduce the loss and thereby protect the party somewhat. With a standard deviation of 12, for example, party X would get 56 per cent of the seats with 52 per cent of the votes and 47 per cent of the seats with 49 per cent of the votes – a loss of seats much more commensurate with its loss of votes.[12]

Gudgin and Taylor have generalised this with a simple diagram, which suggests that the best situation for a party with regard to the variation in its vote percentage across the constituencies will depend on its mean vote (Figure 2.10). Where a party has either a small or a large mean percentage of the votes cast (i.e. the left- and right-hand ends of the top diagram, respectively), the standard deviation is unlikely to affect the number of seats that it gets. It will probably win either none at all if its mean is less than around 30 or all of them if it is 70 or more. With means in either the 40s or the 60s, a low standard deviation is desirable since this produces stability in the allocation of seats. A small drop in the party's share of the votes will not produce a precipitate drop in its share of the seats. (This is shown in A and C in the bottom section of Figure 2.10; the larger the standard deviation, i.e. the 'flatter' the frequency distribution, the larger the proportion of the distribution, i.e. the larger the percentage of the seats, involved with a small shift in the party's mean percentage, shown by the shaded area.) Finally, with means close to 50, a relatively high standard deviation is best at delivering such stability – as the example discussed in the previous paragraph shows. (In Figure 2.10B, the

Figure 2.10   The effect of changes in the standard deviation on the stability of election results

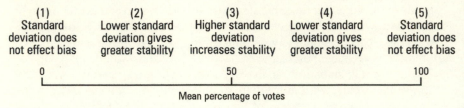

(1)	(2)	(3)	(4)	(5)
Standard deviation does not effect bias	Lower standard deviation gives greater stability	Higher standard deviation increases stability	Lower standard deviation gives greater stability	Standard deviation does not effect bias

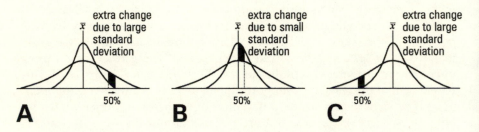

Source: Gudgin and Taylor, 1979, 69 – reproduced with permission of Pion Ltd.

larger standard deviation – the flatter distribution – is associated with a smaller shift in the number of seats when the party's vote share changes.)

Non-normal distributions

These 'theoretical' exercises provide an excellent appreciation of why the geography of support for a party is crucial to the votes-into-seats translation process under the UK's electoral system, but they make assumptions which we need to relax in order to bring the exercises closer to the situation 'on the ground'. The most important of these is the requirement that the distribution of vote percentages for a party be normal. Many distributions are asymmetrical, or skewed in one direction: a positive skew occurs when the right-hand 'tail' of the distribution is more elongated than the left (as in Figure 2.11A); a negative skew is the reverse situation, with a more elongated left- than right-hand 'tail' (Figure 2.11B). The examples in Figure 2.11 show that the impact of a skewed frequency distribution is greatest when the party's vote share is relatively close to 50 per cent of the total – assuming just two parties. Thus in Figure 2.11A the positive skew, with the mode (or peak) of the distribution to the left of the party's average of 50 per cent, less than half of the constituencies are to the right of that figure, and it wins a smaller share of the seats than the votes – its votes are over-concentrated in the relatively small number of constituencies where it performs very well. On the other

Figure 2.11 The effect of skewness on election results

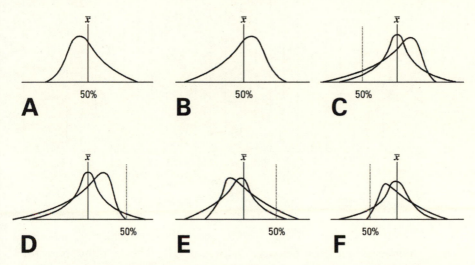

Source: Gudgin and Taylor, 1979, 69 – reproduced with permission of Pion Ltd.

hand, Figure 2.11B shows that with a negative skew the party gets a larger percentage of the seats than of the votes – where it loses (the left-hand 'tail'), it loses badly. Where the party's mean share of the votes is much greater than 50 per cent, a negatively skewed distribution means that it wins slightly fewer seats than with a normal distribution (Figure 2.11C: the proportion of the curve to the left of the 50 per cent point is smaller for the normal curve). Similarly, where the party's mean is well below 50 per cent, it gets slightly more seats with a normally-distributed vote share across the constituencies (Figure 2.11D).

Figures 2.12 and 2.13 show that such skewness characterised the pattern of voting for two of the UK's main political parties at the 1997 general election. The Conservatives' distribution was negatively skewed. Its mean constituency percentage (30) was to the left of the modal categories (i.e. the most common percentages were 36–40), but there was a much more precipitate drop from that mode to its right than to its left; there were very few constituencies where the Conservatives performed very well, compared to the

Figure 2.12 The frequency distribution of the Conservative party's percentage of the votes cast, by constituency, at the 1997 general election (Great Britain only)

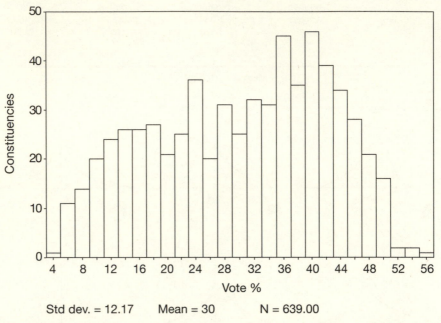

Std dev. = 12.17   Mean = 30   N = 639.00

larger number where they compared relatively badly. The distribution for the Liberal Democrats, on the other hand, was positively skewed, with a very long right-hand tail.

As with the variation around the mean, the impact of skewness varies according to the mean value. In a two-party system, for a party with a mean below 50, the smaller the standard deviation, the greater the advantages accruing from a positive skew, since this gives the party a majority of the votes in a larger proportion of the constituencies than would be the case if the distribution were normal. A party with a mean above 50, on the other hand, benefits from a negative skew, since this gives it a larger number of constituencies where it has a majority than would be the case with a normal distribution. With a negative skew, it wastes relatively small numbers of votes in the constituencies that it loses, whereas with a positive skew it builds up large surpluses in some of those which it wins.

Malapportionment and gerrymandering

The idealised examples used in this chapter so far have been developed to illustrate why geography is crucial to the relationship between votes won and seats won in the UK's electoral system. If you want to win elections, and win them

Figure 2.13 The frequency distribution of the Liberal Democrat party's percentage of the votes cast, by constituency, at the 1997 general election (Great Britain only)

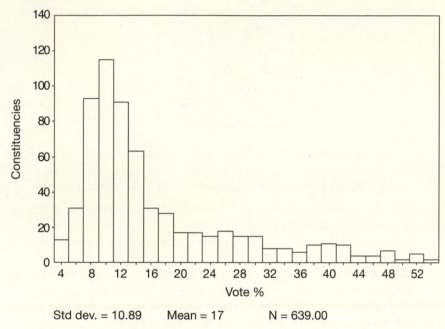

Std dev. = 10.89   Mean = 17   N = 639.00

well, it is not only important to win votes; where you win them is also important. Two particular features of that geographical argument can be stressed:

1 That differences in constituency sizes (in their number of voters) can influence the outcome of an election, given a certain distribution of votes between the two parties; and
2 That differences in the distribution of a party's votes across a set of building blocks from which constituencies are defined can also influence an election's outcome, given the allocation of votes between the two parties.

Our illustrations of these two features have employed neutral criteria. We have shown that different resolutions of the same problem can produce different election results (which of the two pairs of constituencies in Figure 2.1 to select, for example), hence the choice of a solution can have a strong influence on an election outcome.

One obvious consequence follows from this conclusion. If the choice of constituencies can influence an election result, then political parties (and other interested groups) will want to affect that choice, in order to promote their electoral interests. They can do that in one of two ways:

1 by so determining the criteria against which constituencies are defined (i.e. which of the options available will be chosen by those entrusted with the

Figure 2.14   An example of malapportionment, using the vote distribution shown in Figure 2.4A

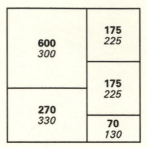

task), that their interests are likely to prevail over those of their opponents; and/or

2 by seeking direct involvement in the constituency-definition process.

Both have been employed in most countries where this type of electoral system is used, including the United Kingdom.

Much of the discussion of such constituency-defining strategies focuses on two electoral abuses.

Malapportionment involves constituencies of different sizes, arranged so that one party is strongest in the constituencies with smaller electorates (and hence gets a good 'return' for its votes), whereas the other is strongest where the constituency electorates are larger (which means a poorer return, because the effective number of votes needed for victory is larger). This can be brought about in one of two ways:

1 by deliberately defining constituencies of different sizes; or
2 by not redrawing constituency boundaries after a period of population change, whereby some constituencies become much smaller than others (either relatively or absolutely).

The former can be illustrated by returning to our earlier example of 25 building blocks to be aggregated into five constituencies (Figure 2.4). Party X is the larger of the two but, as discussed earlier, its support is concentrated into a relatively small number of the building blocks, in the northwestern quadrant of the map. By creating one large constituency there with 900 voters, and four smaller ones elsewhere (one with 600, two with 400 and one with 200) in the areas where Y has most support, it is possible to create a situation where X wins just one of the five seats and Y, with a minority of the votes, has a clear majority of the seats (Figure 2.14). Furthermore, those are all relatively safe seats. It would take a swing of 6.5 per cent for Y to lose any of the four that it won (those where it has 225 votes to X's 175). Party X has one very large seat with a very substantial majority, but its chances of winning more are relatively slight unless there is a major shift of support away from Y.

Figure 2.15 Two examples of gerrymandering, using the vote distribution shown in Figure 2.4A

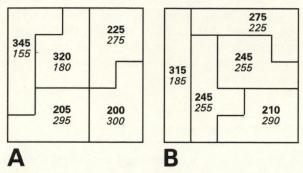

A   **B**

Gerrymandering involves carefully drawing constituency boundaries so that as many of them as possible have a majority of votes for a given party. This may involve constituencies with odd shapes, but not necessarily so. Within the general strategy, there are two main variants:

1 Creating a *stacked (or packed) gerrymander*, which involves concentrating the opposition party's support into a few safe seats (where it builds up large numbers of surplus votes), while diffusing one's own party's support across a larger number of seats. Figure 2.15a shows how this could be done by party Y, using the template from Figure 2.4. There are five equal-sized constituencies, in two of which X has large majorities (190 and 140 votes, respectively) and three where Y has smaller majorities (100, 90 and 50 votes), but none of which would be lost with a swing of less than 6 per cent away from it. (Such a strategy has been common in the United States in recent decades in states where districts have been drawn to ensure black majorities.)[13]

2 Creating a *cracked gerrymander*, by making the opposition waste a lot of votes as the loser in a substantial number of seats. Figure 2.15B shows how party Y could do this; X has one seat with a large majority, though smaller than either of its majorities under the packed gerrymander scheme (130 votes), and Y has four, one with a majority of 80, one with a majority of 50 and two with majorities of just ten. In the short term, this cracked gerrymander brings Y a greater advantage than the packed gerrymander, a victory by 4:1 rather than 3:2, but in the longer term it is more risky. If only six voters in each of the constituencies with a majority of ten changed their minds and shifted their support to X, then X would win a majority of the seats.

Both of these strategies have been widely employed in the United States, where malapportionment was outlawed as unconstitutional in the 1960s, but political parties have continued to practise packed gerrymandering wherever they have power over the redistricting process.[14]

What is important to stress here, however, is that election results consistent with either or both of malapportionment and gerrymandering can come about without any deliberate strategy by, or on behalf of, interested parties. As the previous sections of this chapter have shown, geography matters; a party can be disadvantaged or advantaged in the contest for seats because of where its votes are won, as a straightforward consequence of the geographical constraints to constituency building.

Two further assumptions relaxed

The examples used above to illustrate our basic contention that geography matters in the translation of votes into seats under the UK electoral system have been based on a number of assumptions. Several have been relaxed as that discussion progressed, and in this final section we relax two more, thereby bringing our discussion closer to the 'real world' with which the rest of the book deals.

Multi-party contests

All of our examples so far have been of an election contested by two parties only, who share the votes between them. As Table 1.2 shows, this has certainly not been the case in the UK in recent decades. Increasingly a number of smaller (or third) parties has won a substantial proportion of the votes cast.

How do these 'third parties' influence the result of the contest between the two main parties? Again, the answer depends on the geography. Assume there is only one 'third party' in the system (party Z), which contests all of the constituencies and wins 10 per cent of the votes. If half of those votes would have been won by party X if party Z had not been involved in the election, and the other half would have been won by Y, then there is no change in the allocation of seats, but there is in the seats:votes ratios. This is illustrated in Figure 2.16A, which uses the 25 areas of Figure 2.4 as 25 separate constituencies. Party X wins 46.6 per cent of the votes to Y's 43.4 per cent, but they win 10 and 14 of the seats, respectively (one is tied), giving seats:votes ratios of 0.86 for X and 1.29 for Y. (Recall that with their original vote percentages their ratios were 0.78 and 1.24, respectively.) In other words, the introduction of a third party, which wins votes but no seats, means that the two largest parties get an increased return on their votes; their vote shares fall, but their seat shares remain the same.

But what if party Z takes votes unequally from the other two parties? In Figure 2.16b, 60 per cent of party Z's votes are drawn from party Y's supporters, and the remainder from party X's. This gives X 1190 votes (47.6 per cent) which, with 44 per cent of the seats (it wins the one that was tied in Figure 2.16A), produces a seats:votes ratio of 0.92; Y gets 42.4 per cent of

Figure 2.16 The constituency-definition problem with three parties

A

65/25/10	65/25/10	65/25/10	40/50/10	40/50/10
65/25/10	60/30/10	60/30/10	35/55/10	40/50/10
65/25/10	55/35/10	55/35/10	35/55/10	35/55/10
60/30/10	35/55/10	35/55/10	40/50/10	45/45/10
35/55/10	35/55/10	40/50/10	35/55/10	25/65/10

B

66/24/10	66/24/10	66/24/10	41/49/10	41/49/10
66/24/10	61/29/10	61/29/10	36/54/10	41/49/10
66/24/10	56/34/10	56/34/10	36/54/10	36/54/10
61/29/10	36/54/10	36/54/10	41/49/10	46/44/10
36/54/10	36/54/10	41/59/10	36/54/10	26/64/10

C

63/27/10	63/27/10	63/27/10	38/52/10	38/52/10
63/27/10	58/32/10	68/32/10	33/57/10	38/52/10
63/27/10	53/37/10	53/37/10	33/57/10	33/57/10
58/32/10	33/57/10	33/57/10	38/52/10	43/47/10
33/57/10	33/57/10	38/52/10	33/57/10	23/67/10

D

69/29/2	68/28/4	68/28/4	43/53/4	43/53/4
69/29/2	60/30/10	60/30/10	35/55/10	40/50/10
69/29/2	55/35/10	45/25/30	25/45/30	35/55/10
64/34/2	35/55/10	25/45/30	30/40/30	45/55/10
38/58/4	38/58/4	43/53/4	38/58/4	25/65/10

the votes, 14 seats and a ratio of 1.32. Apart from the decision on the formerly tied seat, the new distribution of party Z's votes favours party Y for two reasons. In the seats that Y wins, its majority over X is reduced and so it has fewer surplus votes (an average of 14 per seat won compared with 17 in Figure 2.15a); and in the seats that it loses to X, the latter's majorities are larger, so that X's surpluses increase, to an average of 34 per seat won instead of 32 as previously.

If party Z attracts 70 per cent of its support from those who would otherwise have voted for X, and only 30 per cent from Y, the allocation of seats does not change, but X benefits most because its number of surplus votes per seat won falls (Figure 2.16C). In the ten seats that it wins in both cases, its average majority in the first is 35 (Figure 2.16B), whereas in the second it is 29. The better the performance of the third party in the seats won by X rather than those won by Y, the greater the benefit to X. This outcome seems somewhat counter-intuitive: the party that loses most votes to Party Z benefits most. This is because its votes become more efficiently distributed. Its majorities over the other main party are reduced in the seats that it wins, so generating fewer surplus votes and the other party's majorities where it wins are increased, so X's wasted votes there are reduced. So a third party's entry to the electoral contest can advantage the party it takes most support from so long as it does not erode it too far, either winning seats itself or letting the other main party win.

But what if the third party wins more support in some areas than others? Here, the range of possibilities is enormous. Only one is shown in Figure 2.16D, where party Z wins almost half of its votes in just four constituencies – it gets 30 each in them, plus ten each in nine others nearby, four each in eight more and two each in the remaining four on the western edge of the map. Its votes are taken equally from X and Y in each constituency. The majority of its support is in constituencies that are won by party Y, whose majorities in many of them are substantially reduced, compared to the situation in those won by X where Z makes very few inroads. Thus, whereas in Figure 2.16C party Y wins 14 seats with 45.4 per cent of the votes, giving a seats:votes ratio of 1.23, in Figure 2.16D it wins the same number of seats with 42.6 per cent of the votes – a ratio of 1.31. (X's ratios are 0.90 and 0.84 for the two maps, respectively.) Thus party Y benefits substantially in relative terms from Z's success in the constituencies in the middle of the map, and X suffers relatively from Z's failure to win converts where X is strong.

These examples are sufficient to make the basic point. A third party can make seats easier to win, especially if its votes are concentrated in constituencies won by one of the two main parties rather than the other. It reduces the number of votes needed for victory in a constituency (i.e. the number of effective votes) and can see the winning party's number of surplus votes reduced too. Once again, geography is crucial to the election outcome; for any party, it depends on not only where your votes are cast, but also where your opponents' are.

Abstentions

One final assumption to be relaxed is that all electors actually vote; this has been implicit throughout our discussion here, with all 100 electors in each of the small areas in Figure 2.4 casting a vote for one of the parties. This is rarely the case of course. Turnout varies by country and by type of election – unless it is compulsory, in which case (as in Australia and Belgium) it is usually close to 100 per cent. In the United Kingdom, for example, it has been below 80 per cent at every general election since 1951, and fell to its lowest level, just over 71 per cent, in 1997. In general, turnout there is lowest at elections which one party appears certain to win by a substantial majority. It also varies substantially across constituencies, as illustrated in detail in Chapter 7. In 1997 for example, the lowest turnout was 51.9 per cent in Liverpool Riverside and the highest 86.1 per cent in Mid Ulster (the highest in Great Britain was 82.2 per cent in Brecon & Radnor).

The impact of abstentions on disproportionality and bias is exactly the same as that of third parties – except that abstainers can never win seats! Thus the examples in the previous section apply just as readily to abstentions, as do the conclusions drawn; simply replace third party votes by abstentions in the examples. Thus:

1 The greater the number of abstentions in a constituency, the smaller the number of effective votes needed for victory there.
2 The greater the number of abstentions across all constituencies, the larger the seats:votes ratios for the parties.
3 If abstentions are drawn unevenly from those who otherwise would have voted for one of the two parties, this will benefit the party which loses most votes to abstentions – so long as the loss is insufficient to result in its opponent winning the seat; it gets fewer surplus votes in the seats that it wins.
4 If abstentions are unevenly distributed across the constituencies, this will probably be of greatest benefit – in terms of the seats:votes ratios and our bias measure – to the party which is strongest in the areas where abstentions are greatest.

In other words, the geography of abstentions, like the geography of third party support, is crucial to the election outcome – in particular to its bias towards one or other of the two main parties. By reducing the number of votes necessary for victory in a constituency, abstention can make it easier for one party rather than another to win seats.

Third parties and abstentions

Finally, and very briefly, these two additional factors probably both operate together. Certainly in the UK over recent decades there has been both a high level of abstention and substantial support for third parties, with both varying substantially across the country's constituencies. If abstention rates are highest where third party support is also strongest, the two could combine to reduce the number of effective votes needed in certain constituencies very substantially, which could very significantly benefit one of the main parties if its support is strong there. Alternatively, the two may counter each other. Abstentions may be high where third party support is low, and vice versa, with the possibility that one party will benefit from the former and the other from the latter.

The impact of third parties and abstentions on election results – both separately and together – is, in effect, a form of malapportionment. Because some of the electors in each constituency – or smaller area used in the construction of constituencies – in effect disenfranchise themselves, either by not voting at all or by voting for a third party whose chances of victory are relatively slim, they reduce the number of votes that 'count' and therefore the number required for victory. Constituency size is in effect reduced by the number of abstentions and third party votes, and disproportionality and bias are likely consequences if this has an uneven impact on the pattern of victories by the two main parties.

Conclusions

The core argument of this book is that dispropotionality and bias in UK election results over the second half of the twentieth century are consequences of geography – of the distribution of support for the two main parties (Conservative and Labour) and the various third parties (particularly the Liberals and the nationalist parties in Scotland and Wales), and of abstentions across the country's constituencies. In this chapter, we have used small and relatively simple examples to show how this occurs. It results from the construction of a map of constituencies – of defined territorial segments – which have different levels of support for the parties. How that map of constituencies is constructed can significantly affect the outcome of an election, assuming that the geographies of party support and abstentions are not affected (which they are of course, as we will see when we turn to analyses of the 'real world' in later chapters).

All of these causes of disproportionality and bias can be subsumed within the two 'classic' electoral abuses – malapportionment and gerrymandering – whether or not they are being practised. As Gudgin and Taylor have shown in their seminal work on *Seats, Votes and the Spatial Organisation of Elections*, results that are consistent with the two strategies are almost inevitable consequences of the UK's electoral system, in which geography is so deeply implicated in a variety of ways. Our simple examples here have illustrated why that is so. In the remainder of the book, we look at malapportionment and gerrymandering – both intentional and unintentional – in the operation of that system and its geography.

Notes

1   The large literature on disproportionality involving comparative studies of different electoral systems includes Rae (1971), Gudgin and Taylor (1979), Taagepera and Shugart (1989) and Lijphart (1994).

2   When these constituencies were eventually abolished there were 12 of them, two

each for Oxford and Cambridge, one for London, two for the combined other English Universities, three for the Scottish Universities, and one each for the University of Wales and for Queen's University, Belfast.

3   For a detailed discussion of the nineteenth-century reforms, see Rossiter, Johnston and Pattie (1999).

4   There may be cases with only a single solution, but this is very unlikely.

5   Again, it is possible, though highly unlikely, that every solution will produce the same outcome.

6   In three of the 4006 cases, A would get four seats and B one, whereas in six others, A would get only one and B would get four. The search for all possible solutions is done by an updated version of a computer program first published in Rossiter and Johnston (1981). We cannot be certain that we have found all of the solutions, but did run the program five million times!

7   Formally, the mean is the average value of a set of numbers (i.e. the total divided by the number of observations). The standard deviation is the square root of the average squared difference between each individual observation and the mean; the larger those differences, i.e. the broader the frequency distribution, the larger the standard deviation.

8   The hypothetical normal distribution is based on an infinitely large number of observations. These figures show that even with 2000 observations, the empirical distributions, even when produced by random number generators devised to produce the defined mean and standard deviation, only approximate to the normal curve for those parameters.

9   For this, as in the previous simulations, we used the normal distribution random number generator in the SPSS for Windows statistical package.

10 Gudgin and Taylor (1979, Ch. 2).

11 The exceptions occur when a party has a mean percentage of the votes only just over 50, but a large standard deviation.

12 Statisticians have identified a 'cube law', which shows that the ratio of seats won by parties A and B is the cube of the ratio of the votes that they win – so that, for example, if A won 55 per cent of the votes and B 45 per cent, A would get 65 per cent of the seats. This only operates, however, if the distributions of A's and B's vote shares are normal across all constituencies, with standard deviations of 13.7 percentage points. For a brief introduction, see Johnston (1979, 58–62).

13 There is a massive literature on racial gerrymandering in the United States: see Kousser (1999).

14 On malapportionment and its outlawing, see Dixon (1968); for an example of packed gerrymanders, see Morrill (1973). For overviews, see Johnston (1979) and Taylor and Johnston (1979).

3

Defining Parliamentary constituencies in the UK

Having discussed the process of constituency definition in general terms in Chapter 2, we turn now to an outline of how it is currently undertaken in the United Kingdom. As noted earlier, until the nineteenth century every Shire and most of the incorporated Boroughs each sent two elected representatives to the House of Commons, whose size was thus largely determined by the number of Boroughs and its composition by the preferences of their electorates. Before the first set of reforms in 1832, 465 of the 658 MPs represented Boroughs, many of which had very small electorates; only seven had more than 5,000 for example, and 56 (the so-called 'rotten boroughs') had less than 50. Most of the County electorates were much larger, however, producing both malapportionment and the equivalent of gerrymandering. Electoral power was largely in the hands of the small number of enfranchised urban property owners.

The primary purpose of the three main nineteenth-century electoral reforms was to expand the franchise in response to public agitation. The electorate of England and Wales was only 435,391 in 1831 and this was increased to 652,777 by the 1832 Reform Act, but it was still less than 5 per cent of the adult male population. Subsequent Acts increased the electorate from 1.1 to 2 million (the 1867 Act) and then from $c.3$ million to $c.5$ million (the 1885 Act). Many of the newly enfranchised lived in urban areas, but not necessarily within the incorporated Boroughs, most of which were in rural southern England well away from the main centres of burgeoning industrialisation and urbanisation. Thus alongside the franchise extensions there were Redistribution Acts, whose main goals were to remove at least some of the malapportionment by taking seats from the small Boroughs and reallocating them either to rapidly growing Boroughs elsewhere or to Counties where there was massive population increase outwith the Borough boundaries (without increasing the size of the House of Commons). Increasingly, this involved the creation of single-member constituencies as divisions of Boroughs or Counties, a task undertaken by specially-appointed Boundary Commissions – although under clear instructions from Parliament which involved de facto gerrymandering (as with the 1885 instruction that 'special regard shall be had to the pursuits of the population' as well as the clear separation of urban from rural areas and electorates which are 'proximately equalised') in order to create constituencies that favoured one party over another.[2]

The next major reform came towards the end of the First World War, when the electorate was approximately tripled with the enfranchisement of all adult (i.e. over 21) males plus all females over 30; there was a further extension in 1928, when the age threshold for women was reduced to that for men. The former extension was accompanied by another redistribution, which involved clear rules to remove malapportionment: no Borough with a population of less than 50,000 was to be separately represented, for example, and the multiple of one MP per 70,000 residents was proposed for the allocation of constituencies to Counties and Boroughs. The Commissioners were also asked to follow the nineteenth-century practices of containing constituencies within individual Counties and Boroughs as far as possible, and of using smaller administrative areas (small boroughs, urban districts, rural districts and, if necessary, civil parishes in Counties; electoral wards in Boroughs) as the building blocks to create constituencies that were 'approximately equal' in population. The outcome was County constituencies in England having average populations of 68,287, with all but nine of the 310 having populations between 50,000 and 90,000, and 125 between 60,000 and 75,000. Borough constituencies had similar averages (72,871 in London and 73,644 elsewhere), but slightly greater variation.

Variations in constituency size are a normal consequence of population change: they may produce the equivalent of malapportionment if the areas of population decline generally favour one party whereas those of population growth favour another. This happened in the decade after the 1918 redistribution, and by 1936 an MP was complaining in the House that constituency electorates varied between 30,00 and 150,000. He pressed for a further redistribution, but the government's response was that although there were clearly some extreme cases ('striking anomalies') only 38 constituencies in England and Wales deviated by more than 50 per cent from the average electorate of *c*.50,000 voters. Furthermore, the government did not wish to conduct a redistribution while it was considering changes to local government boundaries, so the issue was not pressed (a repeat of the situation two years earlier when a Private Member's Bill proposing a redistribution with a permanent Electoral Distribution Commission and clear rules for constituency definition was neither debated nor voted on). Thus the constituencies created in 1918 remained in place until 1949.

The creation of a permanent structure for regular reviews of constituencies

The first official move to change constituencies after 1917 came as part of a wider concern with electoral matters during the Second World War. In preparation for post-war elections, a committee on the country's electoral machinery was established, chaired by the Registrar-General, Sir Sylvanus Vivian. The Vivian Committee's terms of reference included a request: 'To examine the technical problems involved in any scheme of redistribution of Parliamentary seats by way of preparation for consideration of the principles on which any scheme should be based'.

The Committee's general response to this (Vivian Committee, 1942, 14) was:

> The fundamental considerations giving rise to a need for the redistribution of seats, though elementary, are so important that we make no apology for recapitulating them. The essential basis of representative Government in this country is that the main representative body of the legislature should consist of persons elected under conditions which confer upon them an *equal representative status*. It is also a fundamental principle of our Parliamentary system that representation (with the exception of University constituencies) should be *territorial*. Both these features appear to us to be of the greatest importance. It follows from them that seats must be assigned to a series of local areas or communities each of which contains as equal as may be a share of the total number of persons to be represented.

Furthermore, the Committee recognised that 'population is at all times in motion', which calls for regular reviews of constituencies to ensure that disparities from the equality requirement do not become too great. Within this equality requirement, it then identified a number of principles on which redistribution should be based:

1 The need for a *quota*, or 'average of the number of persons to be represented per member' (para. 77), to serve as a standard for both evaluating the pre-existing situation and creating new constituencies.
2 The extent of the *limits of toleration* around that average, recognising that 'trifling' departures (para. 79) from the quota should not trigger a redistribution and arguing that no clear rule can be formulated – 'What degree of departure is to be accepted is in fact determined by the formulation of such limits. But in the application of both the quota and the limits of toleration rigid or artificial precision is not necessary or invariably possible' (para. 79).
3 The need for *continuity of constituencies* – 'we believe to be the general opinion that, other things being equal, the continuity of constituencies is a good thing' (para. 80). Change should only be proposed where necessary, and even then continuity should if possible be maintained by minor

adjustments only, for 'changes in any particular constituency can rarely fail to affect other adjoining constituencies; and the adjustment of even a single constituency may be found to react upon the surrounding constituencies over a gradually widening radius like the ripples from a stone thrown into a pond'.

4 The requirement to *conform to local government boundaries*, which was justified because these are 'the only defined, ascertained and recognised local boundaries which can be used for the demarcation of Parliamentary constituencies' (para. 83); because such boundaries are frequently adjusted, however, this will almost certainly require substantial redistributions of Parliamentary seats, if such events are undertaken at long time intervals.

5 The *assignment of seats* to the separate parts of the United Kingdom had been left to 'the fluid working of the quota and the limits of toleration' (para. 85) in 1918, within a prescribed maximum, but the number for each separate part (i.e. England, Northern Ireland, Scotland and Wales) could be prescribed: if it was not so determined, then 'it is imperative, of course, that the quota and the rules for its operation should operate uniformly throughout the whole area covered' (para. 87).

One issue on which the Committee disagreed was interpretation of the phrase 'the total of the persons to be represented', which could refer to either total population or qualified electorate. With a universal franchise the difference between the two should be slight, except for areas with large proportions of their population under the minimum voting age (then 21), but it claimed that the choice between the two definitions 'may have some small effect upon the allocation of seats as between England and Wales and Scotland' (para. 87).[3]

The Committee then addressed the operationalisation of these principles, arguing that a procedure should be established with three components: legislative enactment of the major principles, such as the electoral quota and the limits to toleration; statutory rules to determine how the principles are applied; and the appointment of an independent administrative body to undertake the redistributions, non-partisan in its composition but with the Speaker of the House of Commons as the nominal chair in order to provide a link with Parliament.[4] It also recommended that a review should be undertaken during the lifetime of each Parliament, i.e. at least once every five years. Such reviews should include the publication of provisional proposals for consultation, with 'local hearings … to enable representations or suggestions' as a probably necessary consequence.

The government's response to Vivian's recommendations was to establish a Speaker's Conference to prepare resolutions on the redistribution of seats (among other matters) on which legislation could be based.[5] It produced two main sets of recommendations, regarding the machinery for undertaking redistributions and the rules that would be applied. These became the basis of the 1944 *House of Commons (Redistribution of Seats) Act*.

Box 3.1   The recommendations of the 1944 Speaker's Conference regarding the machinery for constituency redistributions

Separate Commissions
There should be four separate Boundary Commissions:-one for England; one for Scotland; one for Wales and Monmouthshire; and one for Northern Ireland.

Chairman of the Commissions
The Speaker should be ex-officio Chairman of all four Commissions.

Deputy-Chairman
The Speaker should nominate one of the members of each Commission as Deputy-Chairman of the Commission

Party representations
Each separate Boundary Commission should sit (its Deputy-Chairman presiding) to hear any representations from the Chief or National Officers of the Party organ-isations with respect to the Commission's provisional proposals for redistribution.

Periodic reviews
Each Boundary Commission should be required to undertake, at intervals of not less than three years and not more than seven years, a general review of the rep-resentation in the House of Commons of that part of the United Kingdom with which it is concerned.

Special reports
The Boundary Commissions should, in addition, have authority to submit special reports at any time recommending changes in respect of any particular con-stituency or group of constituencies.

Action
The reports of the Boundary Commissions should be submitted to the Secretary of State concerned, and the Secretary of State should be required to lay every such report before Parliament, together with an Order in Council giving effect to any recommendations (with or without modification) for redistributions, and provid-ing for any consequential or incidental matters. Any such draft Order should be subject to affirmative resolutions.
There should, however, be a special provision that when the Boundary Commis-sions have made their first general reports with respect to the whole of the United Kingdom, effect should be given to this first comprehensive scheme by Bill, and not by Order in Council.

Box 3.1 shows the Conference's proposed machinery, which incorporates virtually all of Vivian's recommendations (on the frequency of reviews, however, it would not have been feasible to hold a review during the lifetime of each Parliament, because Parliament can be dissolved at any time during its five-year life). There were additional items, too, such as the establishment of separate Commissions for each of the four countries within the United Kingdom. The reason for this becomes clear from the proposed Rules (Box 3.2), which stipulate that there should be no reduction in the number of MPs representing Scotland and Wales (including Monmouthshire).

McLean (1995) has investigated the reason for this and discovered that it was at the direction of the Speaker. The Conference Minutes recorded that:

> It was pointed out that a strict application of the quota for the whole of Great Britain would result in a considerable decrease in the existing number of Scottish and Welsh seats, but that in practice, in view of the proposal that the Boundary Commissioners should be permitted to pay special consideration to geographical considerations, it was...unlikely that there would be any substantial reduction. It was strongly urged that ... it would be very desirable, on political grounds, to state from the outset quite clearly that the number of Scottish and Welsh seats should not be diminished. The absence of any such assurance might give rise to a good deal of political feeling and would lend support to the separatist movements in both countries.

Most of the Scottish and Welsh populations live in urban-industrial conurbations. Application of the 'special geographical considerations' provision (which the members intended to refer to sparsely populated, inaccessible areas) would therefore not prevent a reduction in Scottish and Welsh representation if a single electoral quota were applied to the whole of Great Britain. Hence the political decision to guarantee the current number of number of seats for Scotland and Wales, while capping the total for Great Britain – in effect, guaranteeing over-representation for Scotland and Wales (see below).

Box 3.2 The recommendations of the 1944 Speaker's Conference regarding the rules for constituency redistributions

Total number of MPs
The total number of Members of the House of Commons for Great Britain shall remain substantially as at present (i.e. 591, excluding University seats).

Special provision for Scotland and Wales
There shall be no reduction in the present number of Members of the House of Commons for Scotland or for Wales and Monmouthshire.

Redistribution basis
Redistribution shall be effected on the basis of the qualified electorate

Quota
The standard unit of electorate for each Member of the House of Commons for Great Britain shall be a quota ascertained by dividing the total electorate in Great Britain by the total number of seats in Great Britain (other than University seats) existing at the time the Boundary Commissioners report.

Limits of toleration
The Boundary Commissioners shall not be required to modify an existing constituency if its electorate falls short of or exceeds the quota by not more than approximately 25 per cent.

Double-member constituencies
Constituencies at present returning two Members shall be abolished, except where after local inquiry by the Boundary Commissioners it is found in any particular case that abolition is undesirable.

The local government template
The boundaries of Parliamentary constituencies shall, where convenient, coincide with the boundaries of local government administrative areas.

City of London
The City of London shall continue, as at present, to return two Members. (This Resolution was passed by a majority - Ayes 15; Noes 13.)

Northern Ireland
It shall be an Instruction to the Boundary Commissioners for Northern Ireland, in applying the foregoing rules, that there shall be no change in the present number of Members of the House of Commons for Northern Ireland, and that the quota for Northern Ireland shall be ascertained by dividing the total electorate by twelve (that is, the number of Northern Ireland seats, other than the University seat).

Discretionary Powers for the Boundary Commissioners
The Boundary Commissioners may depart from the strict application of these rules if special geographical considerations (including the area, shape and accessibility of a constituency) appear to them to render such a course desirable.

University constituencies
Nothing in the foregoing rules shall apply to University constituencies.

These proposals were embodied in a Bill which passed through Parliament with very little debate. The Act established the Commissions and its Third Schedule set out the Rules that they were to apply (Box 3.3). As well as establishing minimum levels of representation for Scotland and Wales, plus an inferred maximum for England (591 less the 106 allocated to Scotland and

Wales) and a fixed number for Northern Ireland, these incorporated two main redistribution principles:

1 a clearly specified electoral quota (Rule 8(1)) and limit of tolerance around that (Rule 4); and
2 a clear statement that constituencies should be contained within the major local government territories (Rule 5).

The Commissions were given the freedom to depart from these rules where 'special geographical considerations' suggested that they should (Rule 6).[6] In addition, the First Schedule to the Act set out the general procedure of public consultation to be employed during the redistribution process (Box 3.4). The Commissions were required to advertise what they were doing, but any further action (notably the holding of public inquiries) was discretionary.

Box 3.3   Rules for the Distribution of Seats, set out in the Third Schedule to the *House of Commons (Redistribution of Seats) Act 1944* and as amended in 1947

1 The number of constituencies in the several parts of the United Kingdom set out in the first column of the following table shall be as stated respectively in the second column of that table–

Part of the United Kingdom	*No. of Constituencies*
Great Britain	... Not substantially greater or less than 591
Scotland	... Not less than 71
Wales	... Not less than 35
Northern Ireland	... 12

2 (1) A two-member constituency within the meaning of the next following rule which is not divided or required to return a single member as therein provided shall, subject to any adjustment of its boundaries made in accordance with that rule, continue to return two members.
  (2) Every other constituency shall return a single member.

3 (1) Any two-member constituency, the electorate whereof is less than approximately thirty-seven twentieths of the electoral quota or more than approximately two and a half times that quota, shall be divided into or among two or more other constituencies:
  provided that, where the electorate of the constituency is less than approximately one and a quarter times the electoral quota, the constituency may, instead of being divided as aforesaid, be required to return a single member.
  (2) Any other two-member constituency shall be divided as aforesaid unless the Boundary Commission concerned, after causing a Local Inquiry to be held, are satisfied, having regard to any particular circumstances affecting the constituency, that it is undesirable so to divide it.

(3) Where the boundaries of a borough as last defined for the purpose of ascertaining the boundaries of a two-member constituency –

(a) do not include an area which is included within the boundaries of the borough as defined for local government purposes on the enumeration date; or

(b) include an area which is not included within the boundaries of the borough as so defined for local government purposes;

then-

(i) in reckoning the electorate of the constituency for the purpose of paragraph (1) of this rule, that area shall be included on or excluded from the constituency, as the case may be; and

(ii) if it is determined under paragraph (2) of this rule that the constituency shall not be divided as aforesaid, the boundaries of the borough shall be redefined, for the purposes of ascertaining the boundaries of the constituency, so as to include or exclude that area, as the case may be.

...

4   So far as is practicable having regard to rule 1 of these rules, the electorate of any constituency returning a single member shall not be greater or less than the electoral quota by more than approximately one quarter of the electoral quota.

5   (1) So far as is practicable having regard to the foregoing rules –

(a) in England and Wales,—

(i)   no county or any part thereof shall be included in a constituency which includes the whole or part of any other county or part of a county borough or metropolitan borough;

(ii) no county borough or any part thereof shall be included in a constituency which includes the whole or part of any other county borough or the whole or part of a metropolitan borough;

(iii) no metropolitan borough or any part thereof shall be included in a constituency which includes the whole or part of any other metropolitan borough;

(iv) no county district shall be included partly in one constituency and partly in another.

(b) in Scotland,—

(i)   no county or burgh shall be included partly in one parliamentary county and partly in another, or partly in a parliamentary county and partly in a parliamentary borough;

(ii) no burgh other than a county of a city shall be included partly in one constituency and partly in another.

(c) In Northern Ireland, no county district shall be included partly in one constituency and partly in another.

...

6   A Boundary Commission may depart from the strict application of the last two foregoing rules if special geographical considerations, including in particular the size, shape and accessibility of a constituency, appear to them to render a departure desirable.

7   Nothing in rules 2 to 6 of these rules shall apply to the City of London, but that City as constituted at the commencement of this Act shall continue to be a sep-

arate constituency, and shall return either two members or a single member as may be provided by the Act giving effect (whether with or without modifications) to the recommendations contained in the reports submitted by the Boundary Commissions under section three of this Act.

8 (1) For the purposes of these rules—

  (a) the expression 'electoral quota' means –

    (i) in the application of these rules to a constituency in Great Britain, a number obtained by dividing the electorate for Great Britain by the number of constituencies in Great Britain existing on the enumeration date, or, in applying these rules for the purposes of section three of this Act, by the number of such constituencies existing at the commencement of this Act, namely five hundred and ninety-one; and

    (ii) in the application of these rules to a constituency in Northern Ireland, a number obtained by dividing the electorate for Northern Ireland by the number of constituencies in Northern Ireland existing on the enumeration date.

  (b) the expression 'electorate', in relation ... to Great Britain or Northern Ireland, means the aggregate electorates as hereinbefore defined of all the constituencies therein.

These procedures and rules largely followed what had been done at previous redistributions (notably in 1885 and 1918), and codified the recommendations of the Vivian Committee (plus the 1934 Bill which was never voted on). Malapportionment was to be avoided by regular reviews and application of an electoral quota with prescribed tolerance limits; and gerrymandering precluded by delegating the task to an independent body (which might consult the public and political parties). Malapportionment was clearly considered the most important issue to be addressed by the Commissions, since it was addressed in Rule 4, the first to apply to single-member constituencies, and Rule 5, which makes fitting constituencies into the local government template conditional on meeting the electoral quota and tolerance limit. The Commissions' task, it seems, was to be governed by matters of arithmetic.

One aspect of the evolving procedure that was omitted from the legislation, however, concerned the building blocks for the constituencies: what spatial units within the Boroughs and Counties were to be used to define the constituencies? The Commissions decided to continue the established practice of using electoral wards as their building blocks (in fact they had no alternative, since – other than parishes, civil or ecclesiastical – no other units were available), but there is no requirement for that. The 1944 legislation (and the Speaker's Conference that preceded it) also included nothing that took account of the Vivian Committee's third principle (see above), regarding the continuity of constituencies. There was no constraint on the Commissions to limit the amount of change proposed.

Box 3.4   Aspects of the procedure to be adopted by the Boundary Commissions, set out in the Third Schedule to the *House of Commons (Redistribution of Seats) Act 1944*

...

3   Where a Commission have provisionally determined to make recommendations affecting any constituency, they shall publish in at least one newspaper cir-
culating in the constituency a notice stating –
   (a) the effect of the proposed recommendations and (except in a case where
      they propose to recommend that no alteration be made in respect of the
      (constituency) that a copy of the recommendations is open to inspection at
      a specified place within the constituency; and
   (b) that representations with respect to the proposed recommendations may be
      made to the Commission within one month after the publication of the
      notice;
      And the Commission shall take into consideration any representations duly
      made in accordance with any such notice.
4   A Commission may, if they think fit, cause a local inquiry to be held in respect
    of any constituency or constituencies.

....

   1 Subject to the foregoing provisions of this Schedule, each of the Commissions
      shall have power to regulate their own procedure.

Evolution of the legislation

The Boundary Commissions were established after passage of the 1944 Act, and immediately began work. They soon encountered difficulties with Rules 4 and 5, however, as later reported by the Boundary Commission for England (1947, 4, para. 8):

> The difficulties we encountered during our review of constituencies under the provisions of the Act of 1944 arose in the main from the fact that Rule 4 prescribed that the electorate of a constituency should not be greater or less than the electoral quota by more than approximately one quarter. We found that it was not practicable to give effect to this rule, having regard to the limiting provisions of rule 1, without disturbing the unity of local government areas, and in a number of instances, e.g. where the electorate or a borough was too large for a single member but too small to justify two members, we found it necessary to detach part of the borough and add it to an adjoining area ... .

The Commission (and its Welsh counterpart) convinced the Speaker that Rule 4 should be relaxed because, according to the then Home Secretary (cited in Butler, 1963, 84):

... in endeavouring to keep all constituencies within 25 per cent of the quota the Boundary Commissions had been forced to recommend the complete dismemberment for parliamentary purposes of many unified communities; the rules guiding the Commissioners would, therefore, have to be relaxed to allow them to preserve localities intact, although they would, of course, still aim to maintain approximate numerical equality.

The Act was thus amended, despite opposition charges of gerrymandering. Rule 4 was removed (Box 3.3), Rule 5 became Rule 4, and a new Rule 5 was introduced:

5A.–(1) The electorate of any constituency shall be as near the electoral quota as is practicable having regard to the foregoing rules: and a Boundary Commission may depart from the strict application of the last foregoing rule if it appears to them that a departure is desirable to avoid an excessive disparity between the electorate of any constituency and the electoral quota, or between the electorate thereof and that of neighbouring constituencies in the part of the United Kingdom with which they are concerned.

(2) For the purposes of this rule a constituency returning two members shall be treated as two constituencies.

This clearly downgraded the equal electorates requirement of the original Act, and elevated what one member referred to as the organic requirement – that constituency MPs should represent distinct communities as defined by local government areas – over the arithmetic.

The Commissions then produced their recommendations in 1948, when there were further opposition charges of partisan gerrymandering. The English Commission, it was revealed, had informed the Home Secretary of its concern regarding the under-representation of several large Boroughs, and the recommendations transmitted to Parliament had been modified by him accordingly, to incorporate a further 17 seats (all in large Boroughs and most likely to return Labour MPs). Another 12 amendments, proposed by individual MPs to alter the composition of seats in areas that they currently represented (presumably in most cases for their partisan advantage), were also accepted by the Home Secretary and included in the final legislation.

When the Initial Review was complete, the government promoted a new Bill to abolish both the two-member constituencies (hence simplifying the Rules: Box 3.5) and University representation plus remove the special treatment of the City of London. (The latter was a particular concern of Conservatives while businessmen had a separate vote at their place of work as well as at their place of residence; this was abolished in 1948.) The growth of the House of Commons was also recognised by increasing the prescribed maximum for Great Britain to 613. The new Rules, in the Second Schedule to the *House of Commons (Redistribution of Seats) Act 1949* (Box 3.5), provided the context within which the Commissions undertook their First Periodical Reviews, which were reported to Parliament in November 1954.

Box 3.5   Rules for the Redistribution of Seats, set out in the Second Schedule to the *House of Commons (Redistribution of Seats) Act 1949*

1   The number of constituencies in the several parts of the United Kingdom set out in the first column of the following table shall be as stated respectively in the second column of that table –

Part of the United Kingdom   No. of Constituencies
Great Britain   ...   Not substantially greater or less than 613
Scotland   ...   Not less than 71
Wales   ...   Not less than 35
Northern Ireland   ...   12

2   Every constituency shall return a single member.

3   There shall continue to be a constituency which shall include the whole of the City of London and the name of which shall refer to the City of London.

4–(1) So far as is practicable having regard to the foregoing rules –

  (a) in England and Wales, –

  (i)   no county or any part thereof shall be included in a constituency which includes the whole or part of any other county or part of a county borough or metropolitan borough;

  (ii) no county borough or any part thereof shall be included in a constituency which includes the whole or part of any other county borough or the whole or part of a metropolitan borough;

  (iii) no metropolitan borough or any part thereof shall be included in a constituency which includes the whole or part of any other metropolitan borough;

  (iv) no county district shall be included partly in one constituency and partly in another.

  (b) in Scotland, no burgh other than a county of a city shall be included partly in one constituency and partly in another;

  (c) In Northern Ireland, no county district shall be included partly in one constituency and partly in another.

  (2) In paragraph (1) of this rule the following expressions have the following meanings, that is to say: –

  'county' means an administrative county other than the county of London; 'county borough' has the same meaning as in the Local Government Act, 1933;

  'county district' has, in sub-paragraph (a) the same meaning as in the Local Government Act, 1933, and, in sub-paragraph (c), the same meaning as in the Local Government (Ireland) Act, 1898.

5   The electorate of any constituency shall be as near the electoral quota as is practicable having regard to the foregoing rules: and a Boundary Commission may depart from the strict application of the last foregoing rule if it appears to them that a departure is desirable to avoid an excessive disparity between the electorate of any constituency and the electoral quota, or between the electorate thereof and that of neighbouring constituencies in the part of the United

Kingdom with which they are concerned.

6 A Boundary Commission may depart from the strict application of the last two foregoing rules if special geographical considerations, including in particular the size, shape and accessibility of a constituency, appear to them to render a departure desirable.

7 For the purposes of these rules –

(a) the expression 'electoral quota' means –

(i) in the application of these rules to a constituency in Great Britain, a number obtained by dividing the electorate for Great Britain by the number of constituencies in Great Britain existing on the enumeration date;

(ii) in the application of these rules to a constituency in Northern Ireland, a number obtained by dividing the electorate for Northern Ireland by the number of constituencies in Northern Ireland existing on the enumeration date.

(b) the expression 'electorate' means –

(i) in relation to a constituency, the number of persons whose names appear on the register of parliamentary electors in force on the enumeration date under the Representation of the People Acts for the constituency; and

(ii) in relation to Great Britain or Northern Ireland, the aggregate electorates as hereinbefore defined of all the constituencies therein;

(c) the expression 'enumeration date' means, in relation to any report of a Boundary Commission under this Act, the date on which the notice with respect to that report is published in accordance with section two of this Act.

Occurring within seven years of the Initial Review, this first reconsideration of boundaries involved relatively little change in many constituency electorates. Continuity was thus the norm, with the Commissions recommending no changes to 402 of the 625 constituencies: change was least in Wales (with 83 per cent of constituencies unaltered) and greatest in Northern Ireland (only 42 per cent were unchanged – the figures for England and Scotland were 64 and 62 per cent, respectively). Nevertheless, the changes proposed concerned MPs, who felt that boundaries were being moved for relatively trivial arithmetic reasons, causing 'chaos and confusion' for the parties and making it difficult for MPs to develop close links with their constituents. They also claimed that the public consultation procedures were not working well, and called for more justification of their recommendations from the Commissions. These complaints were acted upon by the government, which brought forward amendments in 1958 that increased the period between Reviews from 5–7 to 10–15 years (i.e. on average from *c.*6 to *c.*12 years) and, according to the then Home Secretary, introduced a 'presumption against making changes unless there is a very strong case for them', providing a 'reasonable period of stability' while ensuring that 'gross differences or disparities' do not emerge. The relevant wording was included in the 1949 Act as a new Rule 7, under the title *General and Supplementary*, stating that:

> It shall not be the duty of a Boundary Commission, in discharging their functions under the said section two, to aim at giving full effect in all circumstances to the rules set out in the Second Schedule to the principal Act, but they shall take account, so far as they reasonably can, of the inconveniences attendant on alterations of constituencies other than alterations made for the purposes of rule 4 of those rules, and of any local ties which would be broken by such alterations; ...

The issue of public consultation was addressed by removing much of the Commissions' discretion with regard to the holding of Local Inquiries: the relevant wording (in clause 4 of the Act: Box 3.6) effectively means that

---

Box 3.6   The requirements for public consultation, set out in the *House of Commons (Redistribution of Seats) Act 1958*

4–(1) Where a Boundary Commission revise any proposed recommendations after publishing a notice of them under paragraph 3 of Part III of the First Schedule to the principal Act, the Commission shall comply again with that paragraph in relation to the revised recommendations, as if no earlier notice had been published.

(2) Where, on the publication of the notice...of a recommendation of a Boundary Commission for the alteration of any constituencies, the Commission receive any representation objecting to the proposed recommendation from an interested authority or from a body of electors numbering one hundred or more, the Commission shall not make the recommendation unless, since the publication of the said notice, a Local Inquiry has been held in respect of the constituencies...:

   Provided that, where a local inquiry was held in respect of the constituencies before the publication of the said notice, this subsection shall not apply if the Commission, after considering the matters discussed at the local inquiry, the nature of the representations received on the publication of the said notice and any other relevant circumstances, are of the opinion that a further local inquiry would not be justified.

(3) In the last foregoing subsection, 'interested authority' and 'elector' respectively mean, in relation to any recommendation, a local authority whose area is wholly or partly comprised in the constituencies affected by the recommendation, and a parliamentary elector for any of these constituencies; and for this purpose 'local authority' means the council of any county, or any borough (including a metropolitan borough) or of any urban or rural district.

(4) In the application of the last foregoing subsection to Scotland, for the reference to a borough there shall be substituted a reference to a burgh, and for a reference to an urban or ...

objections from either an impacted local authority (i.e. one within the area covered by the recommendations) or political party became sufficient to trigger a Local Inquiry.

Finally, the 1958 Act dealt with an issue raised by the English Commission. The 1949 Act sets an electoral quota for Great Britain and stipulates a minimum number of seats in each of Scotland and Wales. Because the quota was determined by dividing the Great Britain electorate by the current number of constituencies (including c.100 in Scotland and Wales which were substantially smaller than those in England – the average constituency in England had 56,562 electors after the First Review, compared with 47,990 in Scotland and 50,363 in Wales), the national quota would always suggest a substantial increase in the number of English constituencies. To avoid this (and thereby to ensure the continued over-representation of Scotland and Wales, for so long as their populations continued to grow more slowly than England's), the Rule was changed to require a separate quota for each country (see Box 3.7).

Changes since 1958

The rules and procedures set out in the 1958 Act remain largely in place to the present, and three further Reviews (reporting in 1969, 1983 and 1995) have been completed.[7] The only major changes have been:

1 the very substantial restructuring of local government in the early 1970s, which removed a major tier of administration, simplified Rule 4 (Box 3.5) and as a consequence substantially reduced the 'organic' constraints on the Commissions;
2 the decision in 1979 to increase Northern Ireland's representation, consequent on the failure of devolved government there and the suspension of the Stormont Assembly, from 12 to 16–18 seats; and
3 the decision in 1992 to reduce the time period between Reviews from 10–15 to 8–12 years.

The current Rules were consolidated in the 1986 *House of Commons (Redistribution of Seats) Act* (Table 3.7), and they were still in use for the Fifth Periodic Review, which began in England in 2000.[8] There has been debate about certain aspects of them – as discussed in later chapters – and the *Scotland Act 1998* changes them for the Fifth Periodic Review only (for that review alone, the Boundary Commission for Scotland must use the electoral quota determined by the English Commission, in order to remove Scottish over-representation consequent on the creation of the separate Scottish Parliament, for which the first elections were held in 1999).

One other 'change' during this period concerned an attempt by the leadership of the Labour party to delay the implementation of the Third Periodic

Box 3.7   Rules for the Redistribution of seats, set out in the Second Schedule to the *Parliamentary Constituencies Act 1986*

RULES FOR REDISTRIBUTION OF SEATS

The rules

1–(1) the number of constituencies in Great Britain shall not be substantially greater or less than 613.

(2) The number of constituencies in Scotland shall not be less than 71.

(3) The number of constituencies in Wales shall not be less than 35.

(4) The number of constituencies in Northern Ireland shall not be greater than 18 or less than 16, and shall be 17 unless it appears to the Boundary Commission for Northern Ireland that Northern Ireland should for the time being be divided into 16 or (as the case may be) into 18 constituencies.

2   Every constituency shall return a single member.

3   There shall continue to be a constituency which shall include the whole of the City of London and the name of which shall refer to the City of London.

4–(1) So far as is practicable having regard to rules 1 to 3 –

(a) in England and Wales, –

(i) no county or any part thereof shall be included in a constituency which includes the whole or part of any other county or the whole or part of a London borough,

(ii) no London borough or any part of a London borough shall be included in a constituency which includes the whole or part of any other London borough,

(b) in Scotland, regard shall be had to the boundaries of local authority areas;

(c) in Northern Ireland, no ward shall be included partly in one constituency and partly in another.

(2) In sub-paragraph (1)(b) above 'area' and 'local authority' have the same meanings as in the Local Government (Scotland) Act 1973.

5   The electorate of any constituency shall be as near the electoral quota as is practicable having regard to rules 1 to 4: and a Boundary Commission may depart from the strict application of rule 4 if it appears to them that a departure is desirable to avoid an excessive disparity between the electorate of any constituency and the electoral quota, or between the electorate thereof and that of neighbouring constituencies in the part of the United Kingdom with which they are concerned.

6   A Boundary Commission may depart from the strict application of the rules 4 and 5 if special geographical considerations, including in particular the size, shape and accessibility of a constituency, appear to them to render a departure desirable.

General and supplementary

7   It shall not be the duty of a Boundary Commission to aim at giving full effect in all circumstances to the above rules, but they shall take account, so far as they reasonably can –

(a) of the inconveniences attendant on alterations of constituencies other than alterations made for the purposes of rule 4, and

(b) of any local ties which would be broken by such alterations.

8 In the application of rule 5 to each part of the United Kingdom for which there is a Boundary Commission -

(a) the expression 'electoral quota' means a number obtained by dividing the electorate for that part of the United Kingdom by the number of constituencies in it existing on the enumeration date,

(b) the expression 'electorate' means—

(i) in relation to a constituency, the number of persons whose names appear on the register of parliamentary electors in force on the enumeration date under the Representation of the People Acts for the constituency; and

(ii) in relation to the part of the United Kingdom, the aggregate electorates as defined in sub-paragraph (i) above of all the constituencies in that part,

(c) the expression "enumeration date" means, in relation to any report of a Boundary Commission under this Act, the date on which the notice with respect to that report is published in accordance with section 5(1) of this Act.

In this Schedule, a reference to a rule followed by a number is a reference to the rule set out in the correspondingly numbered paragraph of this Schedule.

Review by challenging the Boundary Commission for England's work. The challenge was lost in the Court of Appeal, but the earlier judgment in the Queen's Bench did claim that the rules up to Rule 7 were 'guidelines only', whereas the wording of Rule 7 made it mandatory for the Commissions to take account of the criteria set down there – the disruptions that might be caused by changes to constituency boundaries, and the community ties that might be broken. Although the Commission was aware of this when it conducted the Fourth Periodic Review, there is little evidence that it had a major impact on its work – nor on the Scottish Commission's, whose Deputy Chairman questioned the ruling in the 1980s. (For further information, see Chapter 5.)

Differences between the countries

The Rules set out in the 1986 Act apply across the whole of the United Kingdom, with a few small exceptions regarding the local government template. In Scotland the 1970s local government reforms abolished the Counties and Burghs, replacing them by nine Regions, divided into Districts, plus three separate Island Authorities. The original wording in the *Local Government (Scotland) Bill 1973* was that 'no region or part thereof shall be included in a constituency which includes the whole or part of any other region' but the

Scottish Grand Committee argued against this, because the new regional boundaries cut across many existing constituencies and so there would be much disruption at the next redistribution. Thus the wording of the final Act merely stated that 'regard shall be had to the boundaries of local government areas', a much weaker requirement than in England and Wales. In Northern Ireland, the six Counties were also abolished in those reforms, being replaced with a single tier of Districts. These are not mentioned in the *House of Commons (Redistribution of Seats) Act 1986*, however, where the only reference is to wards, which should not be subdivided.[9] This gives much greater flexibility to the Boundary Commission for Northern Ireland than to the other three. In effect, it has to treat the entire Province as a single area, which creates problems when deciding which parts of it should be covered by different Local Inquiries.[10]

Local government reforms in the 1990s created totally new structures in Scotland and Wales, plus a mélange in England. In the first two, the existing structure was entirely removed, being replaced by a set of unitary authorities (32 in Scotland and 22 in Wales). There were no consequential amendments to the *House of Commons (Redistribution of Seats) Act 1986* in the *Local Government (Scotland) Act 1993*, so it must be assumed that the Boundary Commission for Scotland is merely required to have regard to those new boundaries. For Wales, however, the Boundary Commission for Wales pointed out that it would face great difficulties if required to use the new local government map as the template for allocating constituencies; and the *Local Government (Wales) Act 1993* retained the eight existing Welsh Counties solely for the purpose of allocating constituencies: they are termed the 'preserved counties'. In England, a Local Government Commission was given the task of reviewing the local government structure in the non-metropolitan 'Shire Counties' in the light of public opinion. Although the government's expectation was that in most Counties the two-tier structure would be replaced by unitary authorities, in most parts of the country the original structure was retained; only the Counties of Avon, Berkshire, Cleveland and Humberside were dissolved and replaced by series of unitary authorities. Elsewhere, 46 large urban areas were created as unitary authorities and separated from their former Counties, the Counties of Hereford and Worcester were split into their former separate parts, and the County of Rutland was recreated (as a unitary authority). Again, there was no consequential legislation amending the *House of Commons (Redistribution of Seats) Act 1986*, and for its Fifth Review the Boundary Commission for England is treating those new unitary authorities as separate areas for the allocation of constituencies (except the six created from what was formerly Berkshire since they, unlike the remainder, have not been designated as county equivalents).

These differences between the four constituent countries of the United Kingdom are operational, and have little effect on the disproportionality and bias in election results. But there is one major difference that does have such an impact, and this is largely because of Rule 1. This

1 sets minimum representation for Scotland and Wales;
2 sets both a minimum and a maximum for Northern Ireland; but
3 makes no mention of England and sets only a general target for Great Britain, including the imprecise term 'not be substantially greater or less than 613'.

A consequence of the first and third of these could be that the number of seats in England is determined (or at least strongly influenced) by the decisions of the Scottish and Welsh Commissions, although this does not appear to have been the case. The English Commission has operated independently of the other two.

One further consequence, however, has been an increasing gap between England, on the one hand, and Scotland and Wales, on the other, in their average constituency electorates. This has developed because of three inter-acting factors: the minima specified for Scotland and Wales; the faster growth of the English electorate; and the operation of Rules 6 and 8. The result has been that whereas the average English constituency electorate increased by 16.8 per cent between the Initial and Fourth Reviews, the figures for Scotland and Wales are 10.0 and 7.6, respectively. The gap between the average English and Scottish constituency electorates is now 14,057 voters, and 13,067 between the English and Welsh (Table 3.1).

Table 3.1 The average number of electors per constituency*

	Initial	First	Second	Third	Fourth
England	58,734	56,562	58,192	64,873	68,626
		(–3.7)	(+2.9)	(+11.5)	(+5.8)
Scotland	49,620	47,990	47,670	52,904	54,569
		(–3.3)	(–0.7)	(+11.0)	(+3.1)
Wales	51,641	50,363	50,366	55,660	55,559
		(–2.5)	(+0.0)	(+10.5)	(–0.0)
Northern Ireland	71,457	72,913	76,405	61,206	64,082
		(+2.0)	(+4.8)	(–19.9)	(+4.8)

* Excluding University constituencies. The figures in brackets indicate the percentage change in the number of electors per constituency between Reviews.

The importance of Rules 6 to 8 in this comes about because of what Butler and McLean (1996, 25–8) describe as a 'ratchet effect'. Under the 1958 Act, each country has its own electoral quota obtained by dividing the national electorate on the enumeration date by the existing number of constituencies there. As a result, the faster the population growth, the larger the quota – which has operated against England and in favour of Scotland and Wales. In addition,

Commissions are allowed under Rule 6 to invoke 'special geographical considerations' to justify overriding the preceding Rules. This has almost invariably been used to justify creating small constituencies (in terms of electors but not area) in relatively remote and inaccessible areas.[11] The Commissions have been increasingly sparing in invoking this Rule, and in the Fourth Review there was only one additional constituency in each of Scotland and Wales under this Rule, and none in England; there were seven such constituencies in the Third Review, however. These additional constituencies are included in the denominator used in the calculation under Rule 8; thus the more there are, the smaller the quota. It may be that the Commission still decides there is a need for additional constituencies in remote areas (basically Gwynedd in Wales and the Highlands and Islands in Scotland), so that despite the low quota, relative to England's, additional constituencies are justified yet again.

In addition to this aspect of the ratchet effect, Butler and McLean argue that the use of local government areas for the allocation of constituencies, plus the rule requiring that the boundaries of major local government areas not be crossed save in exceptional circumstances,[12] further exacerbates the 'ratchet effect'. Most Counties and Boroughs are entitled to fractional numbers of seats, and there is generally more 'rounding up' than 'rounding down' – in part because of the 'harmonic mean effect'[13] – which adds to the total number even further. This is not the case in Northern Ireland, where a maximum is specified, plus in Scotland, where the rule regarding regional boundaries is weaker (see above) and in its Fourth Review the Commission determined not to increase Scotland's number of constituencies. In Wales, however, the Fourth Review added two further constituencies and the Welsh Commission argued in its final report that a 41st would probably have to be added in the Fifth Review if the rules were unchanged, even if the total electorate remained the same.

As a result of this 'ratchet effect', which Butler and McLean claim has probably been exacerbated by Rule 7, which constrains the amount of change and therefore can lead to the Commissions deciding to retain relatively small constituencies, the number of MPs in the House of Commons has increased from 625 after the Initial Review in 1947 to 659 after the Fourth, 48 years later. This is of only marginal interest to our major arguments here about disproportionality and bias. For us the important issue is that, although most of the growth in representation has been in England (from 506 to 529 constituencies) this has not been commensurate with its relative growth of number of electors – with the consequence being Scottish and Welsh over-representation.

How the Commissions proceed

How do the Commissions operate within these Rules and procedural guidelines? The English, Scottish and Welsh Commissions now work in the following general way:

1 Having decided to conduct a Review, the electoral quota is determined using the figures for the total electorate on what is deemed the 'enumeration date'.[14]

2 This quota is then applied to each local government unit covered by the Rules, to determine its 'theoretical entitlement' in terms of number of seats.[15]

3 If considered necessary, adjacent local government units are then combined to make for more equitable seat allocations.

4 Provisional recommendations are determined for the composition of each constituency in each local government area, using local government electoral wards as the building blocks, in the light of the criteria set out in the rules and, as discussed below, government advice regarding their interpretation – not crossing local government boundaries, achieving electoral equality across constituencies, recognising special geographical considerations and paying heed to the disruption that can follow changes and the undesirability of breaking local community ties;

5. The provisional recommendations are published in the relevant local press and representations are called for – both positive and negative – and, if necessary, a Local Inquiry is held to hear further evidence, conducted by an Assistant Commissioner.

6 The provisional recommendations are reconsidered in the light of the Assistant Commissioner's report, and revised recommendations may be published: if they are, further representations are invited and a second Local Inquiry may be necessary.

7 Final recommendations are drawn up and submitted to the relevant Secretary of State for presentation to Parliament.

The Northern Ireland Commission does not have to undertake the second and third steps; rather it has to decide how many constituencies should be recommended, and then it moves straight to the fourth step. It may decide to change the number of constituencies recommended in the light of representations received and Assistant Commissioners' reports, as may the other three Commissions.

Table 3.2 Redistribution in Cornwall and the Isles of Scilly, 1995

| | Electorate | |
Constituency	1976	1991
Falmouth and Camborne	61,888	71,220
North Cornwall	61,160	76,804
St. Ives	62,114	72,115
South East Cornwall	57,848	73,930
Truro	64,190	75,799

Key to columns: 1976 – 1976 electorate; 1991 – 1991 electorate in finally recommended constituencies.

We illustrate the procedure with reference to four English counties at the Fourth Periodic Review. One of the Commission's easiest tasks was its consideration of Cornwall and the Isles of Scilly. At the Third Periodic Review, these had been allocated five constituencies: they were entitled to 4.67 against the electoral quota of 68,534, and the five had average electorates of 61,440, with the largest deviation from this 3118, 5.1 per cent of the average. (The Third Periodic Review used electoral data for 1976 to determine the electoral quota.) By 1991, these five constituencies differed relatively little in their electorates, with an average of 73,974 and the largest deviation from this only 2830 (North Cornwall: Table 3.2): the difference between the largest and the smallest constituency was 5584 voters, only slightly larger than the 4950 when the constituencies were defined using 1976 data. The Commission decided that this was insufficient to warrant disruptive change, and provisionally recommended that the same constituencies be retained. It received only two representations, one supporting its proposal and the other asking that the Truro constituency be renamed Truro and St. Austell: it conceded the latter point, and no further action was taken.

Northamptonshire had been allocated six constituencies in the Third Review (Table 3.3). Its entitlement increased substantially by the Fourth (from 5.50 to 6.32), but the number of constituencies was six in each case. Five of the six defined in the Third Review were very similar in size according to the 1991 electoral data, so the Commission proposed only small changes to reduce the size of Northampton North. This involved switching six wards from that constituency to neighbouring Daventry, and a compensating shift of three more from Daventry to Kettering. The six provisionally recommended constituencies then varied by 5961 electors, a reduction from 11,326. These proposals stimulated 35 representations and a Local Inquiry was held, after which the Assistant Commissioner recommended that the

Table 3.3   Redistribution in Northamptonshire, 1995

| Constituency | Electorate | | | |
	1976	1991	1991P	1991F
Corby	60,525	69,187	69,187	69,187
Daventry	57,165	72,264	75,148	75,148
Kettering	59,757	68,720	72,383	72,383
Northampton North	60,528	73,395	73,395	73,395
Northampton South	59,317	80,046	73,499	73,499
Wellingborough	64,176	74,291	74,291	74,291

Key to columns: 1976 – 1976 electorate; 1991 – 1991 electorate; 1991P –1991 electorate in provisionally recommended constituencies; 1991F – 1991 electorate in finally recommended constituencies.

provisional recommendations be retained, a course of action that the Commission accepted.

The neighbouring county of Oxfordshire also had six constituencies allocated in the Third Review, against an entitlement of 5.50; its entitlement in the Fourth was 6.06, and six seats were again allocated. By 1991, however, a difference of 14,757 electors had evolved between the largest and smallest constituency (Table 3.4), and the Commission decided to recommend changes to all six to produce greater equality: the range of electorates in its provisional recommendations was 5296, approximately one-third of the pre-redistribution situation. The Commission received 127 representations about these, including six petitions containing 756 signatures. After the Local Inquiry, the Assistant Commissioner suggested changes to all six constituencies, which met most of the issues raised but increased the disparity in electorates to 11,526, which the Commission considered 'acceptable' though 'not as good as in our provisional recommendations'. It implemented them all in its revised recommendations, which stimulated a further 30 representations, of which eight questioned some of the proposed changes involving the City of Oxford. The Commission decided that no new points had been raised that were not considered at the Local Inquiry, however, and recommended no further changes.

Table 3.4   Redistribution in Oxfordshire, 1995

| Constituency | Electorate | | | |
	1976	1991	1991P	1991F
Banbury	58,010	72,322	67,959	69,577
Henley	58,128	65,192	69,305	66,340
Oxford East	61,372	63,585	73,255	68,309
Oxford West and Abingdon	63,286	72,377	71,459	77,866
Wantage	58,262	68,237	69,490	68,237
Witney	62,629	78,342	68,587	69,746

Key to columns: 1976 – 1976 electorate; 1991 – 1991 electorate; 1991P –1991 electorate in provisionally recommended constituencies; 1991F – 1991 electorate in finally recommended constituencies.

Finally, Wiltshire had been allocated five constituencies in the Third Review (its entitlement then was 5.43). By 1991 its entitlement against the new quota was 6.21, and the Commission decided to allocate it an additional seat. Much of the growth had been in the town of Swindon and its surrounding villages, and the sixth seat was placed there, involving two Swindon constituencies (Table 3.5). Inserting a new constituency had a domino effect through the rest of the County, and the provisional recommendations involved changes to each of the other four. These stimulated 171 representations, most of them objecting to some aspect of the recommendations, together affecting all six constituencies. After a lengthy Inquiry, the Assistant Commissioner recommended changes to all six, which the Commission accepted, even though they increased the disparity between the largest and smallest electorate from 5689 to 11,664. (The smallest of the six constituencies were those designated for Swindon, presented to the Commission as the 'fastest growing industrial town in Western Europe'.) A further 512 representations were received, most of them focusing on either inclusion of the small town of Cricklade in the North Swindon constituency or including the towns of Calne and Melksham in Devizes constituency rather than keeping the former in North Wiltshire and the latter in Westbury. Again, the Commission was unconvinced, and its final recommendations were unaltered.

Table 3.5   Redistribution in Wiltshire, 1995

Constituency	Electorate			
	1976	1991	1991P	1991F
Devizes	77,717	90,208	70,122	75,555
North Wiltshire	70,284	83,347	72,456	71,312
Salisbury	70,072	76,194	74,333	76,194
Swindon	67,686	90,343	–	–
North Swindon	–	–	72,776	64,530
South Swindon	–	–	68,644	68,197
Westbury	71,548	88,185	71,946	74,489

Key to columns: 1976 – 1976 electorate; 1991 – 1991 electorate; 1991P – 1991 electorate in provisionally recommended constituencies; 1991F – 1991 electorate in finally recommended constituencies.

These four brief examples illustrate the procedure that the Commissions undertake, without exhausting all of the scenarios. In two other Counties, for example, the English Commission found it necessary to hold a second Inquiry before finalising its Fourth Review recommendations. In general, the result of the public consultation process was that inter-constituency disparities were increased; the average deviation between a constituency electorate and the County or Borough average in the provisional recommendations was 3.62 per cent, for example, with a standard deviation of 3.08; in the final recommendations the average was 4.22 and the standard deviation 3.22. Most of the changes resulted from arguments regarding local ties and minimising disruption to constituencies. In Nottinghamshire, for example, the Commission provisionally recommended that six of the county's constituencies should be unchanged, with minor changes to the other five. The public consultation convinced it that all 11 should be unchanged, increasing the average deviation around the average electorate for all eleven from 1.90 to 3.40 per cent.

Just as the Commissions are bound to recommend substantial changes in Counties which are to receive additional constituencies, so major disruption is inevitable where the entitlement to constituencies declines – mainly in Metropolitan Counties and the London Boroughs. To cater with this, both before and after the public consultation process, the Commissions have increasingly recommended crossing the major local government boundaries covered by Rule 4 (Box 3.7). In Scotland, for example, the Commission was determined not to increase the total number of constituencies at the Fourth Review (for reasons discussed further in Chapter 5), and this led it to create two pairs of Regions (Border and Lothians, and Central and Tayside). Three provisionally recommended constituencies crossed Regional boundaries, but this was reduced to two in the final recommendations. In England, two constituencies were created which crossed Borough boundaries within the Metropolitan Counties in the Third Review. This was increased to 13 in the Fourth Review, stimulating many representations. In addition, London Borough boundaries were crossed in eight cases.

The geographical and electoral constraints of redistribution

As a generalisation, the Commissions' provisional recommendations are constructed to reduce the disparity between constituency electorates, within the constraints of the local government template and recognising the need to minimise disruption and not break community ties. The public consultation process, on the other hand, pays relatively little attention to the issue of electoral equality, and concentrates almost exclusively on community ties and minimising disruption. This is because the main participants in that process – especially at the Local Inquiries conducted by Assistant Commissioners – are the political parties and their allies. Their goal is to achieve as many constituencies as possible which they believe that they can win at general elections – in effect, to gerrymander. They can only do that by convincing the Assistant Commissioner that one configuration of wards into constituencies is better than any other, and by using arguments that are non-electoral (i.e. they cannot say that we prefer this because we are more likely to win there: they must use other arguments, based on the criteria set out in the Rules – which could include constituency size, but rarely do). Other groups and private individuals do submit representations, and some appear at the Local Inquiries. Evaluation of the process suggests that the oral arguments at the Inquiries are much more effective than written representations, and that the Inquiries in particular are dominated by the parties, who increasingly (as we shall see below) have researched the situation extensively and employ barristers to present their case and cross-examine those presenting others. (The other substantial group of participants at the Inquiries are local government officers, most of whom are presenting arguments for

particular sets of constituencies determined by the politicians who control their authorities.)

Both the Commissions and the participants in the public consultation process are operating under the same geographic constraints – of the type illustrated with the theoretical examples in the previous chapter. For whichever area they are dealing with, they have a set of wards to combine into a smaller number of constituencies. Those constituencies should comprise a set of contiguous wards, be as equal as practicable in their electorates, and as similar as possible to the constituencies currently being used. For the Commissions, this means that there is a limited (though possibly large) number of possible constituency configurations that meets their criteria, from which they must choose. For the political parties, those alternatives are also assessed for their likely electoral consequences.

We illustrate these geographic constraints with a further set of brief examples, selected from the Second Review because we have better political information about the building blocks used then. In 1979, the general election was held on the same day as the local government elections in many parts of the country. As a consequence, turnout at the local elections was very much higher than the norm, and with a small number of exceptions the result in each ward is a good indication of the general pattern of support for the parties there.

To start with, we consider Sheffield, which consisted of 27 wards that had to be grouped in six constituencies. Labour was by far the strongest party there, getting some 65 per cent of the votes at the 1979 election. Its support was greatest in the central, eastern and northern parts of the city, however, and it was very much weaker in the west (Figure 3.1: the Liberal party had little support in 1979, apart from a small number of wards in the northwest).[16] How many different sets of six constituencies could be produced for Sheffield? This question was initially posed by Graham Gudgin and Peter Taylor, who developed a computer algorithm to identify a random selection of all possible sets of constituencies within a city, and was extended by David Rossiter and Ron Johnston, who wrote a program to identify all of them within given constraints, such as a maximum deviation from the average constituency electorate.[17] For Sheffield, 15,937 different solutions were identified, with a maximum deviation from the electoral quota in each case of 12 per cent. (This was chosen because the Commission's provisional recommendation had a maximum deviation of 10.9 per cent.)[18]

Clearly, the Commission would not have evaluated more than a very small proportion of this total. Inspection of a sample showed that many involved one or more constituencies with very odd shapes, and so a shape index was devised that measured the compactness of each set of six constituencies: the larger the index, the more compact all six constituencies.[19] Of the 15,937 potential solutions identified, 774 had an index of 901 or greater, of which 11 had an index exceeding 1000. The solution recommended by the Commissions had an index of 950.

Figure 3.1 Sheffield's wards in 1979, showing the estimated percentage of votes won in each by the Labour party

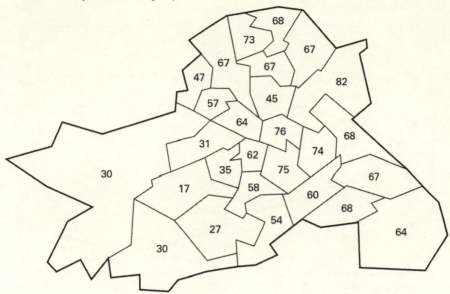

For the political parties, the most important issue is neither electoral equality nor shape, of course, but electoral outcome. What, given the overall level and geography of support shown in Figure 3.1, would have been the electoral outcome of the different constituency configurations? The geography of Labour's support shown in Figure 3.1 suggests that one seat at least would almost certainly have gone to the Conservatives, given its strength in the southwest of the city. On the other hand, it would be difficult for the Conservatives to win more than one, because of their weakness over most of the rest of Sheffield; the situation reflects a packed rather than a cracked gerrymander (using the terms introduced in the last chapter). Indeed, Labour would win five of the city's six seats in 12,327 of the 15,937 solutions identified, with a further 2913 indicating a 4:2 division and the remaining 697 having Labour win all six seats. (The Commission's final recommended solution resulted in five Labour victories at each of the subsequent elections.)

Of course, the prudent political party is interested not only in what number of seats it would win with a set percentage of the votes, but also how that might change if it won either more or less votes. To evaluate this for Sheffield we have estimated the number of seats for Labour with swings both to and away from it of up to 4 percentage points, uniformly across all of the city's wards. Figure 3.2 shows the results as the percentages of the solutions that would give Labour 3, 4, 5 or all 6 seats. At the existing vote distribution (i.e. a zero swing on the horizontal axis) Labour would win five of the six seats in almost 80 per cent of the solutions. If there were a swing of 4 points to the

Figure 3.2   The percentage of seats that would be won by the Conservatives and Labour in Sheffield at different levels of swing away from the position indicated by the 1979 local election results

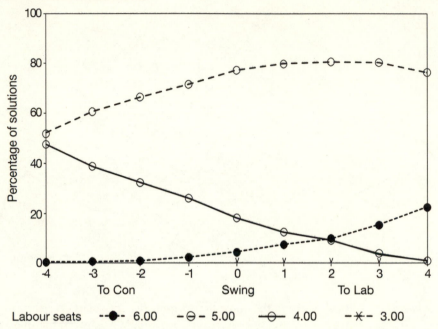

Conservatives (i.e. to the left-hand edge of the diagram), however, then there would be an almost equal chance of Labour getting four or five seats (assuming that each of the 15,937 solutions has an equal chance of being selected); just under 50 per cent of the solutions would have given Labour four seats, and slightly more would have given the party five. As the swing to Conservative declines, so the chances of Labour getting only four seats fall rapidly (about 25 per cent of the solutions with a one per cent swing, for example), while those of it getting five increase (and the miniscule chance of the seats being divided three each disappear: of the 15,937 solutions, 35 give Labour only three seats with a 4 per cent swing to the Conservatives, as do just five with a 3 per cent swing and three with a 2 per cent swing). Furthermore, with a swing to Labour its chances of winning all six seats increase. With a 4 per cent swing to Labour (i.e. the far-right edge of the diagram), 22 per cent of the solutions give Labour all six seats, and a further 76 per cent give it five.

The geography of Sheffield makes a packed gerrymander-like solution very probable, therefore: although Labour had just below two-thirds of the votes it was very likely to win 5/6ths (83 per cent) of the seats. In three other cities, however, a cracked gerrymander was more likely. Hull and Leicester each had three constituencies, made up from 21 wards in the first case and 16 in the

Figure 3.3 Hull's wards in 1979, showing the estimated percentage of votes won in each by the Labour party

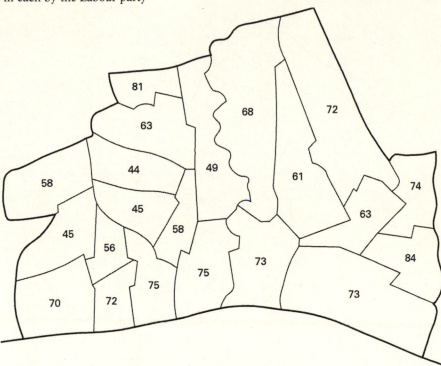

second (Figures 3.3 and 3.4); Labour won 68 per cent of the votes in Hull in 1979 and 59 per cent in Leicester. In terms of its vote share, therefore, Labour was 'entitled' to two of the three seats in each city. In Hull, however, it was bound to win all three, even if there was a 4 per cent swing away from it. The geography of Hull indicates why (Figure 3.3). Labour is weak in the northwest of the city, but even there it is impossible to create a constituency comprising seven wards with an overall majority of votes for Labour's opposition. (There are four with Labour having below 50 per cent, but if all four are in the same constituency, so too must wards where Labour has 81, 63 and 58 per cent support, giving Labour approximately 55 per cent overall. Note that Labour is much stronger in its weakest areas in Hull than in Sheffield; in Hull its minimum percentage of the ward vote is 44, compared to 17 in Sheffield.)

In Leicester, too, the likelihood is that Labour would win all three seats (in 160 of the 214 separate solutions identified) at the given vote percentage. Again, the map shows why (Figure 3.4). Labour has less than majority support in five of the 16 wards, but these are in three separate parts of the city: one to the east of the centre, two in the south; and the other two in the west. But the cracked gerrymander that gives Labour all three seats could see it lose one of them with a shift of support away from it: if the Conservatives got 3

Figure 3.4   Leicester's wards in 1979, showing the estimated percentage of votes won in each by the Labour party

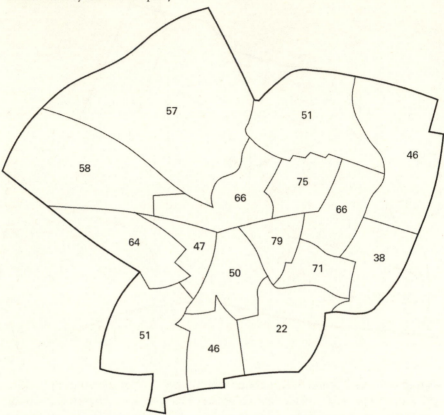

more percentage points share of the votes, they would win one seat in 118 of the 214 solutions (and with a 4 point swing they would win a seat in 127 of the solutions). Clearly, in arguing cases before the Boundary Commission, the Conservatives would want to press for one of those solutions.

Finally, Coventry's electoral geography also makes a cracked gerrymander situation likely (Figure 3.5). In a city with 18 wards to be combined into four constituencies, Labour had 57 per cent of the votes cast, and a majority in ten of the wards. Again, the areas where its support was weakest were not spatially concentrated in one part of the city, unlike the case in Sheffield. Of the 244 separate solutions identified, 193 would have given Labour three seats; 43 of the others would have given it all four, and the remaining eight would have produced a 2:2 split. A swing to Labour of more than 2 percentage points would have made a 4:0 victory for it much more likely, however (in 189 of the 244 cases). On the other hand, a 4 point swing to the Conservatives would have made a 2:2 division of the seats very much more likely – in 96 of the solutions, with 142 giving Labour three seats and only six giving it

Figure 3.5 Coventry's wards in 1979, showing the estimated percentage of votes won in each by the Labour party

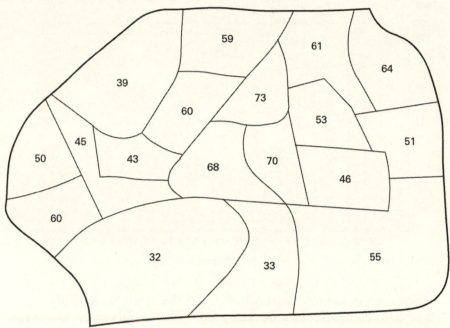

all four. A constituency based on the two southwestern wards where Labour won only 32–33 per cent of the votes would have been the core of one of the Conservatives' victories; another based on those where it got 39, 43 and 45 per cent could have given it another with a small swing of votes. For the Conservatives, therefore, the ideal solution in Coventry would have avoided grouping its strongholds in the southwest and northwest into a single constituency, producing a cracked gerrymander with the potential of two victories. For Labour, the safest solution would group several of the western wards together (i.e. those where Labour's vote percentage was 32, 43, 45, 50 and 60), producing a packed gerrymander-like situation with one safe Conservative seat and three others that were virtually safe for Labour.

Several conclusions can be drawn from these four examples. The first, and most important, is that it is very likely in each separate area considered by a Boundary Commission that the party with most votes will win an even greater proportion of the seats. Secondly, however, this conclusion has to be tempered by the recognition that the detailed geography of each party's support within the area is crucial to determining how many seats it would win there: the Conservative party's concentrated strength in southwest Sheffield served it relatively well there, whereas its much more diffuse geography served it less well elsewhere, especially Hull and Leicester. In most cases, however, there was the possibility of a different result, depending on either or both of the particular

Figure 3.6 Frequency distribution of the number of seats in each of the areas used by the Boundary Commissions in England, Scotland and Wales during the Fourth Periodic Review

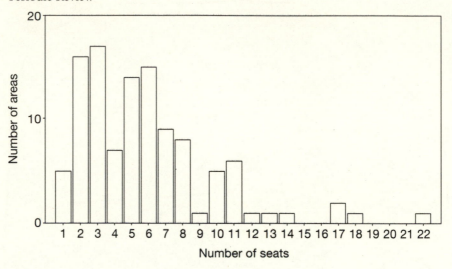

configuration of constituencies selected and the actual share of the votes between the parties. Thus the Boundary Commissions' procedures encourage the parties to try and achieve the equivalent of a gerrymander, to convince the Assistant Commissioners, and then the Commission itself, to adopt a configuration that is favourable to them and unfavourable to their opponents.

All four of the examples shown here involve Boroughs with a small number of constituencies, and the one with most (Sheffield) had the greatest range of possible electoral outcomes. This is normal, however. Very few of the London and Metropolitan Boroughs have many constituencies, for example, and this is so in most of the Counties. Figure 3.6 shows the frequency distributions after the Fourth Review; the modal number of constituencies per area is just three and two-thirds of the areas (74 of 110) have six or less. The main exceptions are a few large cities (notably Birmingham which had 12 constituencies respectively after the Fourth Review) plus the Strathclyde region in Scotland (which had 22 constituencies) and a small number of English Counties: Essex and Hampshire each had 17 constituencies, and Kent had 18. (In addition, because it is no longer divided into Counties, Northern Ireland has 18 constituencies to allocate within one unified area.)

Even in the areas with an above average number of seats, however, the geography of support can severely constrain the options. We illustrate this using 1979 voting data for Derbyshire where, as is the case in all Counties until recently, though much less so with Boroughs, there is a substantial number of wards where one or both of the two large parties did not field a candidate. Apart from the eleven wards where it did not field a candidate, Labour has a

Figure 3.7a Frequency distribution of the percentage of the votes cast in wards at the 1979 local government elections in Derbyshire won by the Conservative party

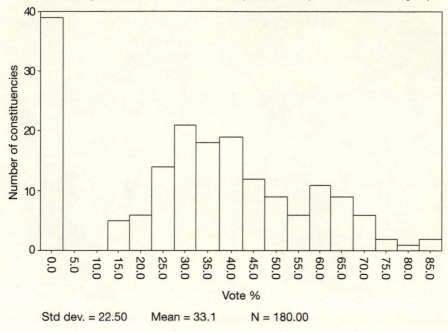

Std dev. = 22.50   Mean = 33.1   N = 180.00

Figure 3.7b Frequency distribution of the percentage of the votes cast in wards at the 1979 local government elections in Derbyshire won by the Labour party

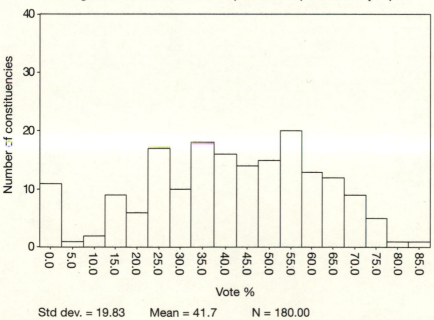

Std dev. = 19.83   Mean = 41.7   N = 180.00

Figure 3.8 The geography of support for the Conservative, Labour and Liberal parties, by ward, at the 1979 local government elections in Derbyshire

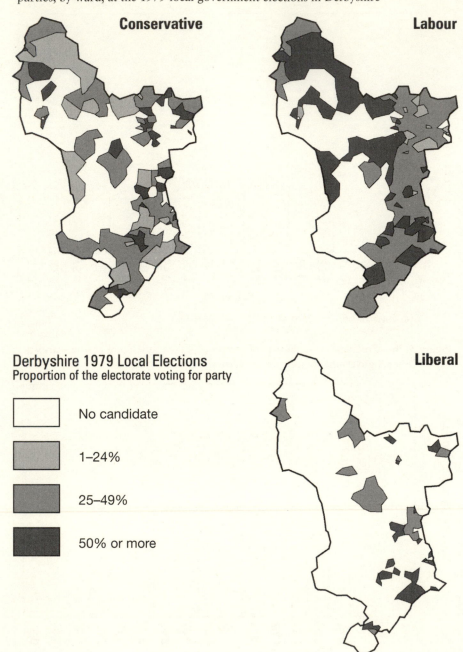

Conservative

Labour

Derbyshire 1979 Local Elections
Proportion of the electorate voting for party

No candidate

1–24%

25–49%

50% or more

Liberal

fairly normal distribution of vote share around its mean of 41.7 per cent (Figure 3.7a). The Conservatives, on the other hand, failed to field a candidate in 39 of the 180 wards (where we can assume that their support would have been relatively small, save in a few cases where there was an independent candidate who was a Conservative in all but name). In the other 141, the frequency distribution was more skewed than Labour's, with a small number of seats where the Conservative vote share was substantial and a much larger number where it was clearly in the minority (Figure 3.7b). This suggests the likelihood of a cracked gerrymander-like situation when the 180 wards were combined into ten constituencies in the Third Review, a situation made even more certain by the geographies of the two parties' support: Conservative support is concentrated in fewer areas than Labour's (Figure 3.8). The outcome was as expected. The Third Review constituencies were first used at the 1983 general election. Labour won 41.8 per cent of the votes in Derbyshire, to the Conservatives' 35.3 – with Labour getting six of the seats and Conservatives the other four.

The more skewed the distribution the more likely that a packed gerrymander-like outcome will result for a smaller party in an area. This is illustrated here

Figure 3.9 Frequency distribution of percentage votes for Liberal Democrat candidates at the 1997 Non-Metropolitan County Council elections in England, by ward

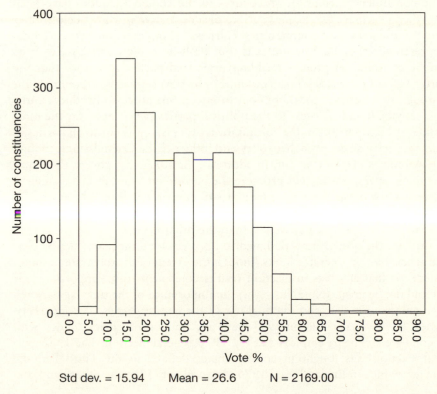

Std dev. = 15.94   Mean = 26.6   N = 2169.00

by the voting figures for County Council wards (on average several times larger than the District Council wards used for constituency building) at the 1997 elections in the English Shire Counties only – where elections were held on the same day as the 1997 general election. The distribution for the Liberal Democrats is highly skewed (Figure 3.9). As well as not fielding a candidate in over 250 of the 2169 wards (where we assume its support would have been small if a candidate had been contesting the seat), its mode was in the 15–20 per cent area and it gained more than 40 per cent in a small number of wards only. Its chances of winning Parliamentary seats thus depended on several of the latter wards being clustered together in particular constituencies, where the remaining votes were split between two other candidates. In fact, with 20 per cent of the votes cast in the 39 Counties it obtained just 7.6 per cent of the seats. Labour's distribution was also skewed (Figure 3.10a), but with 38.1 per cent of the votes in total it won 47.6 per cent of the 330 seats whereas the Conservatives, with a more skewed distribution (Figure 3.10b), obtained almost as many seats (44.5 per cent) with fewer votes.

Conclusions

The constituency-definition procedures in the United Kingdom have been designed to achieve two major goals: to ensure relative equality of electorates and representation for communities. Fairness to both individual voters (equal representation) and communities is thus built-in to the procedure, with its public consultation process enabling interested parties to ensure that the latter aspect of fairness is taken account of by the non-partisan Commissions through statements of local opinion. In effect, this process introduces partisan activity. It adds fairness to the political parties (who are by far the most influential participants in the consultation process) – it is fair to all parties in that they have an equal chance to try and influence the Commissions, though the outcomes may not be fair. In addition, the Rules that govern the Commissions' operations further promote the parties' interests, in that change to meet the first of the main goals (equality of electorates) should be avoided if it disrupts local organisations and communities too much: continuity of representation is given greater weight than the other factors.

In sum, the procedure is designed to keep electoral inequality across constituencies within tolerable limits (though the extent of the toleration is undefined), so that any bias in election results equivalent to malapportionment should not be great. (Note, however, the importance of the time lag between the enumeration date and the final use of the constituencies. The First Periodical Review was based on 1953 data, and the constituencies defined with them were still being employed at the 1970 general election. The 1992 general election was fought in constituencies defined in the Third Periodic Review, which in England used 1976 electoral data.) On the other hand, the

Figure 3.10a Frequency distribution of percentage votes for Labour candidates at the 1997 Non-Metropolitan County Council elections in England, by ward

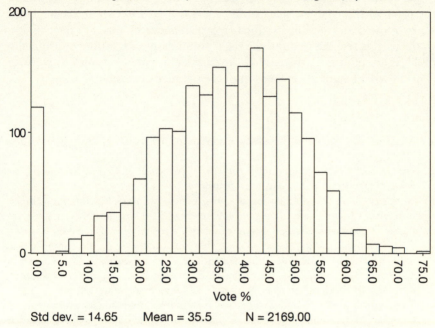

Std dev. = 14.65   Mean = 35.5   N = 2169.00

Figure 3.10b Frequency distribution of percentage votes for Conservative candidates at the 1997 Non-Metropolitan County Council elections in England, by ward

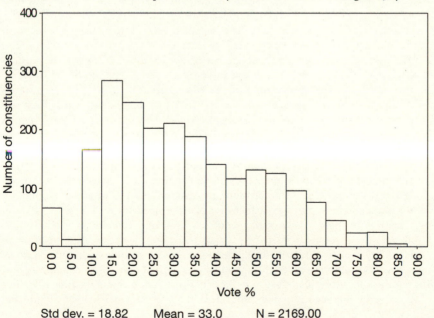

Std dev. = 18.82   Mean = 33.0   N = 2169.00

procedure both provides a structure within which outcomes equivalent to ger-rymandering are very likely (as the examples in this chapter have illustrated, the party with the largest share of the votes will very likely get a much larger share of the seats), and invites further gerrymandering through the activities of the parties seeking to influence the Commissions. Thus disproportionality and bias are built in to the UK's electoral system – in effect, into its constitu-tion. To what extent is the focus of the remainder of this book.

Notes

1 Much of this chapter is based on material from Rossiter, Johnston and Pattie (1999).
2 On de facto gerrymandering during the 1867 and 1885 redistributions, see Roberts (1999) on the role of Lord Salisbury.
3 Note that there was no mention of constituencies comprising contiguous blocks of territory (save where islands are involved) and this has never been a require-ment. The last non-contiguous constituencies were abolished in 1949, however, and there has been no suggestion since that constituencies should comprise non-contiguous areas. (The Tyne Bridge constituency comprises wards from Gateshead and Newcastle upon Tyne, however, which are separated by the river and only joined by the bridges between the two cities – hence the name!)
4 Presentation of the Commissioners and Assistant Commissioners as non-partisan (and their staffs) reflects the requirement that they should have no political affilia-tions. Given their class backgrounds – almost all are lawyers – it might be expected that they are pro-Conservative, but interviews with most after the Fourth Periodic Review found no evidence of partisan leanings in the way that they undertook their roles; nor was there any evidence of partisanship among the Commissions' staffs.
5 A Speaker's Conference became the established way of introducing major consti-tutional changes during the twentieth century.
6 The rules also covered the small number of two-member Boroughs, the particu-lar case of the City of London, and the separate representation of the Universi-ties, which were not dealt with until the 1949 legislation.
7 Although the Commissions reported in 1969, the constituencies that they rec-ommended then were not used in the 1970 general election. The 1983 reports were delivered to the relevant Secretaries of State in 1982, but their formal pre-sentation to, and acceptance by, Parliament was delayed by Court proceedings until February 1983 (see Chapter 5). The parties had assumed that they would be accepted and planned for the next general election accordingly, however; it was held in May 1983. The Commissions are also empowered to undertake Interim Reviews, where population changes suggest the need for a local redistribution. Only one of these of any consequence has been undertaken (other than minor alterations to the boundaries of existing constituencies after local government boundary changes). In 1990 the English Commission recommended an additional seat for the Milton Keynes area, and this was used at the 1992 election.
8 The Fifth Review had not begun in the other three countries at the time when this book was completed (summer 2000). It is likely to start in 2001 in Scotland and 2002 in Wales and Northern Ireland.

9 Since the later introduction of multi-member constituencies for Northern Ireland local government, the District Council wards have become redundant, being grouped together into District Electoral Areas. The Boundary Commission for Northern Ireland continues to use the District wards, however.

10 See Rossiter, Johnston and Pattie (1998).

11 The main exception was the English Commission's use of Rule 6 to defend its decision not to pair the Isle of Wight with Hampshire: as a consequence, the Isle of Wight was the largest constituency in the Fourth Review, with 101,784 electors.

12 In Scotland, the Commission is only required to 'have regard to' such boundaries (see above).

13 The 'harmonic mean effect' comes about because of the requirement that constituency electorates be as close to the quota as possible. Take, for example, the situation where the quota is 50,000. An area with a population of 122,000 would be entitled to 2.44 seats, which should be rounded down to 2.0. In that case, it would have two constituencies with 61,000 electors each, deviating from the quota by 10,500 voters (or 21 per cent). If, however, it were allocated three constituencies, each would have an electorate (assuming exact equality could be achieved!) of 40,667, with each deviating by 9333 (or 18.67). Rounding up would better fit the rules, even though the fractional entitlement were less than 0.5, and the likelihood, therefore, is that there will be more rounding up rather than rounding down. (For more details see Rossiter, Johnston and Pattie, 1999, 184.)

14 Electoral registers are compiled in the autumn of each year, with a closing date for registration in early October. They become current on 16 February in the following year – which the Commissions take as their enumeration date.

15 Because the Scottish Commission is only required to 'have regard to' the boundaries of local government areas, its members stressed to us that as a consequence the concept of a 'theoretical entitlement' has less validity there and is nothing more than a guideline.

16 In line with our calculations of bias when the two main parties have equal vote shares, all of the voting data in Figures 3.1 and 3.3–3.5 are estimates of what the Labour vote would have been if the two parties had achieved equal vote shares nationally (see Johnston and Rossiter, 1982, 132).

17 The original algorithm was described in Taylor (1973); for the Rossiter–Johnston algorithm, see Rossiter and Johnston (1981, 1983) and Johnston *et al.* (1984).

18 Further details of this and the subsequent examples of Coventry, Hull and Leicester can be found in Johnston and Rossiter (1982).

19 The index is derived in Johnston and Rossiter (1981).

4

From theory to practice: the components of bias in UK general election results

The previous three chapters have set out the extent of disproportionality and bias in UK general election results since 1950 and detailed the processes by which this may have been produced. Chapter 2, for example discussed the nature of the constituency-building problem in single-member constituency electoral systems and Chapter 3 examined the UK legislation and administrative practices put in place in the mid-twentieth century as the local resolution to the problem. The rules and guidelines are far from unambiguous, and their implementation seems very likely to result in election results that reflect the main constituency-building abuses – malapportionment and gerrymandering – even if this is unintentional.

The next three chapters explore the extent of those outcomes through analysing in some detail the results of all UK general elections between 1950 and 1997 in the context of the bias measure introduced in Chapter 1. A major benefit of that measure is not only that it is expressed in a readily appreciated metric – the number of seats difference between the two main parties if they had an equal share of the votes cast – but also that it can be decomposed into various contributory causes. Those separate component measures are the focus of the next three chapters. This brief linking chapter between the theory and practice introduces them.

The causes of bias

As already noted, there are two main sources of electoral bias in single-member constituency systems associated with electoral abuses – malapportionment and gerrymandering. Both abuses have been widely practised in the United States. Malapportionment was outlawed in the 1960s by a series of Supreme Court rulings, but gerrymandering, first observed in 1819, continues to this day, with the Courts finding it very difficult to identify objective standards against which it may be judged.[1] Although malapportionment was widespread in the UK until the late nineteenth century, and there were frequent charges of gerrymandering then also, the abuses there have never been on a comparable scale to the American. Nevertheless, as the hypothetical examples in Chapter 2 show, even without deliberate intent, electoral consequences equivalent to those associated with malapportionment and gerrymandering can occur in any single-member system. Hence these form the basis of our decomposition of the bias measure introduced in Chapter 1.

Malapportionment

Malapportionment influences election outcomes when one party is advantaged over another, because its votes are concentrated in smaller constituencies (defined by the number of voters, not their area). Variations in constituency size do not necessarily produce bias, however; it only occurs when there is a differential geography of support for the parties according to constituency size. For example, a system might comprise ten constituencies, four with electorates of 500 each and the other six with electorates of only 200. If party A had 60 per cent of the votes in each of the six smaller constituencies and 25 per cent of the votes in each of the four larger ones, it would win six of the ten seats with a total of just 38.125 per cent of the votes cast. If party B received all of the remaining votes, on the other hand, it would get just four of the ten seats despite getting 61.875 per cent of the votes.[2] If party A had 51 per cent of the votes in three of the six small constituencies, however, with party B getting 51 per cent in the other three, and each party got 51 per cent of the votes in two of the large constituencies, then A and B would both have half of the votes and half of the seats. There would be no disproportionality (or bias) in the latter case, because neither party's support was concentrated in the smaller constituencies. But the former example would be both disproportional and biased. If the vote share were equalised, this would involve transferring 11.825 per cent of the votes away from B; with half of the votes, it would still get four seats, with A retaining six.

Malapportionment results when the two main parties in an electoral system have their support unequally distributed across constituencies of different sizes. It can be brought about in one of three ways:

1 deliberately defining constituencies such that they are on average smaller in areas where one party dominates than in areas where the other party is electorally strongest;
2 deliberately defining constituencies so that they are smaller in some parts of the system than others, on criteria other than those involving electoral interests and outcomes, but which may correlate with party strength; and
3 through the process of population change, whereby constituencies that were once relatively equal in size become increasingly unequal.

The first of these is deliberate malapportionment, which has not been practised in the UK since passage of the *House of Commons (Redistribution of Seats) Act 1944.*[3] The other two may produce malapportionment-like effects, however, if the procedure allows either constituencies of different sizes in different areas or such differences to evolve through population change.

The UK legislation and practices described in Chapter 3 clearly incorporate the second malapportionment strategy, because they ensure different-sized constituencies in each of the four countries. Over-representation of Scotland and Wales is built in to the Rules, and the 1958 amendments ensured that electoral quotas are lower there. As a result, their constituencies are much smaller on average than they are in both England and Northern Ireland (Table 3.1). If one of the main UK parties (Conservative and Labour) has stronger electoral support in one or both of those countries than in England, this should result in a biased outcome in its favour.

Whereas Scotland and Wales have been over-represented in the House of Commons throughout the period being analysed here, Northern Ireland was under-represented for the first three decades. Its allocation of seats was a fixed number (12) until 1978, when it was increased to a varying number (16–18, though with a proviso that it should be 17 unless a strong case was made otherwise: Box 3.7).[4] The average Northern Ireland constituency was thus much larger than its English counterpart, let alone those in Scotland and Wales (Table 3.1: after the Second Periodical Review, for example, the Northern Ireland average was 76,405, compared with 58,192 in England, 50,366 in Wales and 47,670 in Scotland).

Regarding the third malapportionment strategy – which might be termed *creeping malapportionment* – the UK's procedures were clearly defined to prevent this becoming a major issue. Regular reviews – every 6–8 years according to the original legislation, every 10–15 years after the 1958 amendments and then every 8–12 years after the *Boundary Commissions Act 1992* – were legislated for in order to prevent major inequalities developing, even though the relative importance of removing inequalities was downgraded by the 1947 and 1958 amendments to the original legislation and the tolerance limit recommended by Vivian and the Speaker's Conference was removed. Nevertheless, substantial population redistribution can occur during a ten-year period, potentially introducing temporary biases if one party is stronger than the other in the areas with increasingly small constituencies – especially at an election held late in the redistribution cycle.[5] They can be exacerbated to favour one party over another if the period between reviews (and especially their implementation) is either extended or reduced (on which see below).

There are two potential sources of malapportionment-like bias in the UK: first, that resulting from different average constituency sizes in the different countries, because of the varying national electoral quotas implicit in the legislation; secondly, that resulting from inequalities in constituency size, both those in place from the outset, because the Commissions are only required to produce constituencies 'as equal as practicable' (Box 3.7), and those which develop because of population changes.

Gerrymandering

Gerrymandering as a deliberate strategy is not part of the UK system, because redistribution is undertaken by independent commissions that take no account of the possible electoral consequences of their actions. The Commissions are explicit with regard to this, as in the Boundary Commission for England's statement in the booklet produced during its Fourth Periodic Review (Parliamentary Boundary Commission for England, 1991, 9): 'The Commissions are an independent and totally impartial body. They emphasise very strongly that the results of previous elections do not and should not enter their considerations when they are deciding their recommendations. Nor do the Commission consider the effects of their recommendations on future voting patterns'.

Election results that are equivalent to gerrymandering can come about in the United Kingdom, however, for two reasons:

1 because the geographies of support for the political parties differ, so that one's votes are more efficiently distributed across the constituencies than the other's (as illustrated by the hypothetical examples in Chapter 2 and the case studies of particular Boroughs in Chapter 3);
2 because the parties are able to influence the precise definition of constituency boundaries through the public consultation process, to promote their own electoral interests (even though they cannot do that explicitly).

Thus part of the bias in UK election results identified in Figure 1.4 may result from one or both of these, producing a gerrymander effect (or an efficiency effect, since it will come about if one party's votes are more efficiently distributed than the other's).

Reactive malapportionment

The two components of electoral disproportionality and bias discussed above are based on contests between two political parties only, in which all of the electors vote. But many do not. Turnout at UK general elections fell from highs of 82 per cent at each of the 1950 and 1951 elections (the first two in the sequence analysed here) to an average of about 75 per cent thereafter. 1997 had the lowest turnout rate – 71.2 per cent – but there is no evidence of a secular decline since the 1960s. Furthermore, an increasing number of those who do turn out vote for 'third parties', i.e. parties other than the Conservatives and Labour.

Both turnout rates and support for third parties vary across constituencies and can have potential impacts on both the results in individual seats and the overall level of bias. This was illustrated by the hypothetical examples in Chapter 2, which showed that:

1 The more votes won by a third party, the greater the return to the main parties. Their seats:votes ratios would increase (as would the overall system disproportionality) because they would get the same proportion of the seats with a smaller proportion of the votes.
2 If the votes won by a third party were concentrated in certain constituencies, this could advantage one party over another, thereby contributing to a biased outcome.

Both effects come about because a third party reduces the number of votes needed to win a constituency. If two parties are competing for 100 votes, then one of them needs 51 to ensure victory in the constituency if there are no abstentions. If the third party (or parties) wins 20 of the 100, however, then the two main parties are only competing for 80 votes, and 41 are sufficient for victory. The geography of the third party's support is crucial to whether it has a differential impact on seat winning by the two main parties, and thus contributes to the bias. If it wins 20 votes in each of the five constituencies where A is strongest, it reduces the maximum number of votes needed to win in each of those by 10, but if it wins no votes in the seats where B is strongest, B still needs on average 51 votes to be sure of victory. Party A is advantaged because the third party makes the constituencies where it is strong easier to win.

There may be a downside, however. What if the third party does well enough to win in a constituency? In such a case, the party that would otherwise have won (and is probably in second place) is disadvantaged. It may well have many more votes than the other main party, but they do not bring victory. Thus, if a third party is stronger in the constituencies where party A on average wins more votes than party B, this will be to A's advantage if the third party merely reduces the number of votes necessary for victory, but to B's advantage if the third party wins, denying A of an otherwise additional seat. Thus the third party bias effect has two components, depending on whether it wins in constituencies.

The discussion in Chapter 2 showed that abstentions have the same impact as third party votes in a constituency; they reduce the number of votes needed for victory. Thus abstentions can have a differential impact on the seats:votes ratios if they are greater in the constituencies won by one of the parties than in those won by the other. Just like the third party voters, the abstainers reduce the number of votes needed for victory without changing the number of seats won. Abstentions can thus contribute to the bias measure, in exactly the same way as malapportionment does. And, unlike third party voters, they cannot eventually have a negative impact – abstainers can never win a constituency!

We have termed these two impacts on the bias *reactive malapportionment*. The outcome is the same as that produced by malapportionment – a party benefits because it is stronger in the constituencies where fewer votes are needed for victory. But this does not come about because constituency boundaries are drawn to produce smaller constituencies in those areas. Instead, it is a consequence of voter and party reaction to the geography. Voters are more likely to vote for a third party and/or abstain in some areas than others, and parties do not campaign for votes with the same intensity in every constituency. The result is equivalent to that produced by malapportionment.

Measuring the bias components

We have identified three main potential sources of bias in the UK electoral system, therefore, all of which are geographical. They involve the geography of constituency boundaries and the size of constituencies, the geography of support for the various political parties and the geography of abstentions. Two of these three sources can be divided into identifiable sub-sources, giving six bias components in all:

1 *Malapportionment*
   (a) inter-country differences in electoral quotas; and
   (b) intra-country variations in constituency sizes.
2 *Gerrymandering*
   differences in the relative efficiency of the geography of support for each of the two main political parties.
3 *Reactive malapportionment*
   (a) differences between the two main parties in the impact of votes for third parties;
   (b) differences between the two main parties in the impact of victories by third parties; and
   (c) differences between the two main parties in the impact of abstentions.

In addition, a separate bias component has been identified for the special case of Northern Ireland, where one of the two main parties – Labour – never contested general elections during the period studied here.[6] Until the 1970 election, however, the main Unionist party was allied with the Conservatives, giving the latter a bias there equivalent to the number of seats won by the Unionists – whatever the movement of votes between Conservative and Labour to obtain equal vote shares, the Conservatives would always win those seats which its Unionist allies held. After 1970, this component was zero, because neither of the two main Great Britain parties contested any of the seats there.

One of the benefits of the Brookes measure of bias that we introduced in Chapter 1 is that it can be decomposed into these six components.[7] The algebra for this is set out in the Appendix. Each of the components can be interpreted in the same way as the overall bias index – as the difference in the number of seats between the two parties when they have an equal share of the votes cast, because of the particular component. Each, too, can be either positive or negative – a positive figure indicates a bias towards the Labour party according to the method of calculation employed here, whereas a negative figure indicates a bias towards the Conservatives.

The positive and negative biases may cancel each other, at least in part – a party may gain from some components but lose on others, so that the total bias figure shown in Figure 1.4 is a net figure. The total volume of bias may be much greater, as was the case at each of the elections studied here. Table 4.1 shows both total bias, the sum of the various components irrespective of sign, and net bias, the sum incorporating sign.[8] Figure 4.1 shows that the total bias increased substantially over the first two decades. It fell back during the 1970s, before increasing again, regaining its 1970 level at the 1987 and 1992 elections before going on to its highest ever figure at the 1997 contest. By then, total bias was some 165 seats – out of a total of 659, or some 25 per cent of the total.

Table 4.1   The bias components at UK general elections, 1950–97, assuming that the Conservative and Labour parties obtained equal shares of the votes cast (a positive bias is pro-Labour; a negative bias is pro-Conservative)

Election	NEQ	CSV	NI	G	TPV	TPW	A	TB	NB
1950	3	–6	–10	–23	–7	–4	–2	55	–51
1951	4	–5	–10	–39	0	–4	–4	66	–59
1955	4	–8	–10	–13	–3	–4	1	43	–34
1959	6	1	–12	–29	–11	–3	1	63	–51
1964	6	13	–12	–13	–25	4	10	83	–24
1966	6	21	–11	–13	–22	4	17	94	–3
1970	7	39	–8	–39	–14	4	17	128	2
1974F	5	19	–	11	–32	5	16	88	18
1974O	6	19	–	–28	–17	2	17	89	–3
1979	8	31	–	–1	–20	1	12	73	26
1983	10	13	–	–28	–19	12	12	94	–5
1987	14	23	–	–34	–24	13	10	118	–6
1992	12	29	–	–7	–30	20	19	117	38
1997	11	13	–	48	–36	33	24	165	82

Key to bias components: NEQ – national electoral quotas; CSV – constituency size variations; NI – Northern Ireland; G – gerrymander (or efficiency) ; TPV – third party votes; TPW – third party wins; A – abstentions; TB – total bias (irrespective of sign); NB – net bias. (Note that the net bias is not the sum of the bias components because the interaction terms are excluded from this table.)

Apart from a lull in the 1970s and early 1980s, therefore, the operation of the UK electoral system has become increasingly biased over the 50-year period

Figure 4.1 Total and net bias, 1950–97

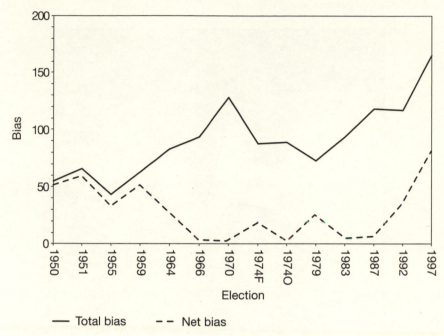

studied here. This trend in total bias has not been paralleled by that of net bias (Figure 4.1). At the first four elections in the sequence, net bias was almost the same as total bias, because one party – the Conservatives – was advantaged on just about all of the bias components (Table 4.1). From 1959 on, however, net bias fell because the Conservative advantage in the efficiency and third party vote components was increasingly countered by a Labour advantage on the other components (notably constituency size variations and abstentions: Table 4.1). From 1966 until 1987, the different bias components favouring the two parties generally balanced each other, producing only a small net bias. But the net bias increased substantially over the last two elections, when the pro-Labour abstentions component doubled. Finally, between 1992 and 1997 there was a substantial shift in the gerrymander (or efficiency) component – from a small pro-Conservative figure in 1992 to a large pro-Labour one five years later.

Figure 4.2 shows the relative importance of the three main groups of bias components as percentages of the total bias (where all biases are treated the same, irrespective of sign). The percentage contribution of the malapportionment group (national electoral quotas, constituency size variations and Northern Ireland) increases quite substantially over the first two decades, whereas the gerrymander component falls in relative importance – from nearly 60 per cent of the total volume of bias in the 1950s to about 25 per cent in 1997 (and much less than that in 1979 and again in 1992). The malapportionment contribution varies in its relative importance in the last

Figure 4.2   The contributions of the three main groups of bias components to total bias, 1950–97, as percentages of the total

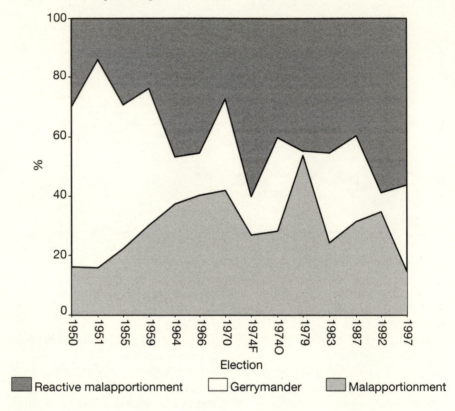

two decades, being highest in 1979 and 1992 (both the last years of a redistricting cycle. As discussed in the next chapter). Finally, the third – reactive malapportionment – group (comprising abstentions, third party votes and third party wins) increased in relative importance, from around 30 per cent in the 1950s to over half of the total at the last two elections. Overall, therefore, the malapportionment and reactive malapportionment components have replaced the gerrymander equivalent as the dominant source of electoral bias in the United Kingdom over the 50 years, with reactive malapportionment dominant at the end of the period.

To illustrate these changes further, Figure 4.3 plots the separate relative contributions of the three main groups of bias components to the overall total shown in Figure 4.1. The main variation among those related to malapportionment is in the relative importance of constituency size variations, from virtually zero in 1959 to over 40 per cent in 1979, and then back to 10 per cent in 1997 (Figure 4.3a). National electoral quotas contribute around 10 per cent at each election, and of course the Northern Ireland contribution

Figure 4.3a   Trends in the three malapportionment bias components, 1950–97, as percentages of the total

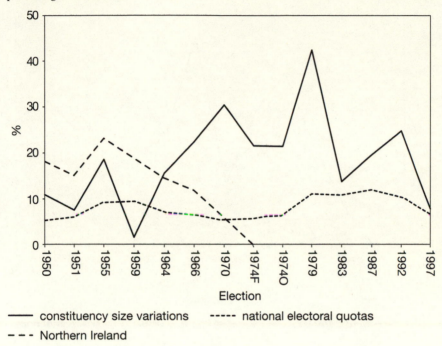

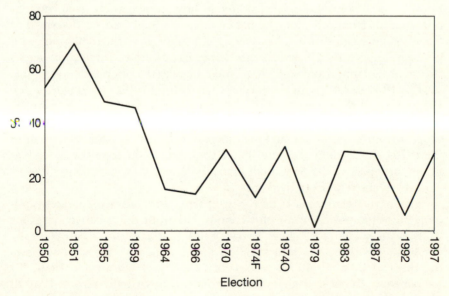

Figure 4.3b   Trends in the gerrymander bias component, as a percentage of the total, 1950–97

Figure 4.3c   Trends in the reactive malapportionment bias components, 1950–97, as percentages of the total

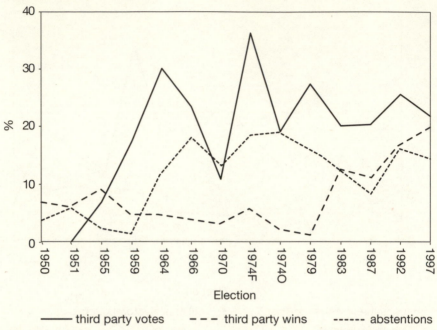

falls away in the middle of the period. The single gerrymander component (Figure 4.3b) contributed around half of the total bias at the first two elections, but then fell substantially, although the decline was far from continuous. Indeed, from 1970 on the pattern may perhaps best be described as 'trendless fluctuation' around an average contribution to the total of some 20 per cent. Finally, the general feature of the last group of three components ('reactive malapportionment') is of their increased importance over time, starting 20 years later with abstentions than with the other two (Figure 4.3c). For both third party votes and third party victories, the increases from less than 10 per cent in the 1950s reflect the third parties' growth in electoral support from the 1960s on and their increased success at winning seats after the 1970s. Abstentions also contributed very little to the total volume of bias in the early part of the period but increased after 1959, averaging some 15 per cent of the total from then on.

What of the relative biases for the two parties, obtained by separately summing all of the positive biases for Labour and all of the negative biases for Conservative? Figure 4.4 shows two very different patterns. Whereas for the Conservatives there has been trendless fluctuation, with the various biases together worth some 40–60 seats to it at every election since 1950, for Labour there has been a substantial increase, from virtually zero in 1950 to

Figure 4.4 Trends in total bias for the Conservative and Labour parties, 1950–97

over 130 in 1997. The procedure for producing the constituency system has been largely unchanged over the 50-year period, but its impact on Labour's seat-winning ability has hugely changed, from less than ten seats at the first four elections through around 40–60 (the same as for the Conservatives) in the 1970s and 1980s to 80 in 1992 and then well over 100 in 1997. Why Labour has increasingly benefited from the system's operation is the focus of the next three chapters.

In summary

Biased outcomes can result from three sets of factors operating within the UK's single-member constituency electoral system. These reflect processes of malapportionment, gerrymandering and reactive malapportionment – and can occur even without any deliberate attempt to create them. All three sets have made substantial contributions to an increasing volume of bias over the suite of elections from 1950 to 1997 inclusive, although for much of the central part of that period the biases favouring the Conservative party and those favouring Labour tended to counteract each other, producing a relatively small net bias. The origins of those biases have changed in relative importance over time, and those changes have almost entirely favoured the Labour party. Whereas its opponents have experienced the same amount of bias over the 50 years, Labour benefited from it much more in the later than the more recent decades, having had virtually no advantages in the first decade.

Notes

1   See Grofman (1998) and Kousser (1999).
2   Party A would get 120 votes in each of the six small constituencies and 125 in each of the four largest, giving 1220 votes in total. There are 3200 votes in total across the ten constituencies.
3   It was practised more recently in the Republic of Ireland, however (Paddison, 1976).
4   For an interpretation of this proviso, see Rossiter, Johnston and Pattie (1998).
5   If the changes create large differences between constituencies, the Commissions have the power to conduct Interim Reviews and recommend changes (though these are subject to Parliamentary approval). This has occurred only once, however, when two seats were created to replace one in Milton Keynes in 1990, which suggests that the Commissions are unlikely to act save in situations where either population growth or decline has been very substantial.
6   Indeed, it is not possible to join the Labour party if you live in Northern Ireland.
7   In addition, it is possible to calculate interaction terms, which identify the joint effects of two or more of the components – such as the impact of third party votes according to constituency size. With six components there is a large number of these (15 two-component interactions, 20 three-component interactions, 16 four-component interactions, 6 five-component interactions and 1 six-component interaction). These have not been identified separately here.
8   Note that the net bias shown in the table is not the sum of the various components because we have not shown the various interaction terms between the components.

5

Malapportionment: UK style

The first set of components producing bias in the UK electoral system is akin to the practice of malapportionment. As indicated in the previous chapter, it comes about in two main ways: because of differences in the treatment of the constituent countries of the UK in the rules operated by the Boundary Commissions since 1944, and because of differences in constituency size within countries. Both only have an effect if one party has its support concentrated to some extent in the areas with smaller constituencies, whereas its opponent's support is relatively concentrated in the larger constituencies – either in the country with the larger constituencies or in the larger constituencies within any one country, or both. In this chapter, we evaluate the relative importance of these two sources of bias.

Differences in national electoral quotas

As already described, the Rules introduced in the *House of Commons (Redistribution of Seats) Act 1944* and amended in 1958 not only treated the four constituent countries of the United Kingdom differently in the allocation of House of Commons seats but in effect created over-representation for Scotland and Wales relative to England (we deal with Northern Ireland in a later section). This was because Scotland and Wales (a) were each guaranteed a minimum number of seats, irrespective of the UK-wide national electoral quota before 1958 and then (b) were given separate quotas by the 1958 amendments. Together, these have ensured not only that Scotland and Wales have smaller average constituencies than England, but also that the differential between them has widened over time.

This is shown by the data for the average constituency size in each country at each of the five Reviews, using the electoral data employed by the Commissions (Figure 5.1). The average constituency size declined in all three countries between the Initial and First Reviews. From then on, the average English constituency increased substantially, from 56,562 at the First Review

Figure 5.1   Average constituency electorates in England, Scotland and Wales after each Boundary Commission Review

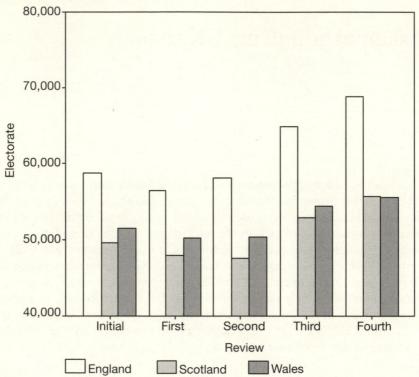

to 68,626 at the Fourth – an increase of 21.3 per cent. Scottish and Welsh constituency averages both declined in size between the First and Second Reviews (a period during which the Scottish electorate declined slightly and the Welsh electorate was virtually unchanged). By the time of the Fourth Review, their averages had increased by 14.5 and 10.3 per cent, respectively, over their nadir, much less than the comparable change in the English situation.

These differences have produced a bias in favour of Labour at each of the elections in the sequence from 1950 to 1997 (Figure 5.2: in all of the figures showing the bias components, we use a consistent vertical scale, with a positive bias being pro-Labour and a negative bias being pro-Conservative). In terms of the total amount of bias shown in the previous chapter, the contribution of this component has been relatively small, though with only just over 100 constituencies involved in Scotland and Wales, a contribution of 14 seats to the 1992 total is far from insignificant. The general trend over the 50-year period was for the pro-Labour bias to increase, it being worth four times as many seats to the party in 1997 as it was in 1950.

The reason for this is made very clear by the diagrams showing support for the parties in each of the countries. In Scotland (Figure 5.3), the Conservative

Figure 5.2 Bias in the general election results 1950–97 due to differences in national electoral quotas

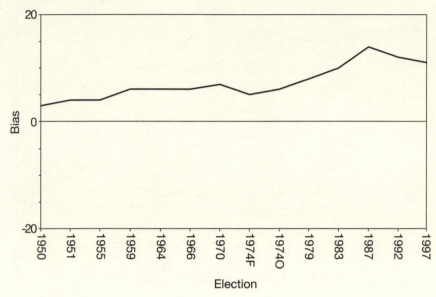

Figure 5.3 Party performance at general elections in Scotland, 1950–97

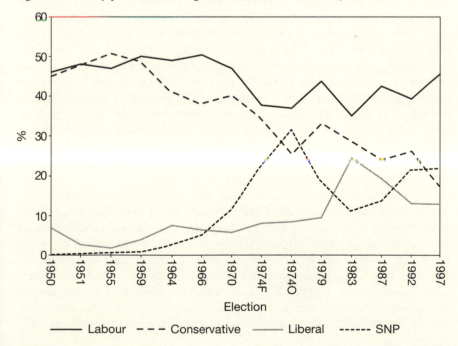

Figure 5.4 Party performance at general elections in Wales, 1950–97

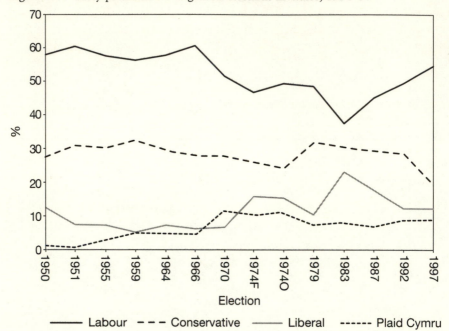

and Labour parties obtained very similar shares of the votes cast over the first four elections in the sequence. From 1964 on, Labour had a clear lead, and this became much wider after 1979. By 1997, Labour had 28 percentage points more of the votes than the Conservatives, who had fallen into third place behind the SNP. In Wales, on the other hand (Figure 5.4), Labour has always had a substantial lead over the Conservatives. It was less than 10 percentage points at only one of the 14 elections (1983), the sole occasion on which Labour failed to gain at least 40 per cent of the votes cast there. Finally, in England (Figure 5.5) the two main parties were very even in their support until 1979, when the Conservatives opened a substantial lead, which was extended in 1983 before Labour regained ground. By 1997, Labour had a 10-point advantage over its main rival, but this was much smaller than the situation in either of the other two countries.

The bias towards Labour in Scotland and Wales shown in Figure 5.2 is thus a clear consequence of its relative strength there in comparison to England. Increase in the size of that pro-Labour bias reflects a combination of two factors: the growing differential between Scotland and Wales on the one hand and England on the other in the relative size of their constituencies (Figure 5.1), and the growing relative strength of Labour in the former countries, especially the bigger (Scotland), over the period. Whether such a malapportionment effect is a result of deliberate political manipulation or merely the serendipitous consequence of rules that differed between the

Figure 5.5 Party performance at general elections in England, 1950–97

countries for other reasons can ultimately only be a matter of conjecture. It was of course the 1944 Speaker's Conference which introduced the differential treatment by recommending a minimum number of seats for Scotland and Wales (page 55). Some have suggested for Scotland this was because it had been guaranteed a certain number of seats by the Act of Union, but McLean has shown that this was not so.[1] His study of the Minutes of the Conference identified that it was a political decision made to ensure that Scotland and Wales did not lose seats, justified at least in part because – according to one of the MPs who was a member of the Conference – 'Scotland and Wales should have a larger representation than their population entitles them to ... because we considered that the two smaller nations should have a larger representation because they were smaller' (Parker in *Hansard*, vol. 582, 11 February 1958, col. 266). The Home Secretary at the time the 1944 Act was passed (Herbert Morrison) later told the House of Commons that their minimum representation had not been 'conceded to them for all time', but rather for 'this time' only (though what 'this time' meant is not exactly clear (*Hansard*, vol. 448, 17 February 1948, col. 1114)).

Since then, the issue of Scottish and Welsh over-representation only became an issue of concern when devolution came to prominence on the political agenda of the 1970s, and then again from the late 1990s on. The proposals to create devolved assemblies for Scotland and Wales developed by the Callaghan administration in 1978 (and which were eventually defeated at referendums in 1979)[2] included no consequential measures to reduce Scottish and Welsh representation at Westminster (although the removal of Northern Ireland's devolved Assembly in 1972 led to it being allocated further seats at Westminster in the late 1970s, very much as part of a political deal between the Callaghan government and the Ulster Unionist party, designed to win the latter's support for the minority Labour government). In 1997, when devolution to Scotland and Wales was again proposed, the issue was raised once more and a measure was introduced to reduce Scottish representation, by requiring the Boundary Commission for Scotland to apply the English national quota at its Fifth Periodic Review. This will probably result in the number of Scottish MPs being reduced from 72 to 60, although almost certainly not until after the first two general elections of the twenty-first century.[3] No similar provision was made to reduce Welsh representation at Westminster, on the apparent grounds that the Welsh Assembly has less power than the Scottish Parliament; nor was there any discussion of reducing Northern Ireland's representation after reinstatement of a devolved Assembly there in 1999.

The representation of Scotland and Wales relative to England appeared briefly on the political agenda during an inquiry into aspects of the redistribution process conducted by the House of Commons Home Affairs Committee during the 1986–87 Parliamentary session, soon after passage of the *Parliamentary Constituencies Act 1986*. Its main concern was with the continued growth of the House of Commons because of the ratchet effect discussed in Chapter 3, and it recommended that set denominators should be used to determine future electoral quotas.[4] This was rejected in the Government's Reply to the Committee's report because it would introduce uncertainty; statistical analysis, it was reported, revealed that 'the divisors they recommend would *not* reproduce the status quo on most occasions' (Government Reply, 1988, 3) and so a 'fixed divisor would be a most unwelcome addition to our electoral law'. Regarding Scottish and Welsh over-representation in the House of Commons, a memorandum to the Committee from the Home Office stated blandly that reducing Scottish MPs by 12 and Welsh by 6, while increasing the English complement by 19, 'would be completely unacceptable in Scotland and Wales' (Home Affairs Committee, 1986–87, 10), and an Under-Secretary from the Scottish Office claimed in oral evidence that 'Scotland, like Wales, as a small nation should be given special treatment vis-à-vis her bigger national neighbour' (p.35). A member of the Boundary Commission for England at the time (Judge Newey) contested this, arguing that (p.107) 'it is inconsistent with both with the existence of a "union" and with democracy that the votes of electors in two of the constituent parts, Scotland and Wales, should as a matter of course carry greater weight than those of the electors in the remaining parts'. But the Committee disagreed, arguing that (p.vii) 'In our judgement it would not be feasible on political grounds to change the Rules so as to provide a uniform electoral quota for the whole United Kingdom. In essence, we believe that Scotland and Wales would successfully resist any change in the numbers of seats which was sought in the interests of electoral parity'. (It did believe that its proposals for fixed divisors might reduce the disparities, however, and also prevent them becoming wider.) A few years later, Kenneth Clarke, when presenting the *Boundary Commissions Act 1992* to Parliament, rejected the case that Scottish and Welsh representation should be reduced on the grounds that this was a long-standing situation that should be dealt with by primary legislation (as it was by the *Scotland Act 1998*). The government's view was that 'a proposal that solely determined the number of seats in Scotland and Wales would not be useful' (*Hansard*, 15 June 1992, col. 670).

There was an interesting difference between the Scottish and Welsh Commissions during the Fourth Periodic Review. The former determined from the outset that there would be no increase in the number of Scottish MPs, being cognisant not only of the charges of Scottish 'over-representation', but also of the House of Commons' desire that its size should not increase further. Hence it announced its decision that the number of seats should remain at 72, which involved it crossing Regional boundaries in order to ensure relative equity in constituency size. The Welsh Commission, on the other hand, recommended a further two seats. It expressed concern in its report about the contribution that this made to the continued growth of the House of Commons, but argued that its decisions were inevitable given the current rules. Indeed, it suggested that a further seat would probably be recommended in the Fifth Review, even if the Welsh electorate did not grow over the intervening period.

Northern Ireland

One area for which the issue of representation was tackled was Northern Ireland. This has had no effect on relative bias in the UK electoral system towards either Conservative or Labour, because the change came after the relationship between the Conservatives and Ulster Unionists had been dissolved as a consequence of the Heath government's response to the 'troubles' that began in 1969. Before then, as Figure 4.2 shows, Northern Ireland had contributed a small pro-Conservative bias at each election. The Labour party did not contest elections there and so those seats won by the Conservatives' allies would be retained, whatever the switch of votes to achieve equality of vote share between the Conservatives and Labour across the entire United Kingdom. This bias component was worth ten seats to the Conservatives at the first three elections in the 1950s, when Unionist candidates won ten of province's 12 seats. In 1959 and 1964 they won all 12, producing a 12-seat bias to the Conservatives. Their share fell in the next two elections, when the DUP and SDLP won seats; the pro-Conservative bias was 11 seats in 1966 and eight in 1970.

This bias to the Conservatives could have been worth a slightly larger number of seats if Northern Ireland had not been under-represented over that period. The average constituency there had an electorate at the Initial Review of 71,457, compared to 58,734 in England, and after the First Periodical Review the two figures were 72,913 and 56,562, respectively. (If the UK electoral quota had been applied in those two reviews, Northern Ireland would almost certainly have been allocated 15 seats.) Northern Ireland's Westminster representation had been set at 12 by the legislation which established the partition of Ireland in 1922.[5]

In 1977, the Labour government (by then in a minority in the House of Commons and dependent on support from other parties, notably the Liberals but also, when the Lib-Lab pact was dissolved, other minority parties such as those from Northern Ireland and the Scottish and Welsh nationalists) established a Speaker's Conference to consider the issue of Northern Ireland's representation. This resolved that the number of seats should be increased, with the final wording changed from 12 to 'a minimum of 16 and a maximum of 18'. This was resisted by nationalist parties, which wanted the issue of Westminster representation considered as part of a wider settlement of the problems in the province (and also because they feared, wrongly as it turned out, that the Unionist parties would be the major beneficiaries), whereas the Unionist parties – which had many more votes in the House of Commons on which the Labour government might call – lobbied for even more.[6] The proposals were accepted by the House of Commons. They may have won the Labour government a little time before its eventual defeat in 1979, and 17 years later the Unionist votes may have sustained John Major in power, but the extra seats have had no impact on the operation of the electoral system since an entirely separate party system has operated in Northern Ireland from that in the rest of the United Kingdom since the 1970s.

Creeping malapportionment: population change and electoral bias

The classic cases of malapportionment in the United States, starting with the *Baker v Carr* case in 1962, resulted from differential population changes within states with no consequent redistricting to ensure (relatively) equal electorates.[7] The first half of the twentieth century saw very rapid urbanisation of the population in most states, accompanied by rural depopulation. Districts drawn up in the century's first decades became increasingly unequal in size, with large populations in the urban areas matched by small ones in the countryside. The seminal case of *Baker v Carr*, for example, referred to the situation in Tennessee, where by 1960 the largest district for election the lower house of the State Legislature had 42,298 residents and the smallest had only 2340. In general, the rural areas favoured the Republican party and the urban districts the Democrats, so that malapportionment favoured the former. In New York State, for example, the average 1960 population of a district represented by a Republican in the State Lower House was 398,000 whereas that for one represented by a Democrat was 424,000.

Urbanisation characterised the United Kingdom during the first half of the twentieth century as well. By 1934, just 17 years after the previous redistribution that had achieved substantial equality in constituency electorates, MPs were complaining that there were substantial disparities: the largest constituencies had over 150,000 voters in them, whereas the smallest had less than 30,000. Hence the Private Member's Bill introduced that year included a provision for regular reviews of all constituency boundaries at least once a decade. The proposal was not successful, but a decade later the Vivian Committee included regular reviews – once during the lifetime of each five-year Parliament – in its report, and the subsequent Speaker's Conference accepted the spirit of this recommendation. It proposed that each Commission review all constituencies once every 3–7 years and this was incorporated into the 1944 Act, though subsequently amended to every 10–15 years to reflect MPs' concerns about frequent changes to their constituencies (see page 63).

Whereas the first half of the twentieth century was marked by urbanisation, the second half was characterised by suburbanisation and, increasingly, what commentators came to term counter-urbanisation. The inner parts of cities began to lose population, in part because of housing and planning policies which promoted lower density, higher quality provision. Extensive programmes of slum clearance were accompanied by the construction of large suburban estates to which many inner-city residents were relocated, with some moving even further to the New Towns and expanded towns established beyond the Green Belts which encircled most urban areas. Inner-city electorates thus declined, whereas those of the suburbs grew. And then decline began in the suburbs too, as economic activity moved away from the larger urban areas. Between 1951 and 1961, for example, population growth was much greater in suburban areas than inner cities, and then in the following decade inner-city populations began to decline. The 1971–81 period saw a continuation of inner-city decline plus, for the first time, a faster rate of growth in areas beyond the suburban zones of most metropolitan areas – a difference that was accentuated in the following decade.[8]

As constituencies 'age' after a review, therefore, there should be an increase in the disparity in their electorates. This is illustrated in Figure 5.6, which shows the standard deviation around the mean electorate at each of the general elections (note that the two 1974 elections were fought on the identical electoral register). The standard deviation was large in 1950, and was about 1000 voters larger a year later. It then fell very substantially in 1955 – the consequence of the First Periodical Review, whose recommended new constituencies were used in the election then. It fell further by 1959, and then increased by about half between then and the 1970 election, the last to

Figure 5.6   Standard deviations in electorate size for English constituencies, 1950–97

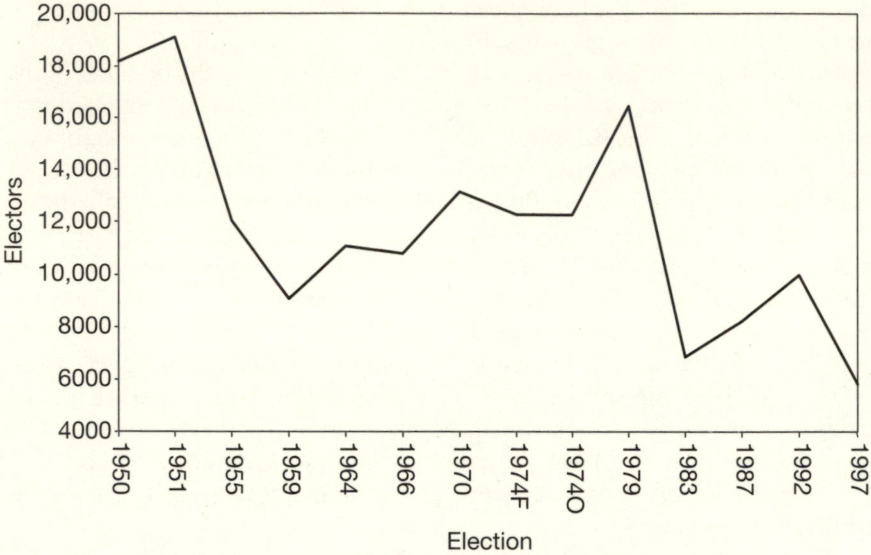

be fought in the constituencies first used a decade-and-a-half previously. The new constituencies introduced after 1970 had a lower standard deviation in 1974, though not by much because the electoral data on which they were based referred to 1964, ten years before the first election in which they were employed. (See below for the reasons for this.) There was then an increase to 1979, and a subsequent substantial fall as a result of the new constituencies recommended in the Third Periodic Review and used for the first time in 1983. (Interestingly, these were defined using 1976 electoral data.) There was then a further increase over the next two elections, and a final decline in 1997, when the constituencies recommended in the Fourth Periodic Review were first employed.

Similar trends are shown for Scotland and Wales (Figure 5.7), where constituencies are on average substantially smaller than they are in England. As well as confirming that disparities in constituency electorates increase over time, however, this figure illustrates another major feature of constituency redistributions in the United Kingdom over the second half of the twentieth century: not only did each Boundary Commission Review substantially reduce constituency electorate disparities, but also the later Reviews produced much greater electoral equality than the earlier ones. In England, for example, the standard deviation in 1950 after the Initial Review was *c.*18,000, voters whereas after the First Periodical Review it was 12,000; it was *c.*7000 after the Third Review in 1983 and even less after the Fourth in 1997. The Initial Review was conducted using 1947 electoral data, when the country's population was still in great flux after the Second World War, but overall the

Figure 5.7 Standard deviations in electorate size for Scottish and Welsh constituencies, 1950–97

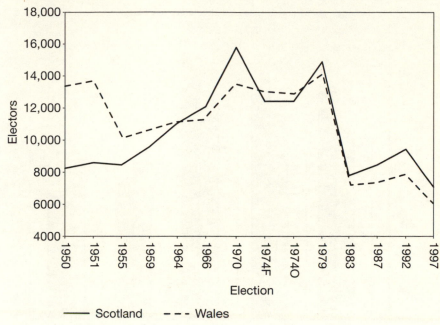

conclusion seems to be very clear: the Boundary Commissions have been increasingly successful at achieving one of the goals set for them: equality of electorates, as far as is practicable. Great precision is not possible, because of the other rules; in addition the building blocks that the Commissions use – wards – are relatively large units, especially in urban areas, and as a consequence disparities are certain. (In 1991, for example, the average ward in an English Shire County had 3229 electors, in a London Borough 6814 and in a Metropolitan District 10,231; in Birmingham, the average ward had 18,905 electors.) Nevertheless, the Commissions appear to have become increasingly adept at producing constituencies with a relatively narrow range of electorates – despite the change in the rules in 1958, which reduced the salience of the electoral equality criterion and the Court judgments in 1982 and 1983 (see below) which suggested that Rule 7 is the most important.

Two indicators of this aspect of the Commissions' work are shown in Figures 5.8 and 5.9. The first shows the average percentage deviation around the electoral quota in each country after each Review, using the electorate data employed by the Commissions. (To calculate these means, the difference between each constituency's electorate and the national quota is expressed as a percentage of that quota, irrespective of sign.) There was a clear shift after the Second Periodical Review. In England, for example, the mean deviation from the quota at each of the first three Reviews was 10–12 percentage

Figure 5.8   Variations in constituency electorates: mean percentage deviations
from the electoral quota after each redistribution

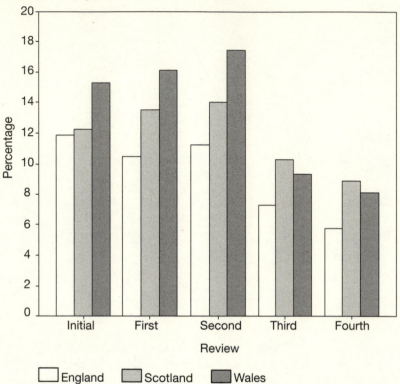

points; at the last two it was 7.3 and 5.8, respectively. Constituencies were
being squeezed into narrower bands, it seems, an interpretation confirmed by
Figure 5.9, which shows the percentage of all constituencies in each country
that were within 10 percentage points of the mean. In England, only about
half of the constituencies were that close to the mean at the first three
reviews, whereas in Wales it was no more than 40 per cent. After the last two
Reviews, the figures for England were 74.7 and 87.0 per cent, respectively,
for Scotland they were 57.0 and 73.7, and for Wales 68.4 and 75.0.

The main reason for this greater equality in electorates after the last two
Reviews is the very significant weakening of the constraint relating to the
local government map in the 1970s. Outside Greater London, where local
government had been reformed in the mid-1960s and the number of boroughs substantially reduced, there was a plethora of separate local authorities until the reforms of the mid-1970s. In England, for example, there were
76 County Boroughs and 44 Counties, with the latter containing 218
Municipal Boroughs, 444 Urban Districts and 271 Rural Districts. Rule
4(1)(a) of the 1949 *House of Commons (Redistribution of Seats) Act*

Figure 5.9 Percentage of constituency electorates within ten percentage points of the national average after each Review

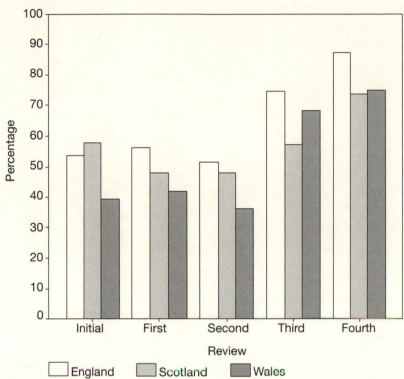

required that 'no county district shall be included partly in one constituency and partly in another', which was a very severe constraint on the Commissions' degrees of freedom in seeking to achieve electoral equality. The Boundary Commission for England had reported after its Initial Review that it could not produce constituencies within 25 per cent of the quota (the original requirement of the 1944 Act) 'without disturbing the unity of local government areas', which led to the removal of the 25 per cent tolerance in 1949 and the elevation of Rule 4 (relating to the local government template) over Rule 5 (electoral equality).

The changes to local government in the 1970s, and the consequent amendment to the *House of Commons (Redistribution of Seats) Act*, very much reduced this constraint. In England, for example, the County Boroughs were abolished, and the 120 separate upper-tier authorities were replaced by two groups of counties: the six Metropolitan Counties, comprising 36 lower-tier Metropolitan Districts, and the 39 Non-Metropolitan Counties, comprising 296 separate County Districts. At the same time, Rule 4 was relaxed, stating for England and Wales that 'No county or any part thereof shall be

Figure 5.10   Bias in the general election results 1950–97 due to differences in constituency electorates

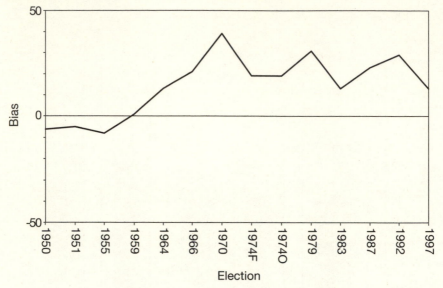

included in a constituency which includes the whole or part of any other county or the whole or part of a London borough'. There was no mention at all of County Districts, and although the Commissions have continued to recommend constituencies whose boundaries conform with District boundaries wherever possible, given the other rules, this is a much less stringent requirement, which has allowed them to achieve much greater electoral equality. (In Scotland, the relaxation was even greater: there the Commission is merely required to 'have regard' to the boundaries of local government areas.)[9]

Electoral equality and bias

We have shown that there were variations within each country in constituency electorates after each redistribution by the Boundary Commissions, although much less so after the last two redistributions than after the first three, because of changes to the local government structure. Furthermore, these variations increased with time from each Review, presumably as a result of population changes, with some constituencies losing electors and others gaining them through natural change (the ratio of new electors qualifying to those dying) and/or net migration. But did those variations produce electoral bias? As shown earlier, this would only occur if one party were stronger than the other in the smaller constituencies and in those that were losing electors compared to those which were gaining.

Figure 4.3a showed that there was indeed a substantial bias resulting from constituency size variations across the full period; its size and direction is shown in Figure 5.10. For the first three elections in the sequence (1950–55) there was a relatively small bias favouring the Conservative party; it was worth six, five and eight seats to it, respectively. In 1959 there was a very small bias to Labour (one seat), which then benefited from this bias component at every subsequent election – by as many as 39 seats (in 1970). The trend in that bias is a jagged one, with a reduction after each redistribution introduced new constituencies – in 1974, 1983 and 1997 – and a subsequent rise as electoral disparities increase again.

Urban:rural differences

Several questions are raised by the pattern in Figure 5.10. The first concerns the direction of the bias: why did it favour the Conservatives in the early years, and then Labour? The answer to this is that the Commissions – more specifically the Boundary Commission for England – changed policy after the first two Reviews. During those, it operated a pro-rural bias, on the grounds, as stated in the report of its Initial Review (Boundary Commission for England, 1947, 5), that 'in general urban constituencies could more conveniently support large electorates than rural constituencies' because of the greater ease of access between constituents and their MPs in the higher density urban areas. (The Commission was 'impressed by the advantages of accessibility they [the urban constituencies] enjoy over widely scattered rural areas'.)

In doing this, the Commission was implicitly using Rule 6 (regarding the use of 'special geographical considerations' to override the equal electorates criterion: see Box 3.7) to overcome what it perceived as the 'difficulties and disadvantages [that would be] attendant upon the creation of large rural constituencies'. (Rule 6 was not mentioned in the report.) As the Conservative party is generally stronger in rural areas, this meant that it was advantaged (albeit only slightly) in the creation of smaller constituencies there.

The Commission continued with this policy in its First Periodical Review, reporting that it 'saw no reason to recede from the view expressed in our initial report' ... [that] ... 'in general, urban constituencies could more conve niently support large electorates than rural constituencies' (Boundary Commission for England, 1954, 5), though it accepted that Parliament wished less disparity between the two groups than had been recommended in its Initial Report. (The House of Commons had been concerned at a number of very large constituencies recommended then and had modified the recommendations to produce a further 17 constituencies, all of them in urban areas.) Hence the continued pro-Conservative bias at the first election held in the new constituencies in 1955. This had been removed by 1959, however, as population decline saw many urban constituencies lose electors, whereas those in many rural areas grew (especially in and beyond the suburban rings around all large cities). As this population redistribution continued, and urban constituencies experienced more haemorrhaging, so the bias towards Labour grew. Its strongholds were in urban areas, which had increasingly small constituencies, whereas the Conservatives were strongest in the growing rural areas. Counter-urbanisation was producing an electoral system biased towards Labour.

Although the Boundary Commissions classify constituencies as either Borough or County (solely because these two types of constituency have different maximum spending limits for general election campaigns), this division into urban and rural is too coarse to illustrate the trends just described. For that we have produced two sets of comparative regions. In the first, we contrast London (the area covered by London County Council until 1964 and the Greater London County Council from then on) with seven adjacent Home Counties – Bedfordshire, Berkshire, Buckinghamshire, Essex, Hertfordshire, Kent and Surrey.[10] In the second, we contrast four major cities in the north of England (Leeds, Liverpool, Manchester and Sheffield: their County Boroughs pre-1974 and Metropolitan Districts thereafter) with five southwestern Counties (Cornwall, Devon, Dorset, Somerset and Wiltshire). For each we have calculated both the average electorate and the ratio of Conservative to Labour votes at each general election.

Figures 5.11 and 5.12 show the London:Home Counties contrasts. Until 1955, there was very little difference between the two areas in their average

Figure 5.11   Average electorates in London and the Home Counties

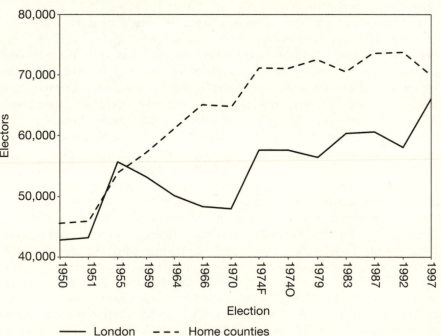

Figure 5.12 The ratio of Conservative to Labour votes in London and the Home Counties

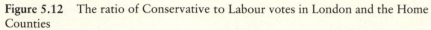

constituency electorates (Figure 5.11). From then on, however, the gap between the two widened, although it was closed somewhat by each Boundary Commission Review – as shown by the slightly narrower gaps between the two trends in 1974, 1983 and 1997.[11] On average, over much of the period London constituencies had as many as 10,000 fewer electors than their counterparts in the Home Counties. Turning to the pattern of votes, Figure 5.12 shows the ratio of Conservative to Labour votes cast in the two areas at each election: a ratio greater than 1.0 indicates that the Conservatives outvoted Labour, whereas one of less than 1.0 indicates that Labour was the larger of the two parties. The Conservatives outpolled Labour at every election in the Home Counties, but at only three of the 14 (1983, 1987 and 1992) in London. The urban area had both the smaller constituencies and, at most elections, a relative concentration of Labour voters.

A very similar pattern with regard to trends in average electorates is shown for the second set of contrasting areas in Figure 5.13, although the gap was only as wide as 10,000 voters between 1974 and 1983. Again, from 1955 on, it was the urban areas that had the smaller constituencies, and the difference between the two areas widened with the increasing age of the constituencies: the average constituency electorate declined in the four cities after each redistribution (which achieved greater equality by reducing the number of seats), whereas it grew in the southwestern counties. (In the latter,

Figure 5.13   Average electorates in four northern cities and five southwestern Counties

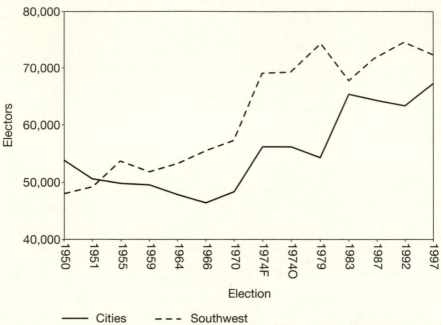

each redistribution reduced the average constituency size slightly by increasing the number of constituencies there.) Regarding voting patterns, Figure 5.14 shows the same urban:rural difference as Figure 5.12, though with a wider gap. The northern cities provided more votes for Labour than the Conservatives at every election, whereas the southwestern counties were very much pro-Conservative; from 1979 until 1992, the Conservative vote there was more than twice Labour's tally, and was four times greater at the apex of Thatcherite Conservatism's electoral successes in 1983.

Manipulating malapportionment

The second of the questions raised by Figure 5.10 relates to the shape of the trend in pro-Labour bias post-1955: why did it reach such a high peak in 1970, relative to 1983 and 1992? The answer lies in the time between redistributions, and political 'interference' with that.

As already noted, the Vivian Committee recommended that there should be a review of constituencies during the lifetime of each five-year Parliament. Because the House of Commons can be dissolved at any time within five years of the date when the Parliament first sat, however, it was not possible to build this recommendation into the legislation proposed by the Speaker's Conference, and instead a time limit of 5–7 years between reviews was

Figure 5.14 The ratio of Conservative to Labour votes in four northern cities and five southwestern Counties

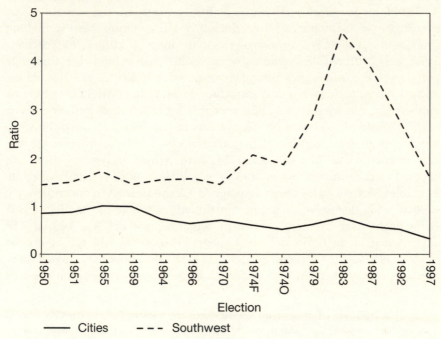

included in the 1944 legislation. The Commissions delivered their Initial Reports in 1947, and so their First Periodical Reports were due by and delivered in 1954.[12] This caused much concern to MPs, who thought that the frequency of change to constituency boundaries would hamper their ability to develop close relationships with their constituents. They expressed this to the Commissions during the Review, and the Boundary Commission for England (1954, 4) included in its Report the statement that 'It was clear from representations submitted to us that the changes recommended, even where they included proposals for additional representation, were not wholly welcome because of the disturbance they would inevitably cause both to the electorate and to their representatives in Parliament'.

The Commissions had, in fact, proposed relatively few changes; the Northern Ireland Commission proposed no change at all to the twelve constituencies there, for example, and the Welsh Commission proposed changes to only six of the 36 seats under its jurisdiction; in Scotland, 44 of the 71 constituencies were altered; and in England 323 of the 506 constituencies remained unchanged after the full procedure had been completed. But many MPs were dismayed by what one called this 'constant chopping and changing' during the debates on the Commissions' proposals in December 1954, and they returned to the issue in 1958, which not only changed the period between reviews to 10–15 years but also added Rule 7, which required the Commissions to take account of the disruptions that changes would cause and of the local ties that might be broken (see page 64).

The Home Secretary in 1958, R. A. Butler, presented the new Rule 7 to the House of Commons as introducing a 'presumption against making changes unless there is a very strong case for them' (*Hansard*, 11 February 1958, col. 230). MPs and parties were against change, and therefore prepared to accept inequalities among constituencies in their electorates. Alterations to constituencies not only introduce uncertainties ('Might they have to apply to stand in another seat, or even apply for re-selection in their current seat?'; 'Would the new seat be safer or less easy to win than the old one?'), but also mean that campaigning organisations have to be restructured. Most constituency parties are amalgams of ward parties and when there are changes to constituency boundaries new combination of wards have to be assembled. Activists who once campaigned for candidate A in constituency *x* suddenly find themselves living in constituency *y*, where the candidate is B (who might have a worse chance of winning than did A). As one MP expressed it in the 1954 debate (Kenneth Thompson, MP for Liverpool Walton: *Hansard*, 15 December 1954, col. 1839), a boundary change may move a party worker out of a constituency, to whose organisation she had contributed very significantly, to:

> ... what is to her a foreign land where there are a lot of people who do not speak her language ... [Such moves break links between MPs and] ... ordinary people who live in the streets and villages of our constituencies. ... Time goes on, and they may not like us very much, they may tolerate us but they do get to know us as their Member or candidate. Something happens in their lives, big or little ... and they think in the first place of their Member of Parliament. If he has done his job reasonably well over the passage of years, it is not difficult for them to recall his name or his face ... Then the Boundary Commission draws a line, and out of their lives completely goes this man or woman.

For the MPs and the parties, of course, the key issue is whether the Commissions' recommended changes make constituencies more or less winnable; their focus is on the electoral arithmetic.

Apart from changing the law, as they did in 1958, is there anything else they can do? Events in 1969 show that there is – and the graph in Figure 5.10 shows its impact: a 39-seat pro-Labour bias in 1970. The Boundary Commissions were due to report by 1969, 15 years after their previous reports in 1954. As the recommendations were being finalised through the public consultation process, it was clear to the Labour party (as expressed in members' diaries and memoirs, such George Brown's, Richard Crossman's and Harold Wilson's) that these could lead to it losing a number of seats – though there were considerable differences in the estimated number (Crossman said as many as 30, whereas Wilson thought only six to eight). It would be desirable to fight the next general election (due by 1971) in the old constituencies, but how could this be achieved, since the relevant Secretaries of State are required to table the Commissions' recommendations before Parliament?[13]

The Conservatives were aware that the Commissions' reports had been delivered in April and in June called on the government to lay them before Parliament.[14] The Home Secretary (James Callaghan) responded by pointing out that a Royal Commission on Local Government in England was soon to report (he was aware of its proposals), and that if its recommendations were enacted this would create considerable difficulties because the new constituency map was based on the old structure. At least a fifth, and perhaps a quarter, of constituencies outside London would be affected, plus half of those in Wales (where a parallel review was being conducted; a Scottish review would be completed later). A new redistribution of Parliamentary constituencies would thus be needed and it would be better to abandon the current one – except for London, where local government was restructured in the 1960s and the new constituencies were the first to take account of that. Callaghan also suggested minor changes outside London, where current constituencies were very large.[15] A Bill was introduced to this end, but it was defeated in the House of Lords. Callaghan then laid the Commissions' proposals before the House of Commons, and moved that they be not approved, on the grounds that 346 constituencies were to be changed, and that they would have to be changed again within three years because of the local government reorganisation (although this would presumably be an Interim Review). The Labour majority in the House voted for this.

Labour thus fought the 1970 general election in the constituencies introduced in 1954, and based on 1952 electoral data.[16] It lost the election, but might have done so by an even greater margin if the new constituencies had been employed. The new Conservative government enacted the Commissions' proposals soon after they were elected, and when the next general election was held in February 1974, the pro-Labour bias because of variations in constituency size was half that it benefited from in 1970.[17] According to Callaghan's biographer (Morgan, 1997, 363), he was embarrassed by this 'cynical political manoeuvre', but Figure 5.10 shows why it was done.

Having successfully influenced the amount of bias in the system in 1970, Labour sought to do so again in 1982 (though only in England), when the Boundary Commissions delivered their Third Periodic Review reports to the relevant Secretaries of State. Once again, it was felt that the new constituencies would harm Labour's cause and benefit the Conservatives – and by now both the parties and political analysts were better able to analyse the recommendations and evaluate their likely political consequences. As Figure 5.10 shows, at the 1979 election the pro-Labour bias was already approaching its 1970 peak, and there were strong expectations that if the next general election (due by 1984) were fought in the old constituencies, then Labour could benefit very substantially from the by then very small constituencies in many of its inner city heartlands.

But Labour was out of office and there was no Parliamentary way to stop the enactment of the Commissions' recommendations. And so the decision was taken to challenge them in Court, before the Secretary of State had laid them before Parliament (only the Boundary Commission for England's recommendations were challenged). A case was brought in the name of four senior party members, including the leader (Michael Foot), that the Boundary Commission for England had, in legal terminology, 'misdirected itself'. Two individuals were instrumental in developing this argument – Edmund Marshall MP and Gerry Bermingham, a Sheffield City Councillor and Parliamentary candidate for St Helens South who had been active for the party at the Local Inquiries held in several parts of the country and who set the foundations for Labour's successful campaign during the Fourth Periodic Review (see page 146). The case was that the disparities between constituency electorates were too large, given the wording of Rule 5, with evidence presented that much greater equality could have been achieved if the Commission had paid more attention to this issue.[18] It is very unlikely that a new set of constituencies with less variation around the electoral quota would have benefited Labour in more than a few cases. Focusing on this issue simply reflected the grounds on which it was considered that a legal challenge had some chance of success. If the Commission were required to rework the review, the next general election would then almost certainly be held in the old constituencies, which would be to Labour's advantage.

This, too, was a manoeuvre designed to promote Labour's electoral advantage; Waller estimated that Labour stood to lose as many as 30 seats because of the redistribution.[19] It received short shrift from the Courts and the case was dismissed in February 1983. The new constituencies were then immediately enacted, in time for the general election called for May of that year (and for which the parties had in any case been preparing). The judgments did create some interest beyond the refusal of Labour's case, however. In particular, it was stressed that the Commissions have very considerable discretion as long as they work to the rules. They were not, in Sir John Donaldson's words in the Court of Appeal, required to 'do an exercise in accountancy': instead, they had to strike a balance between many factors and '... mere demonstration that there is an alternative answer, which also could be put forward consistently with those instructions [the Rules] tells us nothing. There being more than one answer, Parliament has asked the Commission to advise on which, in their judgement, should be adopted'. And, of course, it is Parliament which finally decides, not the Commissions – and it is not for the Courts to override Parliamentary sovereignty in this matter. Furthermore, in examining the Rules, Sir John argued that the wording of Rule 7 in effect makes it the most important; taking account of potential disruptions because of change, and the breaking of local ties that may follow, is more important than electoral equality.[20]

Both the Second and the Third Reviews provoked attempts by the Labour party to influence the timing of their implementation, to promote its electoral interests by having elections fought in an old set of constituencies with a large number of small urban seats where Labour might be expected to win easily – thus producing a pro-Labour bias. And this was not the end of such political cynicism with regard to redistributions. After the 1987 general election, the Conservatives realised that constituency-size variations were once more increasing, and that when the next review reported it would remove them – again, almost certainly to their advantage (the figure of 20 seats was widely cited). Certainly, as Figure 5.10 shows, the pro-Labour bias increased again between 1983, when the new seats were first used, and 1987 and there was no reason to believe it would not continue to do so.

The next review was not due to report until 1997, and indeed did not start (in England) until 1991, and there was little concern expressed during the early years of that Parliament. But the close victory at the 1992 general election convinced some Conservative party members of the need to ensure that the next election was fought in a new set of constituencies (although by then some at least had reduced their expectations; the new set of constituencies might be worth just ten seats to them). One member in particular (Rob Hayward, who had lost his seat in 1992) argued strongly that the government should ensure that the Commissions reported well before 1997 (with a majority of 21, it was quite possible that the government would be forced to go to the country before the end of its five-year term). And so in June 1992, very soon after the election victory, the *Boundaries Commissions Act* was passed, with relatively little protest from the opposition parties (whose main concern was over constitutional niceties). The Home Secretary, Kenneth Clarke, argued that there were already considerable discrepancies between constituency electorates and that these would continue to grow. The next election could be fought in constituencies that were, in effect, twenty years old (the Third Review in England had been based on 1976 electoral data) and so the Bill proposed: (a) to require the Commissions to report on their Fourth Periodic Reviews by December 1994, and (b) thenceforth to report every 8–12 years. This was enacted, and although the Commissions (with the exception of the Scottish) did not meet the 1994 deadline, the new constituencies were in place by the end of 1995. The pro-Labour bias in 1997 was thus substantially less then than it had been five years earlier (13 seats instead of 29).

Conclusions

Malapportionment contributes to bias within an electoral system if either smaller constituencies are established in a part of the country, where one party is much stronger than the other, and/or population redistribution across an established set of constituencies means that one party increasingly obtains an advantage because its support is relatively concentrated in areas where constituency electorates are falling. Both occurred in the United Kingdom during the second half of the twentieth century.

Over-representation of Scotland and Wales was present throughout the period and benefited the Labour party, increasingly the strongest of the two main UK parties in both countries. This was a function of the rules under which the Boundary Commissions operated, and of their alteration in 1958. For the next four decades, governments of neither party were prepared to act on what was clearly an inequitable situation. For Conservatives to have done so would have led to claims of partisanship, and also would have dented their claimed position as the 'party of the Union' in the 1980s and early 1990s; for Labour to have done so would have been to damage the party's chances of electoral victory (it could have lost about 15 MPs as a consequence) – although in 1997 it realised the necessity of doing so once powers (including limited taxation powers not also granted to the Welsh) had been devolved to the Scottish Parliament.

There was substantial population redistribution in the United Kingdom during the second half of the twentieth century, with the inner cities and later the inner suburbs declining. Growth was increasingly focused not only on the outer suburbs, but also on the smaller towns beyond the Green Belts that constrained the outward growth of the main conurbations. The constituencies that lost population were largely Labour strongholds, whereas most of those which gained favoured the Conservatives. Thus Labour benefited from these shifts. Its votes were concentrated in the smaller constituencies where fewer votes were needed for victory than was the case for the Conservatives – and as the constituencies aged and the disparities in their electorates increased, so Labour's advantage grew once the Boundary Commission for England stopped its policy of recommending smaller constituencies in rural areas (which, interestingly, it did in the Second Periodical Review, when Labour was in power).[21]

This malapportionment came about through the natural processes of population change and movement, and the Boundary Commissions' rules were designed to limit it through the regular redistributions – although MPs made it clear that they considered other criteria more important in those reviews, if for no other reason than they offered them the chance to achieve gerrymanders (on which, see the next chapter), and it was only after local government reforms in the 1970s that the Commissions were fully able to implement the 'equal electorates' criterion.[22] The parties could only influence this process by changing either the rules or the timing of reviews. The latter was employed, in one way or another, on several occasions: by the decision to lengthen the period after the First Periodical Review; by the Labour government's successful delay of the implementation of the Second Periodical Review until after the fifth election fought over a period of 15 years; by the failure of the Labour leadership to delay the implementation of the next review; and by John Major's government's decision to shorten the period between reviews again in 1992 in order to promote its re-election chances five years later. As a consequence, the component due to constituency-size variations has been one of the main contributors to the total bias at UK elections over the last half of the twentieth century.

Notes

1 See McLean (1995).

2 In Scotland, a majority of those voting favoured devolution, but the legislation, as a result of amendments introduced by anti-devolution MPs, also required that it receive the support of 40 per cent of the registered electorate – which it failed to do.

3 The Boundary Commissions need not report on their Fifth Reviews until early 2007, 12 years after submission of their last reports. As each Parliament can run for five years, it may well be that the new constituencies are not used until 2007 if elections are held in 2002 and that year. However, many Parliaments in recent decades have been dissolved after four years, which would produce elections in 2001 and 2005, with the new constituencies not being employed until 2009 (or even 2010).

4 The recommended denominators were: England, 523 seats; Scotland, 66 seats; Wales, 26 seats; Northern Ireland, 17 seats (Home Affairs Committee, 1986–87, x).

5 On the decision to allocate Northern Ireland 12 seats then, see French (1978).

6 A strong case is made by his biographers that Enoch Powell, by then MP for South Down, was instrumental in the pressure for the Conference (see Shepherd, 1997; Heffer, 1998)

7 See Dixon (1968).

8 The data from which these brief generalisations have been drawn can be found in Coleman and Salt (1992) and Champion (1994).

9 The Home Office advice to the Commissions, reported by them, was that they should operate within the District boundaries wherever feasible: Rossiter, Johnston and Pattie (1999).

10 The GLC covered an area and population about twice that of the LCC (and the change moved substantial areas that were formerly in the Home Counties into the GLC area). Thus comparisons before and after the 1974 elections (when new constituencies based on the local government reforms involved in the creation of the GLC were used for the first time) are difficult.

11 The smaller gap in 1997 is because for the first time since the 1960s restructuring of the London Boroughs, the Boundary Commission combined Boroughs in order to reduce the electoral disparities.

12 Intriguingly, the Commissions called their first two reviews after the Initial Review Periodical Reviews, and then changed the adjective to Periodic!

13 Several sets of diaries and memoirs recount how the issue was handled: Brown (1972), Callaghan (1987), Crossman (1978) and Wilson (1974).

14 By then, of course, both parties had calculated the likely impact of the Commissions' recommendations, because they had all previously been published and made available to the parties.

15 According to Callaghan's biographer (Morgan, 1997, 362), the Commissions' proposals 'might cost the party up to twenty seats, in view of their rearranging English and Welsh boundaries in favour of growing middle-class areas; in Scotland, on the other hand, Labour might actually benefit'.

16 The Boundary Commission for England announced that it started the review in August 1953, using the roll that became current in March of that year, which was compiled at the end of 1952.

17 By 1974, of course, the constituencies were 22 years old, having been based on 1952 electoral data. If the 1970 election had been held in them, the bias may have been below 19 seats because population change would have been less by then.

18 Interestingly, this case had not been argued by the party's representatives at the Local Inquiries, nor by party officials when they met the Commission.

19 Waller (1983).

20 This reading has been challenged, both by academics (Rawlings, 1988) and by a former Deputy Chairman of the Scottish Commission.

21 On this, see Rossiter, Johnston and Pattie (1999, 165–66).

22 In the Fourth Periodic Review, the Boundary Commission for England decided not to allocate further seats to four counties – Avon, Derbyshire, Norfolk and Warwickshire – according to the harmonic mean rule (Chapter 3, endnote 13) on the grounds that this would violate Rule 7. In this, they were generally supported by the parties, despite some arguments to the contrary from academics in two cases (Rossiter, Johnston and Pattie, 1999).

6

The gerrymandered UK

The determination of constituency boundaries in the UK has been undertaken since 1944 by independent bodies – the Boundary Commissions – acting outside the political arena. No political party has control, or even direct influence, over the Commissions in the way that occurred in the nineteenth century, and hence there has been no gerrymandering, drawing of boundaries by politically motivated groups in order to promote their electoral interests. Such groups, including the political parties, are consulted by the Commissions and can seek to influence their deliberations and recommendations – as will be illustrated below. But all parties are involved in that procedure and hence 'classic' gerrymandering by one party cannot occur.

Nevertheless, the equivalent of gerrymandering does occur, and the outcome of most general elections since 1950 has seen one party benefit over the other because its votes are more effectively distributed across the constituencies that its opponent's. This is illustrated in Figure 6.1, which shows the trend in the gerrymander (or 'efficiency') component of the bias measure that we are employing here. For most of the period, the advantage when vote shares are equalised has lain with the Conservatives, substantially so until the 1970s. Their party had an advantage over Labour of 39 seats because of this bias component in both 1951 and 1970: its advantage was 23 seats in 1959 and 13 at each of the other three. At the two 1974 elections, the direction of the bias shifted: pro-Labour (by 11 seats) in February, but pro-Conservative again in October (28 seats). It remained pro-Conservative over the next four elections, ranging from a low of just one seat in 1979, through 28 and 34 seats at the two 1980s elections, and fell again to seven seats in 1992. There was then a very substantial shift to Labour in 1997, which had an advantage over the Conservatives of 48 seats then.

Why has this come about? Is it just through chance or does it reflect aspects of the electoral system in operation? We show here that it is the latter, that there are strong gerrymander tendencies built in to the procedures operated by the Boundary Commissions, and that these can be manipulated by the parties, both when boundaries are being drawn and during election campaigns.

Figure 6.1   Bias due to the gerrymander component, 1950–91

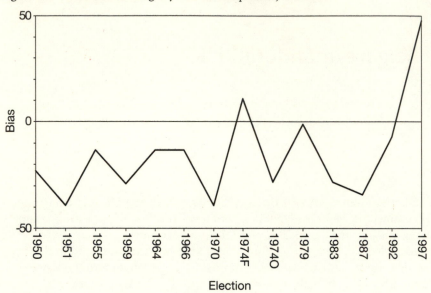

The infrastructural gerrymander

Gerrymander-like outcomes are in-built to the procedure operated by the Boundary Commission – largely because of Rule 4 in the *Boundary Commissions Act 1986* and its predecessors. We term this an *infrastructural gerrymander*, because it is part of the system.

The infrastructural gerrymander comes about because each Commission (with the exception of Northern Ireland's) is required to take account of certain local government boundaries, and not create constituencies which cross those boundaries unless there are special circumstances requiring them to do so. (The requirement is weaker for the Scottish Commission, which is only required to 'have regard to' the boundaries of local governments, than it is for the English and Welsh.) Thus, as we illustrated for a number of cities in Chapter 3, the Commissions have to recommend a set of constituencies for each major local government area which, again as we showed there, is likely to mean that the largest party is advantaged, winning a larger percentage of the seats than it does of the votes.

We illustrate this using the 1983 general election, the first fought in the new constituencies recommended by the Commissions' Third Periodic Reviews.[1] In England, Wales and Scotland there were 124 separate areas to which seats were allocated (the Counties in the first two, and the Regions in Scotland, plus the London Boroughs. In England most of the Metropolitan

Districts were treated separately by the Commission, and they are analysed separately here too, except where the Commission combined two Districts). We have analysed the distribution of seats in these 124 areas to show the infrastructural gerrymander at work.

Most of these areas are small and return few MPs to the House of Commons. Indeed, as the first column of Table 6.1 shows, of the 124 separate areas used by the Commissions the majority (70) had no more than four seats each and only 11 returned more than ten MPs each. The other two columns divide the 124 areas into which of the two main parties won most votes there. In general, the areas in which the Conservatives were the largest party had more constituencies than those where Labour was the largest party The average number of seats in the areas where the Conservatives were the largest party was 5.4, with 14 of the 83 areas having ten or more seats each; in the 41 areas where Labour was the largest party, on the other hand, only two had ten seats or more and the average was 4.5.

As shown by our examples in Chapters 3 and 4, in each of these areas the largest of the two parties is likely to win a larger share of the seats than it does of the votes, especially in the smaller areas where few constituencies

Table 6.1 The number of seats in the areas used by the Boundary Commissions, 1983–92 to allocate constituencies – the final two columns divide the areas into those where Conservative and Labour, respectively, were the largest parties

| Seats | All | Areas | |
		Con largest	Lab largest
1	3	2	1
2	26	15	11
3	24	14	10
4	17	10	7
5	9	8	1
6	19	12	7
7	6	5	1
8	3	2	1
9	0	0	0
10	6	6	0
11	4	3	1
12	2	1	1
15	1	1	0
16	3	3	0
22	1	0	1
Total	124	82	42

Table 6.2 The infrastructural gerrymander in operation: the 1983 general election – the final two pairs of columns divide the areas into those where Conservative and Labour, respectively, were the largest parties

Percentage of seats won	All areas		Con largest		Lab largest	
	C	L	C	L	C	L
0	23	52	4	51	19	1
1–10	0	3	0	3	0	0
11–20	6	5	2	5	6	0
21–30	6	3	4	3	4	2
31–40	11	11	0	9	7	0
41–50	13	13	8	7	5	6
51–60	3	1	3	3	1	1
61–70	7	9	6	1	0	6
71–80	5	6	5	0	0	5
81–90	9	6	9	0	0	5
91–99	1	0	1	0	0	1
100	40	15	40	0	0	15
Total	124	124	82	82	42	42

are involved. This is clearly indicated by the percentage of the seats won by each of the parties across the 124 areas (the first two columns of Table 6.2). In 75 of the areas (fully 60 per cent of them) one or other of the two parties won no seats at all, whereas in 55 one of the parties won all of the seats; the Labour party was more likely to fail to win a single seat in an area where it was the weaker of the two – 52 of the 75 cases – and least likely to win all of the seats where it was the stronger – 15 of the 55 areas only. In the 82 areas where the Conservatives were the largest party (the second pair of two columns in the table), they won all of the seats in 40 cases, with Labour winning none of them in 51. There were only ten areas where the Conservatives won less than half of the seats despite being the largest party – in almost every case because other parties (the Alliance, Plaid Cymru or the Scottish Nationalists) won seats there. (In all eight cases where the Conservatives won 41–50 per cent of the seats, their actual percentage was 50.) Similarly, in the 42 areas where Labour was the largest party (the last two columns), it won 50 per cent or more of the seats in 39 of the cases, with the Conservatives winning none at all in 19 and getting a majority of the seats in only one.

What we have here, therefore, is a series of local gerrymanders. This produces seats:votes ratios which are far from 1.0, as illustrated in Figures 6.2 and 6.3, which plot the seats:votes ratios for each party in the areas where they were largest (i.e. 82 areas in the case of the Conservatives and

Figure 6.2   Conservative seats:votes ratios by Conservative vote percentage and number of seats in areas where the Conservatives were the largest party, 1983

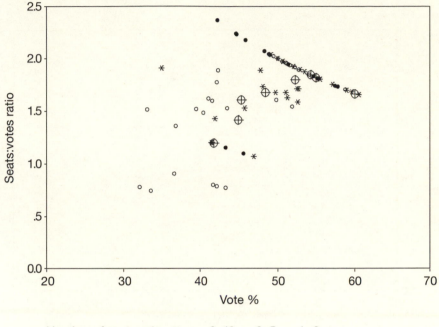

Number of seats   ⊕ >10   * 6–10   ○ 3–5   • 1–2

42 for Labour: Table 6.2) against its percentage of the votes there. For each party, the larger its share of the votes cast, the larger its seats:votes ratio. (The odd, crescent-shaped alignment of the points on the top-right of each diagram reflects the maximum ratio possible at any given vote percentage, given that the maximum seats percentage is 100; with 60 per cent of the votes, for example, the ratio cannot exceed 1.67.) There is no apparent difference in seats:votes ratios according to the number of seats in the area, however.[2] In other words, each party almost invariably gets a larger proportion of the seats than of the votes in the Boundary Commission areas where it is the larger of the two main parties (i.e. a seats:votes ratio greater than 1.0), and the larger its votes share the larger the ratio. (With 50 per cent of the votes, for example, both parties had ratios of at least 1.5 in every area.)

This suggests a clear reason for a pro-Conservative gerrymander in 1983. The Conservative party was the largest in two-thirds of the areas, and in virtually all of them it got a seats:votes ratio well above 1.0 (the average was 1.60). Labour was even more advantaged in the 42 areas where it was the largest party, with an average ratio of 1.70, but this occurred in areas containing just 188 seats in total, compared to 445 seats in the areas where the

Figure 6.3   Labour seats:votes ratios by Labour vote percentage and number of seats in areas where Labour was the largest party, 1983

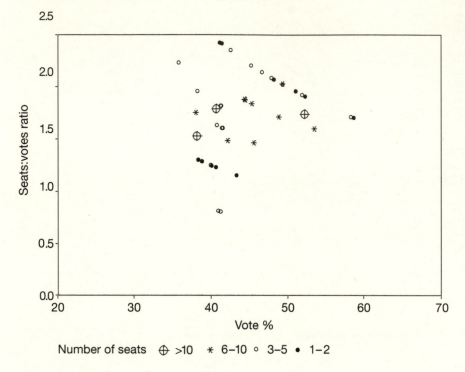

Conservatives were in a majority. The infrastructural gerrymander worked strongly in the Conservatives' favour.

Of course, our bias measure is based on the situation when the two parties have an equal share of the votes cast, so to appreciate the contribution of the infrastructural gerrymander to the bias we need to look at that situation. In 1983, if the votes had been equally shared between Conservative and Labour, the position would have been very different from the actual situation, when Labour obtained its lowest share of the votes cast during the 50-year period being studied.

Of the 124 areas, Labour would have been the largest party in 68 with equal votes shares overall, with the Conservatives occupying first place (of the two main parties) in the remaining 56. This suggests that there should have been a pro-Labour bias, but Labour's strength in a majority of the areas was countered by their relative size: its 68 areas contained 311 of the constituencies, compared with 322 in the Conservatives' 56 areas. Furthermore, the Conservatives got a better return on their votes in those areas than Labour did in its 68; the average Conservative seats:votes ratio in its 56 areas was 1.72 whereas Labour's average in its 68 was 1.62. (The main reason for this difference was that although there was little variation between the two areas in the percentage of the seats won by the largest party – 78.7 for Labour and 75.9 for the Conservatives – there was a much larger difference in the votes won – 47.5 and 43.3 per cent, respectively.) Thus overall the gerrymander bias component favoured the Conservatives because they performed better in winning seats relative to votes in the areas where they were strongest – they won more seats with fewer votes.

Trends in the infrastructural gerrymander

The discussion of the 1983 general election has shown that the infrastructural gerrymander comes about because of the division of the country into areas by the Boundary Commissions, acting according to Rule 4. Within almost all of these areas, the largest party gets a greater share of the seats than of the votes, and hence a seats:votes ratio in each that is substantially larger than 1.0. One party is favoured over the other in each area, therefore. Whether it is favoured over Great Britain as a whole depends on a combination of three factors: the number of areas in which each party is strongest, the number of seats in each of those areas, and the leading party's average seats:votes ratio in each type of area.

To apply this analysis to all elections since 1950, we have calculated the seats:votes ratios (for equal vote shares) in each of the areas employed by the Boundary Commissions. In most cases these areas were clear from their reports, especially those of the Third and Fourth Periodic Reviews; at earlier reviews, we have used the Counties and County Boroughs, plus the London Boroughs.[3] For the last two reviews, we have combined Metropolitan Districts where the English Commission did so, and for the Fourth Review we have similarly combined London Boroughs. This gave us the following number of separate areas for each review:

Review	Elections	Areas
Initial	1950–51	180
First	1955–70	179
Second	1974–79	191
Third	1979–92	124
Fourth	1997	110

Each set of areas was divided into those where the Conservative party had more votes than Labour and vice versa for each of the elections, and we then calculated the number of seats in those areas and the average seats:votes ratio for the largest party.

Table 6.3 shows that, with equal vote shares, at every election the Labour party was strongest in more of the areas employed by the Boundary Commissions than was the case for the Conservatives. It also shows

Table 6.3   The infrastructural gerrymander in Great Britain

Election	Areas C	Areas L	Seats C	Seats L	TotalS C	TotalS L	All C	All L	S:Vstr C	S:Vstr L	S:Vweak C	S:Vweak L
Initial Review												
1950	78	102	3.9	3.0	303	308	65	54	1.62	1.51	0.40	0.26
1951	85	95	3.8	3.0	326	285	61	57	1.50	1.42	0.35	0.32
First Periodical Review												
1955	79	100	3.9	3.1	309	309	63	57	1.65	1.43	0.35	0.27
1959	86	93	4.1	2.9	352	266	65	61	1.62	1.46	0.33	0.29
1964	77	102	4.0	3.1	307	311	68	68	1.74	1.62	0.25	0.26
1966	71	108	4.0	3.1	287	331	70	69	1.71	1.60	0.35	0.26
1970	75	104	4.1	3.0	304	314	59	73	1.72	1.64	0.20	0.29
Second Periodical Review												
1974F	84	107	3.4	3.2	286	337	57	62	1.76	1.71	0.33	0.30
1974O	86	105	3.4	3.2	289	304	57	58	1.75	1.67	0.36	0.25
1979	82	109	3.4	3.2	277	346	63	67	1.71	1.59	0.26	0.22
Third Periodic Review												
1983	56	68	5.8	4.6	322	311	32	44	1.72	1.62	0.41	0.46
1987	56	68	5.6	4.7	315	318	39	50	1.67	1.58	0.39	0.41
1992	54	70	5.5	4.8	296	337	33	50	1.55	1.54	0.36	0.47
Fourth Periodic Review												
1997	47	63	6.3	5.5	294	347	17	41	1.38	1.62	0.37	0.59

Key to columns: Areas – the number of separate areas in which the party (C or L) had the largest percentage of the votes cast; Seats – the average number of seats in the areas where the party (C or L) had the largest percentage of the votes cast; TotalS – the total number of seats in the areas where the party (C or L) had the largest percentage of the votes cast; All – the percentage of areas in which the party (C or L) won all of the seats; S:Vstr – the average seats:votes ratio in the areas where the party (C or L) had the largest percentage of the votes cast; S:Vweak – the average seats:votes ratio in the areas where the party (C or L) had the smallest percentage of the votes cast.

that this advantage was countered in many cases by those areas where Labour was strongest having fewer seats on average than those where the Conservatives were the major party – with the result that at several elections the areas where the Conservatives were the strongest party contained more seats in total than those where Labour was strongest. (The difference between the two types of area was approximately one seat in four of the five groups of elections; only in the 1974–79 period, after the Second Periodical Review, was the difference significantly smaller.) Thus whereas there was always a majority of areas where the infrastructural gerrymander favoured Labour, this advantage was 'watered down' by the small average size of those areas.

The major disadvantage suffered by Labour in the operation of the infrastructural gerrymander, however, came because it performed too well in the areas where it was strongest in terms of vote winning, but no better in terms of seat winning than was the case with the Conservatives in the other areas. In 1950, for example, Labour won on average 52.7 per cent of the votes in the 102 areas where it was strongest and 79.9 per cent of the seats, giving an average seats:votes ratio of 1.51. In the 78 areas where its opponent was strongest, on the other hand, the respective averages for the Conservatives were 52.3, 85.7 and 1.62. With almost exactly the same percentage of the votes, the Conservatives won more of the seats, and so achieved higher seats:votes ratios. The reason for this was that the Conservatives were more likely to win all of the seats in the areas where they were strong than was the case for Labour in its areas: in 51 of the 78 areas for the Conservatives (65 per cent) compared to 55 of the 102 (54 per cent) for Labour. As a result, as Table 6.3 shows, the Conservatives scored a higher average seats:votes ratio in the areas where they were strongest than did Labour in the areas where they were strongest.

This greater likelihood of the Conservatives winning all of the seats in their areas of strength than of Labour doing so where it was the largest party only occurred at the elections held under the first two reviews (Table 6.3); at all of them, the average Conservative seats:votes ratio was approximately 0.1 larger than that for Labour. After the last three reviews, however, Labour won all of the seats in substantially more areas than did the Conservatives – although with the smaller number of areas, and the larger average number of seats per area after the Third and Fourth Periodic Reviews, the probability of a party winning all of the seats in an area fell substantially. Nevertheless, until the last two elections (in 1992 and 1997) the Conservatives had a substantially larger average seats:votes ratio in the areas where they were strongest than was the case for Labour in its stronger areas.

The reason for this is that at most elections the Conservatives tended to win more seats in the areas where Labour was strongest than Labour did in the areas of Conservative strength. This is indicated in the final pair of columns in Table 6.3, which gives each party's average seats:votes ratio in the areas where its opponent was the strongest party. In eight of the cases (all of them before the 1980s), the Conservative ratio was higher than Labour's – even though it got a smaller percentage of the seats than of the votes, it got a larger one than Labour did in comparable circumstances. The graphs in Figures 6.4 and 6.5 show these differences clearly, especially with regard to the seats:votes ratios in the areas of strength (Figure 6.4).

Until 1992, the translation of votes into seats was more effective for the Conservatives in their areas of strength than it was for Labour in the areas

Figure 6.4   The average seats:votes ratios for the Conservative and Labour parties in the Boundary Commission areas where they were the larger of the two parties

where it was the largest party. In addition, for much of the period, the translation of votes into seats was less effective for Labour in the areas where the Conservatives were the stronger party than vice versa (Figure 6.5). After 1979, however, Labour did better in its areas of relative weakness than was the case for its opponent.

These differences between the parties are made clear by looking at the patterns of wasted votes per seat lost and surplus votes per seat won, for individual Boundary Commission areas rather than for the complete country, as in Chapter 1. This is illustrated in Table 6.4 for two areas which each had six seats at the 1983 election: Northamptonshire, where the Conservatives would have won five of the seats with equal vote shares; and Sheffield, where Labour would have won five. (The first two columns show their vote totals after adjustment to achieve national equality in vote shares.) In Northamptonshire, the Conservatives' average surplus votes per constituency won (i.e. their margin of victory over the second-placed party, less one vote) was 5560, compared to an average surplus for Labour in Sheffield of 15,185, almost three times as large. Where Labour won, it won by a much larger margin than was the case for the Conservatives where they won. Furthermore, where Labour lost in Northamptonshire they wasted many more votes per seat than the Conservatives did in Sheffield – because

Figure 6.5   The average seats:votes ratios for the Conservative and Labour parties in the Boundary Commission areas where they were the smaller of the two parties

Labour lost by a smaller margin on average; Labour wasted on average almost twice as many votes per seat lost in Northamptonshire as the Conservatives did in Sheffield.[4]

Both Northamptonshire and Sheffield have infrastructural gerrymanders, but of different types. In Chapter 3 we noted the difference between a *stacked gerrymander*, in which one party wins seats by very large majorities and which it is unlikely to lose unless there is a massive shift in votes away from it, and a *cracked gerrymander*, in which it wins seats by small majorities and is thus vulnerable to relatively small shifts in votes away from it. A cracked gerrymander is more efficient in its distribution of votes than is a stacked gerrymander, i.e. it gives a better return of seats, as indicated by the seats:votes ratio. Sheffield clearly has a stacked gerrymander, with Labour winning five of the six seats by very large majorities. Northamptonshire, on the other hand, has a cracked gerrymander, with the Conservatives getting very many fewer surplus votes in the five seats that they won there than Labour did in Sheffield. Thus if this difference between the two counties in gerrymander types is repeated across the country, with Labour areas having stacked and Conservative areas cracked gerrymanders, this could account for the inter-party variations in seats:votes ratios, and hence for the gerrymander bias.

Table 6.4 Wasted votes per seats lost and surplus votes per seats won at the 1983 general election: Northamptonshire and Sheffield

	CVA	LVA	AV	CS	LS	CW	LW
Northamptonshire							
Corby	17,117	21,368	9,905	0	4,251	17117	0
Daventry	22,568	13,628	13,221	8,939	0	0	13,628
Kettering	19,544	13,797	14,637	4,906	0	0	13,797
Northampton North	19,355	17,042	12,829	2,312	0	0	17,042
Northampton South	22,986	15,370	11,698	7,615	0	0	15,370
Wellingborough	21,700	17,673	12,994	4,026	0	0	17,673
Average				5,560			15,502
Sheffield							
Attercliffe	8,023	26,498	10,241	0	16,256	8023	0
Brightside	4,535	28,884	10,322	0	18,561	4535	0
Central	4,793	27,874	7,969	0	19,904	4793	0
Hallam	22,834	14,479	15,077	7,757	0	0	14,479
Heeley	11,706	28,148	12,813	0	15,314	11706	0
Hillsborough	11,577	25,204	19,355	0	5,848	11577	0
Average					15185	8127	

Key to columns: CVA – Conservative vote total (adjusted to ensure equal vote shares nationally); LVA – Labour vote total (adjusted to ensure equal vote shares nationally); AV – Alliance vote; CS – Conservative surplus; LS – Labour surplus; CW – Conservative wasted; LW – Labour wasted.

A ready test of whether the infrastructural gerrymander is of a different type for the two parties is whether they differ in the average majorities in the seats that they win. Stacked gerrymanders produce safer seats on average than cracked gerrymanders, so the Labour party should win its seats by larger majorities, on average, than its opponent. This is indeed the case. Figure 6.6 shows the average majority for Conservative- and Labour-held seats at each election, if they had equal vote shares nationally: the average Labour majority was generally larger – by as much as 5000 votes on some occasions. But the graphs do converge, notably in 1966–70 and 1979, i.e. at the end of the periods when the constituencies of the Second and Third Reviews, respectively, were in use. By the end of those periods, constituency size variations had increased, with those held by Labour tending to get relatively smaller over time (as shown in the previous chapter). As a result, its majorities would be dropping in absolute terms, whereas its opponent's would have been increasing.

To control for these variations in constituency size over time, Figure 6.7 shows average majorities as percentages of the total number of votes cast.

Figure 6.6 The average majority in Conservative- and Labour-held seats with equal vote shares: 1950–97

The picture is clear: across all 14 elections Labour was winning its seats by larger majorities than were the Conservatives, relative to the number of votes cast in the constituencies won. Furthermore, this gap widened from 1955 on, reaching maxima of 8 percentage points at the October 1974 general election and then 10 points in 1987. Labour was thus substantially disadvantaged by the geography of its support being more concentrated than that of its Conservative opponent. The infrastructural gerrymander produced by the procedures that the Boundary Commissions operate in England, Scotland and Wales and overlaid on the geography of party support, means that Labour has more surplus votes per seat won and more wasted votes per seat lost.[5]

These differences in the operation of the infrastructural gerrymander in the great majority of the Boundary Commission areas produce the better average seats:votes ratios for the Conservatives than for Labour shown in Table 6.3 and graphed in Figures 6.4 and 6.5. Up until 1997, the Conservatives had a more efficient vote distribution than Labour (i.e. the infrastructural gerrymander worked in their favour) because:

1 In the Boundary Commission areas where they were the larger of the two main parties, they tended to win by relatively small majorities so that (a) they had relatively small numbers of surplus votes per seats won and (b) Labour had relatively large numbers of wasted votes per seats lost.

Figure 6.7   The average majority in Conservative- and Labour-held seats, as a percentage of the total votes cast, with equal vote shares: 1950–97

2 In the Boundary Commission areas where the Conservatives were the smaller of the two main parties, Labour won on average by much larger majorities than the Conservatives did in the areas where they were strongest, so that (a) Labour piled up much larger numbers of surplus votes per seat won and (b) the Conservatives had fewer votes per seat lost.

The infrastructural gerrymander worked against Labour because it had too many very safe seats in its areas of electoral strength: it favoured the Conservatives, because their majorities tended to be smaller in the seats that they won – so that they got a better return on their votes (more of their votes were effective. Fewer were either surplus or wasted) than was the case for Labour. But that all changed in 1997 – an issue to which we return below, but which Figures 6.6 and 6.7 suggest was not due to changes in the operation of the infrastructural gerrymander.

The production of the infrastructural gerrymander bias reflects a number of factors which result from the division of each country into separate areas for the allocation of constituencies. In almost all areas, the stronger of the two parties wins a greater percentage of the seats than it does of the votes, but although Labour always had that advantage in more areas than the Conservatives, it was nevertheless disadvantaged overall because:

1 The areas in which it was strongest tended to have fewer seats than those where the Conservatives were strongest.
2 In the first half of the period, the Conservatives were more likely to win all of the seats in the areas where they were strongest than was the case for Labour in the areas where it was strongest.
3 At most of the elections, the Conservatives got a greater percentage of the seats in the areas where Labour was strongest than was the case for Labour in the areas where the Conservatives were strongest.

As a result of the interaction of these three factors, the Conservatives had higher seats:votes ratios in the areas where they were strongest than did Labour in its areas of voting strength, which means that the Conservatives had fewer surplus votes per seat won because of the way the country was divided up for the production of constituencies than did Labour, which suffered from the greater spatial concentration of its support in certain areas (mining constituencies, for example, and inner-city local authority estates).

One election stands out from this general pattern, however: 1997. Labour not only had a higher average seats:votes ratio in its 63 areas of relative strength than the Conservatives had in their 47, but the difference between them (1.62 and 1.38: Table 6.3) was much larger than any difference in the opposite direction over the previous 13 elections. In addition, Labour's average seats:votes ratio in the areas where the Conservatives were the larger of the two parties was not only substantially larger than its opponents' average in the areas of Labour strength, but the gap between the two was much larger than it had ever been previously.

The 1997 general election saw a fundamental shift.[6] This could have been a result of the Fourth Periodic Review, with for the first time Labour advantaged by the Boundary Commissions' work in terms of the patterning of wasted and surplus votes. On the other hand, the pattern of differential majorities did not change, and the movement in the average seats:votes ratios occurred earlier: in 1992. The averages in the areas where the relevant parties were strongest were virtually the same for the first time in 13 elections, and the difference between the two averages in the areas of weakness (which favoured Labour) was larger than at any of the previous elections with one exception – 1950. This suggests that the shift was part of a longer term trend.[7] Both possibilities are the subject of the following sections.

Influencing the infrastructural gerrymander: the parties and the Boundary Commissions

Although the Boundary Commissions are independent bodies and they operate without taking any account of the electoral and political implications of their deliberations (both within the Commissions and at the Local Inquiries conducted by their Assistant Commissioners), nevertheless they are not entirely free from political influence. This is because of the public consultation process that they are required to operate, as recommended by the Vivian Committee and enacted in the *House of Commons (Redistribution of Seats) Act 1944*. This allows political parties, and others, to try and influence the Commission's recommendations for their political/electoral gain, either by urging them not to change their provisional recommendations, despite any arguments to the contrary from others (presumably because they believe they will benefit from them), or by canvassing for changes to the recommendations, whether wholesale or minor, because these should be to their advantage. If they are successful, then they are able to 'bend' the infrastructural gerrymander to their advantage.

These provisions were not widely used in the first two reviews conducted by the Commissions; during the Initial Review, for example, there were only 25 Local Inquiries, and the First Periodical Review a few years later had only seven (all of them in England; the Commissions recommended no changes to 402 of the 625 constituencies at that review, which presumably pleased most MPs and parties). Despite this apparent lack of interest, however, MPs expressed concern over the public consultation procedures, claiming that the Commissions frequently failed to justify their recommendations in any detail, that many representations were dismissed without clear reasons given, and that the criteria for holding Local Inquiries were unclear. As a consequence, their amendments to the Act in 1958 set out clear conditions which, if met, would make a Local Inquiry mandatory. These were that if either an interested local authority (i.e. within the area covered by the provisional recommendations) or 'a body of electors numbering one hundred or more' objected to the provisional recommendations, either in whole or in part, a Local Inquiry must be held. The number then increased substantially: 77 were held during the Second Periodical Review, 117 during the Third and 84 during the Fourth. In their reports on the last of these exercises, the Commissions noted the greater degree of public interest as a consequence of their information campaigns and encouragement to participate. The English Commission reported that whereas some 8000 representations were received during the Third Periodic Review, for example, the number during the Fourth was in excess of 40,000 (Boundary Commission for England, 1995).

The purpose of these Local Inquiries is to ascertain local opinion about the provisional recommendations, and thereby allow the Assistant Commissioner to advise whether they should be altered. Many of the representations received come from the general public – albeit often stimulated by the political parties – but there is no doubt that politicians have most impact on the Assistant Commissioners, either directly or through local authorities, many of which enter representations on the direction of their 'political masters' (the party(ies) which control the authority). Furthermore, it is clear from our detailed analyses of the Inquiries held during the Fourth Periodic Review that the Assistant Commissioners were primarily influenced by the oral evidence presented to them at the Inquiries – which in an increasing number of cases is subject to cross-examination by either a barrister employed by a political party or by a party representative very knowledgeable about both the process and the area being considered. (The English and Welsh Commissions both appoint Assistant Commissioners who do not know the areas they are considering in any detail; the Scottish Commission uses High Sheriffs with local knowledge, which may mean that they are better able to identify spurious cases of claimed local community ties than their English and Welsh counterparts.) The written representations have very little impact; indeed, many of those presenting evidence at the Inquiries argue different cases from those put in their documents, which have to be filed within one month of publication of the provisional recommendations, and in some cases are therefore little more than 'holding statements'.

The dominance of the Local Inquiries by the political parties and those associated with them is shown by two sets of data relating to the Fourth Review. Although 73 per cent of the written representations came from individuals, and only 23 per cent from political parties, MPs and MEPs, local authorities and local councillors (acting as individuals), the situation was reversed at the Inquiries. There only 22 per cent of the time was taken up by individuals, and 72 per cent by the four political categories; the remaining time was occupied by voluntary organisations.[8]

The goal of the political parties and their associates in making representations is to influence the Commissions' final recommendations, in order to promote their electoral prospects. They have become increasingly sophisticated and effective at this. Until the Third Periodic Review it was generally assumed that each redistribution would benefit the Conservative party, largely through the reduction of malapportionment discussed in the previous chapter. The Conservatives were thus fairly complacent about the situation, and Labour saw no reason to become deeply involved, until they realised fully the potential for influencing the infrastructural gerrymander by promoting constituencies that they were likely to win. This occurred at a local, largely unconnected, scale only during the Third Periodic Review, however, largely through the agency of a small number of Labour activists, such as Edmund Marshall, MP for Goole, and Gerry Bermingham, a Sheffield City Councillor.[9] In Sheffield, for example, the Commission's provisional recommendations for six constituencies included four which Labour was almost certain to win and two that would probably be won by the Conservatives. The Labour party and Sheffield City Council argued for an alternative set of constituencies of which Labour would almost certainly win five. Their case made no mention of political or electoral considerations, of course, but focused – as do almost all of the cases argued before the Assistant Commissioners – on the criteria set out in Rule 7 (Table 3.5): the inconveniences attendant on alterations to existing constituencies and the breaking of local (community) ties that would occur if constituency boundaries were changed. The political parties almost invariably use the 'soft and subjective' criteria in Rule 7 rather than the 'hard and objective' issue of electoral equality (Rule 5) when seeking to influence Assistant Commissioners (especially those in England and Wales who have no detailed local knowledge of the areas under consideration). Labour succeeded in that case and thus changed the infrastructural gerrymander in Sheffield even more to the party's favour.

Work such as this laid the foundation for a major Labour party assault on the public consultation process during the next review. In 1987 a party official, David Gardner, was given the task of developing a strategy which would enable the party to maximise its returns from the Fourth Periodic Review. He set five clear goals:

1 to maximise the number of winnable seats for the party (defined as the numbers with Conservative majorities of 15 per cent or less, reduced to 9 per cent after the 1992 general election), consistent with the party obtaining an overall majority;
2 to achieve the maximum possible consensus within the party for this goal;
3 to identify objective arguments to support the party's representations in individual cases, within the criteria applied by the Commissions and likely to command public support;
4 to encourage a positive approach to the exercise throughout the party; and
5 to encourage electoral registration in areas where additional enrolment might lead to the allocation of an additional constituency that the party could win.

This was approved by the party's National Executive in 1989, which set up a Boundaries Strategy Group (chaired successively by leading Shadow Cabinet members such as Frank Dobson, Jack Cunningham, Margaret Beckett and John Prescott) to support Gardner, especially in his negotiations within the party around the country. Gardner then prepared an options paper for each Boundary Commission area setting out possible sets of constituencies there (using ward data), and held meetings in the relevant areas to determine the best option to follow and then ensure complete backing for it locally – in written representations following publication of the provisional recommendations, for example. This latter was sometimes difficult, because in identifying the best set of constituencies for the party across an area as a whole, it may be that some Labour safe seats were eroded somewhat – which the local MP and party did not favour! But Gardner's choice generally prevailed and there was very little public dissent from it, either in writing or at the Local Inquiries.

Labour's preparedness, and plans to maximise its benefits from the infrastructural gerrymander, took the Conservative party by surprise, and it was not until after several Local Inquiries had been held (and dominated by well-prepared and well-presented Labour cases) that the Conservatives became fully aware that their complacent attitude to the review could lead to substantial electoral reverses. By then it was largely too late, however, and Labour continued to prevail in what *The Times* called a 'determined, nationally coordinated campaign' that resulted in that party winning the 'battle of the boundaries'. The infrastructural gerrymander became a focus of political conflict, and although the decision making rested with the independent Commissioners, as advised by their similarly independent Assistant Commissioners who heard the arguments, nevertheless it became much closer to a 'real' gerrymander than had been the case at previous reviews.

In each area, the parties evaluated the Commissions' provisional recommendations against their own assessments of the electoral situation there – in Labour's case against Gardner's preferred option. In a few cases, especially in those counties where no change was proposed, they decided that the recommendations were acceptable and fielded no objections. In others, they sought minor changes only, as illustrated by two examples.

The Boundary Commission for England suggested small modifications to the existing Bristol North West and Bristol West constituencies, in order to achieve greater electoral equality across the county of Avon. This included suggesting that one ward, Lockleaze, be moved from the former to the latter, which needed to be made slightly larger (Figure 6.8). Bristol West was a relatively safe Conservative seat up to and including the 1992 general election, whereas Bristol North West was highly marginal; the Conservatives won it with a majority of 45 in 1992, their second smallest. Labour hoped to win it at the next election, but saw the Commission's recommendation as likely to impede that goal somewhat. Lockleaze is a relatively strong Labour ward, so its removal from Bristol North West would make its task harder. Labour argued that Lockleaze should remain in Bristol North West, with the safe Conservative ward of Westbury-on-Trym being moved instead; Bristol North West would be made more winnable as a consequence. The case for this was made to the Assistant Commissioner on the grounds that Westbury ward had many links with other wards in Bristol West, whereas Lockleaze's main links were with other wards in Bristol North West. The Conservatives opposed the change, but Labour's arguments were accepted by the Assistant Commissioner and the Commission's revised recommendation followed accordingly. The Conservatives then protested vigorously, with the Commission receiving 662 written representations (451 of them versions of a pro forma letter distributed by the party), but their arguments were rejected by the Commission on the grounds that they raised no new issues that had not been covered at the Local Inquiry. The Conservatives had not submitted a single representation favouring the provisional recommendations prior to that, and they were completely outflanked by Labour's well-organised strategy.[10]

Another example of an attempt to influence the infrastructural gerrymander by moving just two wards is provided by the London Borough of Merton (Figure 6.9). This contains two constituencies: one – Wimbledon – was

Figure 6.8   The Fourth Periodic Review in part of Bristol, showing the recommended constituencies of Bristol North West and Bristol West, the two wards whose location in those constituencies was disputed, and estimates of support for the parties in 1992 in the proposed constituencies and the two wards

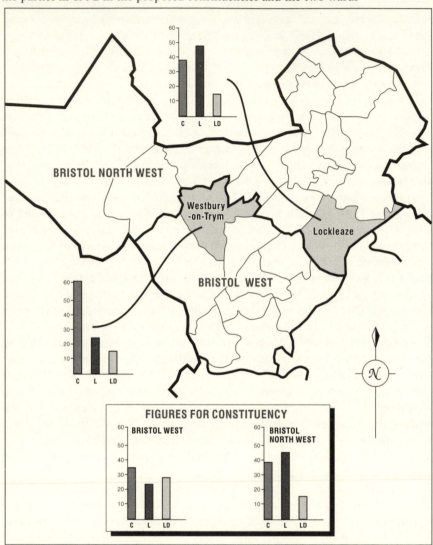

Source: Rossiter, Johnston and Pattie, 1999, p. 345.

relatively safe for the Conservatives at the 1992 general election, but the other – Mitcham and Morden (held by one of the party's Vice-Chairmen, who had responsibility for the party's response to the Review) – was much more marginal. The Commission decided that there was no reason to change

Figure 6.9 The Fourth Periodic Review in part of the London Borough of Merton, showing the recommended constituencies of Wimbledon and Mitcham and Morden, the two wards whose location in those constituencies was disputed, and estimates of support for the parties in 1992 in the proposed constituencies and the two wards

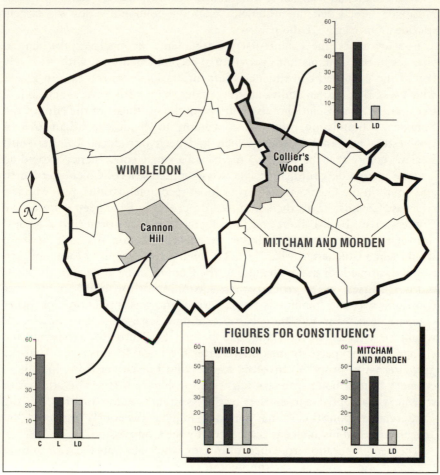

Source: Rossiter, Johnston and Pattie, 1999, p. 254.

the boundaries (they had 1991 electorates of 60,633 and 61,603, respectively). To try to make the latter somewhat safer, while not significantly denting the Conservative majority in Wimbledon, however, the local Conservative party in Mitcham and Morden recommended moving a relatively safe Conservative ward (Cannon Hill) into their constituency, replacing it by the marginal Labour ward of Collier's Wood, arguing that this would, in effect, reconstitute the former Borough of Merton and therefore be more consistent with community ties. (Meanwhile, unaware of this proposal –

further evidence of Conservative complacency – the Wimbledon party's reply to the provisional recommendations was to support them!) Labour also favoured the provisional recommendations, of course, since it wanted to keep Mitcham and Morden as marginal as possible, and the Assistant Commissioner agreed that the argument regarding community ties was largely spurious. Once again, Labour won.[11]

In a few cases, the Labour party's arguments involved very substantial changes to the Commission's provisional recommendations, with relatively few of the proposed constituencies left intact. This was the case in Essex, which was allocated an additional seat under the Fourth Review and so had to experience a substantial redistribution. In the northeast of the county, the Boundary Commission proposed continuing to divide the urban area of Colchester between two seats, which had been introduced by the Third Review; before that the (smaller) town had a single constituency extending into the surrounding rural area. The two proposed seats of Colchester North and South in the Commission's provisional recommendations, plus Maldon and East Chelmsford to the south, would probably have been safe for the Conservatives. Both Labour and the Liberal Democrats preferred a separation of town and country, however, in the expectation that one of them would win a Colchester urban seat. Through a consortium of local authorities, they argued for major changes to the Commission's proposals throughout north Essex on the grounds that: separation of town and country was consistent with the community ties criterion, and was applied in most other comparable cases in England; that allocating a separate seat to Colchester would be a return to the status quo before the Third Review (when the change was unexpectedly introduced after the Local Inquiry); and that the new alternative proposals involved fewer constituencies crossing local government district boundaries (as illustrated in Figure 6.10). The alternative scheme was accepted in its entirety by the Assistant Commissioner (again, the Conservative opposition to it at the Local Inquiry was poorly organised and articulated), and his advice was accepted by the Commission.[12]

The clear implication from these examples, which illustrate the sorts of cases presented and argued against throughout Great Britain, is that Labour 'won' the 'battle of the boundaries' – an argument sustained by our detailed analyses of all of the Inquiries and their outcomes.[13] But how significant was this victory in terms of Gardner's first goal, of maximising the number of winnable constituencies for Labour? His estimate is that he converted ten constituencies from probable Conservative victories (if the new constituencies had been used at the 1992 election) to probable Labour ones – all of them in urban areas – but our overall estimate is that he achieved a net gain of just five. Of course, what we cannot know is what would have happened if the Labour party had not had such a well-planned and well-implemented strategy, especially in the urban areas where Labour was already strong (it made no substantial gains in the rural areas where the Conservatives were the strongest party, in large part because

Figure 6.10   The Fourth Periodic Review in Essex, showing the provisional and final recommendations

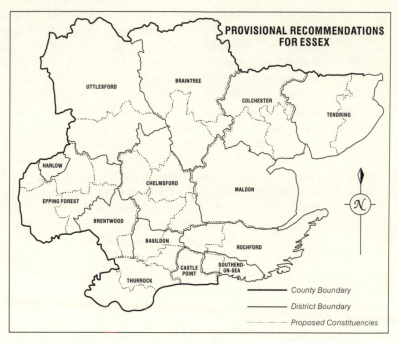

Source: Rossiter, Johnston and Pattie, 1999, p. 254.

the geography made this very difficult there). The Conservatives may well have done much better, as they did at the previous review when Labour had no over-all strategy. Our analyses show a pro-Labour bias of 26 seats at the 1979 general election. If, however, that election had been fought in the new constituencies first used in 1983 there would have been a pro-Conservative bias of six seats – with the difference between the two reflecting the removal of the constituency size component of malapportionment as a result of the Commissions' work. Similarly, the 1992 general election had a pro-Labour bias of 28 seats, which would have been reduced to 21 if it had been fought in the new constituencies first used in 1997 – and for the same reason.[14]

Two conclusions follow from this. The first is that it is clearly possible to affect the infrastructural gerrymander in a large number of areas, and per-haps change the partisan composition of one or two constituencies in each. One final example further illustrates this. Northern Ireland's number of con-stituencies was increased from 17 to 18 by the Fourth Periodic Review. The main political division there is religious: Protestants overwhelmingly support the two main Unionist parties, whereas Roman Catholics are every bit as strong in their support for nationalist parties (the SDLP and Sinn Féin). Thus the parties' goals are to maximise the number of constituencies containing a majority from their religious group.

Before the review, six of the province's constituencies had Roman Catholic majorities (Table 6.5), although nationalist parties failed to win two of them in 1992 because they split the vote between them and allowed a Unionist vic-tory. The Commission's provisional recommendations were to retain 17 con-stituencies, of which only five would have a Roman Catholic majority. This reduction was brought about by their proposals for the southeast where the former constituencies of South Down and Newry & South Armagh both had Roman Catholic majorities and were won by the SDLP in 1992 (Figure 6.11). Most of those Roman Catholics live in the south of the two constituencies that the Commission proposed to reconstitute as one constituency, Newry & Mourne (Figure 6.12), which would have a very large pro-nationalist major-ity as a consequence, whereas the proposed constituencies to the north (Blackwater and Mid Down) would have Protestant majorities. Not surpris-ingly, this was strenuously opposed by the two Roman Catholic-based parties (which included charges of pro-Protestant gerrymandering). The Commis-sion eventually resolved the issue, and others before it, by proposing 18 rather than 17 seats including separate constituencies with Roman Catholic majorities in Newry & Armagh and South Down (Figure 6.13). Overall, there were six seats with pro-nationalist majorities, which led to charges of a pro-Roman Catholic gerrymander. These six were retained in the Commission's final recommendations, however, with the SDLP and Sinn Féin winning five of them at the 1997 general election.[15]

This Northern Ireland example clearly indicates the potential for political parties and associated interest groups to influence the extent of the infra-

Table 6.5 The percentage of Roman Catholics in Northern Ireland constituencies: Fourth Periodic Review

Existing constituencies	%RC	Provisional recommendations	%RC	Final recommendations	%RC
Belfast West	69.9	*Newry & Mourne*	70.2	*Belfast West*	75.6
Foyle	67.4	*Foyle*	67.2	*Foyle*	67.2
Newry & Armagh	59.9	*Belfast West*	64.0	West Tyrone	60.9
Mid Ulster	56.7	*Mid Ulster*	56.6	*Newry & Armagh*	59.9
Fermanagh & South Tyrone	52.3	*Fermanagh & South Tyrone*	54.5	*Mid Ulster*	57.7
South Down	50.4	Blackwater	47.9	*South Down*	55.8
Belfast North	38.4	East Londonderry	35.2	Fermanagh & South Tyrone	49.0
East Londonderry	36.8	Upper Bann	35.1	Upper Bann	35.0
Upper Bann	35.0	Mid Down	34.6	Belfast North	33.3
Belfast South	26.4	Belfast North	32.0	East Londonderry	31.0
North Antrim	24.6	North Antrim	24.6	North Antrim	24.6
Lagan Valley	22.9	Lagan Valley	23.1	Belfast South	24.3
South Antrim	20.0	South Antrim	20.8	South Antrim	20.6
East Antrim	13.0	Belfast East	13.7	Lagan Valley	13.5
Strangford	12.6	East Antrim	12.5	East Antrim	12.6
North Down	7.1	North Down	10.2	Strangford	11.5
Belfast East	5.9	Castlereagh & Newtownards	9.3	North Down	7.9
				Belfast East	5.6

Constituencies named in italics have a Catholic majority. Existing constituencies underlined were won by the SDLP in 1992; finally recommended constituencies underlined were won by either the SDLP or Sinn Féin in 1997. Nationalist parties repeatedly won a majority of votes cast in both Mid Ulster and Fermanagh & South Tyrone, but whereas the Nationalist vote is split between Sinn Féin and the SDLP, agreement between the UUP and the DUP not to stand against each other effectively ensure the return of two Unionist MPs.

Figure 6.11   Parliamentary constituencies in Northern Ireland as defined in the Third Periodic Review

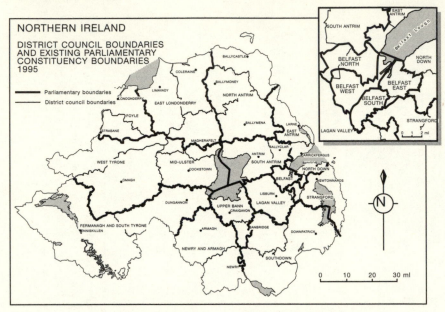

Source: Rossiter, Johnston and Pattie, 1998, 462; reproduced with permission of the Royal Geographical Society.

structural gerrymander within individual Boundary Commission areas. But it also illustrates our second general conclusion, which is that such influence is at the margin only and is only likely to result in the transfer of a single seat from one party to another, save in very exceptional circumstances. Thus while it is important for a party to win the 'battle of the boundaries' in as many areas as possible, this is extremely unlikely to result in very substantial shifts in the number of seats that they win, and certainly not the very significant shift in the gerrymander component of our bias measure identified in Figure 6.1. For that we have to turn to another explanation.

Tactical voting and the wasting of votes

The earlier discussion of differences between the parties in their average majorities suggested that the change in seats:votes ratios in 1997 was not a result of alterations in the operation of the infrastructural gerrymander; Labour still had more surplus votes per seat won than did the Conservatives. Although Gardner's goal in his strategy for the Fourth Periodic Review was to maximise the number of winnable seats, which may have eroded some of Labour's safest constituencies slightly, our analysis of the review and its

Figure 6.12 The provisionally-recommended Parliamentary constituencies in Northern Ireland during the Fourth Periodic Review

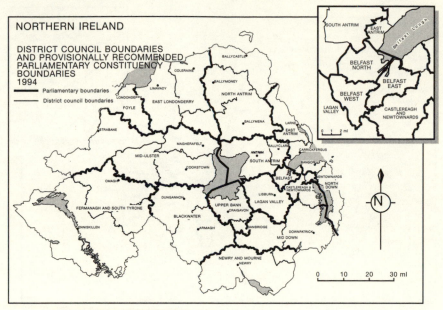

Source: Rossiter, Johnston and Pattie, 1998 p. 463; reproduced with permission of the Royal Geographical Society.

outcomes suggests that this was only a very marginal influence on the seats:votes ratios, at best.[16] Thus we need to look elsewhere to account for the major trend in the gerrymander bias away from the Conservatives from 1987 on.

Our focus here is on tactical voting and wasted votes. Tactical voting is a practice only viable in three (or more) party contests, in which some people vote for their second- rather than first-choice party in order to try to defeat their third choice. Take, for example, a constituency in which at the first election in a pair party A won 45 votes, party B won 35 votes and party C won 20. The votes for both B and C are wasted and will be again at the next election if there is no major shift in voting patterns. But party B could well argue to party C's supporters that if they wish to see party A defeated, the best chance of doing this is to switch their support to B. If 11 of them were to do so, A would be defeated, whereas for C to defeat A would require 26 of B's supporters to vote tactically in order to remove A. By voting for B, those supporters of C who switched would achieve their goal of removing A, even though they must do it by supporting their second-choice rather than their first-choice candidate. The negative goal of defeating A takes priority over the positive goal of electing C, because voters realise that B has a much better chance than C of defeating A.[17]

Figure 6.13   Parliamentary constituencies in Northern Ireland as defined in the Fourth Periodic Review

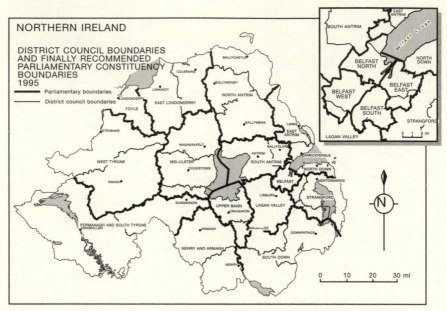

Source: Rossiter, Johnston and Pattie, 1998, 470; reproduced with permission of the Royal Geographical Society.

More generally, anti-government tactical voting (Americans call it strategic voting[18]) occurs when:

1 there are several opposition parties which differ in their strength across the constituencies;
2 there is a strong desire among supporters of those opposition parties to remove the incumbent government;
3 the differences between the opposition parties are insufficient to deter a significant number of people from voting for one of them rather than the other (which is their first choice) on ideological or other grounds; and
4 voters are provided with information by the parties (and perhaps other interested groups) which makes them aware of the potential for tactical voting in their constituencies.

If these conditions hold, then the opposition party which is best placed to defeat the incumbent is likely to attract tactical voters. The third-placed party's vote share would then decline between elections and its number of wasted votes per seat lost would decrease. Thus if there were two opposition parties, each of which was best placed to unseat a candidate of the incumbent government in a proportion of the constituencies held by the latter, then – if the tactical voting strategy is successful and the second-placed party wins seats – each would experience a reduction in its number of wasted votes per seat lost. Furthermore, the more seats won through tactical voting, the more wasted votes per seat lost that the previous incumbent would experience, because many of those constituencies would probably be won by relatively small majorities.

Tactical voting, then, reduces a party's number of wasted votes per seat lost if it is one of the parties involved in the enterprise. In Great Britain the large-scale potential for it has only been in place since the 1970s within the period studied here. Until then, the Conservative and Labour parties won the great majority of the votes cast and 'third parties', notably the Liberals and the nationalist parties in Scotland and Wales, contested few seats and in most of them garnered little support. There was a revival in support for all three at the two 1974 general elections, however; since then, the Liberals (and their successors) have contested virtually every seat in Great Britain and Plaid Cymru and the Scottish National Party have contested every seat in Wales and Scotland respectively.[19]

Third-party politics was given a substantial boost in 1981 by the forma-tion of the Social Democratic Party (SDP), which included by a number of MPs who abandoned the Labour party. The SDP entered an electoral alliance with the Liberals, which lasted through the 1983 and 1987 general elections, in which neither fielded candidates against the other. The two parties then merged in 1989 to form the Liberal Democrats.[20] Voter disillusion with Labour in the early 1980s saw the Alliance gain substantial support, and for a time it led the opinion polls. By the time of the 1983 general election it was in third place, but not far behind Labour in national vote share (they obtained 26.0 and 28.3 per cent of the votes, respectively). The Alliance won few seats (23, compared to 209 by Labour), but occupied second place in a substantial number (311 compared to 133 for Labour). At the 1987 gen-eral election, therefore, voters who wished to remove the Conservative gov-ernment had a tactical choice before them in most constituencies; the Alliance offered them the best chance of attaining their goal in some, as did Labour in others. The Alliance and Labour won 23.1 and 31.5 per cent of the votes respectively then, and 22 and 229 seats. Of the 376 won by the Conservatives, the Alliance occupied second place in 230 compared to Labour's 143. Thus 1992 again offered tactical voting opportunities, and the result once more saw the two opposition parties dividing second place between them.

Between the 1992 and 1997 general elections, the recommendations of the Fourth Periodic Review were implemented, and so the latter contest was fought in a new set of constituencies. The parties and others were able to esti-mate what would have been the result if the 1992 general election had been fought in the new constituencies, however, and thus what the position would be regarding tactical voting in 1997.[21] Our estimates suggested that of the 347 new constituencies notionally held by the Conservative government,

157 had the Liberal Democrats in second place, with Labour in second place in a further 187.

Tactical voting, then, was an important feature of the British electoral landscape during the last two decades of the twentieth century. Analysts have devised a number of ways of estimating how much of it took place and the consensus suggests that about 7 per cent of those who turned out in 1987 voted tactically, as did 9 per cent in 1992 and 10 per cent in 1997.[22] But where did it happen, and did it produce the reduction in wasted votes per seat lost for Labour that we noted in Chapter 1 (and also for the Liberals and their allies)?

Flow-of-the-vote matrices

To answer this question we have analysed flow-of-the-vote matrices which show the gross pattern of inter-party shifts between elections, and are derived from sample surveys in which people are asked immediately after one election both how they voted then and how they voted at the previous contest. We focus here on three of those matrices – for 1983–87, 1987–92 and 1992–97 (Table 6.6). These show, for example, that between 1983 and 1987, some 77 per cent of those who voted either Conservative or Labour at the first of the two contests voted for the same party again at the second. The Alliance retained only 60 per cent of its support, however, with slightly more switching to Labour than to the Conservatives. Those who deserted both the Conservatives and Labour were more likely to shift to the Alliance than to the other main party. Between 1992 and 1997, when the Conservative share of the vote fell sharply and Labour's increased, the former retained the loyalty of less than 60 per cent of its supporters at the first of the contests, compared to 80 for Labour. There were substantial flows from the Conservatives to both Labour and the Liberal Democrats, with only small counter-currents in the opposite direction, and in addition twice as many 1992 Conservative voters decided to abstain in 1997 as was the case with their Labour counterparts.

For the analyses here, we focus on eight of the cells in those matrices which are most relevant to the hypothesised pattern of tactical voting; these are highlighted in Table 6.6. We assume that most tactical voting is undertaken to try and ensure the government's defeat, and therefore our analyses look only at the constituencies won by the Conservatives at the first election of the pair, since they were in power throughout the period 1983–97.[23]

1 First, we look at the percentages of Labour and Liberal supporters who remain loyal across the two elections. If for some of them removing the Conservative incumbent is a prime goal, then there should be fewer Labour loyalists in seats where the Liberals occupy second place and fewer Liberal loyalists where Labour is in second place and most likely to win them.

Table 6.6 Inter-election flow-of-the-vote matrices

	1987				
1983	C	L	D	N	NV
C	77.1	5.1	8.0	0.3	9.4
L	4.3	77.3	7.2	0.7	10.5
D	13.1	15.8	60.0	0.9	10.6
N	5.8	11.1	5.3	60.8	17.0
NV	16.3	14.9	6.7	0.6	61.5

	1992				
1987	C	L	D	N	NV
C	78.2	5.2	7.4	0.4	7.0
L	3.1	78.4	7.7	1.3	7.6
D	16.6	11.9	61.8	1.0	7.5
N	3.1	3.1	3.1	81.3	3.1
NV	25.9	18.8	12.7	1.3	39.0

	1997				
1992	C	L	D	N	NV
C	57.1	9.2	5.4	0.3	25.9
L	1.6	80.6	2.8	0.5	12.5
D	3.2	14.8	58.7	0.6	19.8
N	30.	13.2	1.6	67.9	11.3
NV	11.5	19.1	6.2	1.1	57.9

Key to rows/columns: C – Conservative; L – Labour; D – Liberal (Alliance in 1983 and 1987; Liberal Democrat in 1992 and 1997); N – nationalist parties; NV – did not vote. The cells in italics (highlighted) show the flows employed in the studies of tactical voting. The data are percentages of the two totals (i.e. those who voted for the relevant party at the first election of the pair).

2 Secondly, we look at those who 'deserted' the Conservative party and voted for one of its two main opponents. If their goal was to unseat the incumbent Conservative in their constituency (and, by doing that, hopefully contribute to the Conservatives losing power), then more of them should switch their support to the Alliance/Liberal Democrats where that party was in second place (for the remainder of this discussion we refer throughout to the Liberals to cover both the Alliance and the Liberal Democrats), but to Labour where it was in second place at the first of the two elections.

3 Thirdly, we look at voters who shift their allegiance between the two opposition parties. In order to advance tactical voting, we expect more

people to move from Labour to Liberal, where the Liberals occupy second place than in constituencies where Labour occupies that position, and vice versa for shifts from Liberal to Labour.

4 Finally, we look at those who did not vote at the first contest (either because they abstained or were ineligible to) but who voted either Labour or Liberal at the second contest. We expect more of them to vote Labour where it was second at the first of the two elections, and to vote Liberal where it occupied that position.

To test these four hypotheses, we need data on the flow-of-the-vote in every constituency. Sample surveys are much too small to give us those, and so we employ an estimating procedure which predicts the pattern of flows consistent with the outcome; the number of votes for each party in each constituency must equal their tally at the actual election, and the overall pattern of flows across the whole of Great Britain must be the same as that shown in the matrices in Table 6.6.[24]

The diagrams in Figures 6.14–6.17 confirm all of our hypotheses, showing the expected differences for all eight flow types and all three inter-election

Figure 6.14a   Labour loyalty in Conservative-held seats according to second-placed party

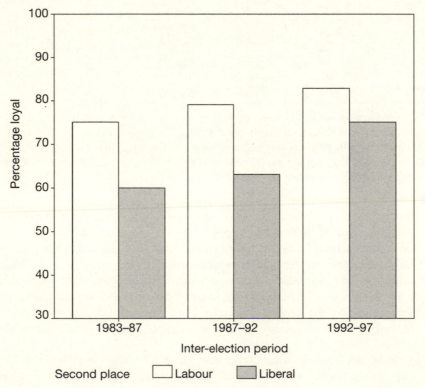

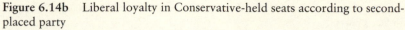

Figure 6.14b Liberal loyalty in Conservative-held seats according to second-placed party

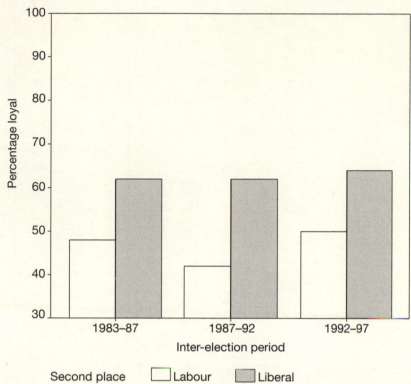

pairs. The first two diagrams relate to party loyalty. For the Labour party in the first two cases, there was a difference of some 15 percentage points in the level of loyalty between Conservative-held seats in which Labour came second at the previous election and those where the Liberals occupied that position (Figure 6.14a); the difference was somewhat less for 1992–97 at some 10 percentage points, but still in the expected direction. Average Liberal loyalty also varied substantially (15–20 percentage points) between seats where it occupied second place and those where Labour did (Figure 6.14b). For each party, therefore, more of its supporters in seats that the Conservatives won at one election voted for it again in the second election of the pair where it was in second place and had the better chance of defeating the incumbents. Where it occupied the third (or even fourth) place, fewer were loyal; they were more likely to shift their allegiance between elections, presumably because they felt that the party they voted for on the first occasion had little chance of winning in the constituency at the next.

Relatively small percentages of those who voted for the Conservatives at an election over most of this period (1983–92) shifted their support to one of the

Figure 6.15a   Conservative–Labour flows in Conservative-held seats according to second-placed party

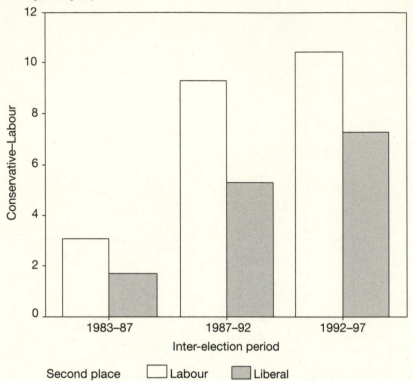

Second place   ☐ Labour   ▨ Liberal

other two parties between contests. Between 1983 and 1987, for example, less than 4 per cent on average shifted from voting Conservative to Labour (Figure 6.15a), but more of them did so in seats where Labour was second. The average shift from Conservative to Labour more than tripled at the next two inter-election pairs, but again with substantially more doing so in constituencies where Labour was in second place. Shifts from the Conservatives to the Liberals averaged over 7 per cent over the first two pairs and around 5 per cent between 1992 and 1997; as expected, the shifts were substantially larger where the Liberals were in second place – almost twice as large as in seats where Labour occupied that position in 1992, for example (Figure 6.15b). Thus voters who decided to shift their support away from the government party were more likely to move to one of its two main opponents if its candidate had come second at the last election in which they voted Conservative; they not only deserted their party of choice at the first contest, but they were also most likely to shift support to the party most likely to beat it in their home constituency.

Patterns of shifts between the two main opposition parties were also consistent with tactical voting. Voters were more likely to switch their support from Labour to the Liberals in constituencies where the latter came second

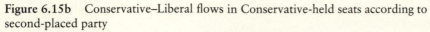

Figure 6.15b Conservative–Liberal flows in Conservative-held seats according to second-placed party

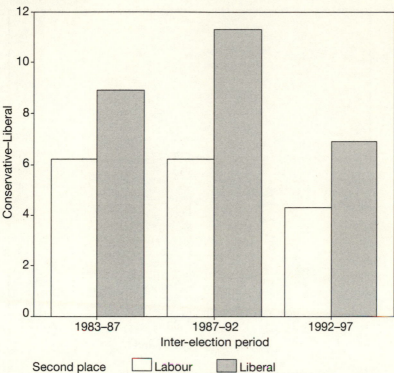

to a Conservative victor than they were in seats where Labour came second (Figure 6.16a). The differences between the two types of seat were very substantial during 1983–87 and 1987–92, with almost three times as many making the shift where the Liberals came second in 1987, for example. The average flow from Labour to Liberal was much less in the third period (1992–97) – no doubt reflecting Labour's greater prospects overall, even in seats where it came third in 1992 – but again almost three times as many shifted to the Liberals where they came second in 1992 (*c.*6 per cent) than where Labour came second. Similarly with flows in the opposite direction, voters were more likely to change their allegiance from Liberal to Labour in Conservative-held constituencies where Labour was in second place (Figure 6.16b). The difference was approximately two-fold in each case: between 1983 and 1987, for example, on average just under 20 per cent of Liberal supporters at the first election shifted their support to Labour at the second in seats where Labour came second in 1983, as compared to just over 10 per cent in seats where the Liberals came second. Again, these two patterns show clear evidence of tactical voting. Supporters of one of the two opposition parties in seats held by the governing Conservatives were much more likely

Figure 6.16a   Labour–Liberal flows in Conservative-held seats according to second-placed party

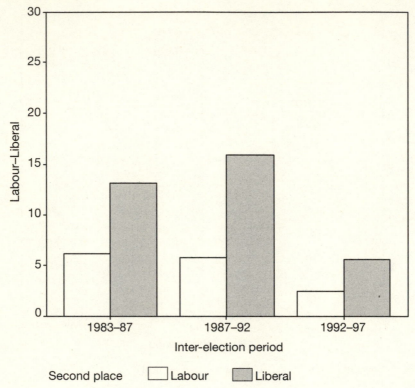

to shift their support to the other at the next election if it occupied second place at the previous contest and was thus best able to mount a viable challenge to the government's candidate.

Finally, the pattern of shifts from non-voting at one election to support for one of the two opposition parties at the second is again entirely consistent with the tactical voting argument (Figure 6.17a and b). On average, more non-voters shifted to Labour in seats where Labour came second at the election when they did not vote, and to the Liberals in constituencies where they came second (although very few non-voters in 1987 voted Liberal in 1992).

These averages provide very strong evidence of tactical voting at the last three elections in our sequence, therefore. In Conservative-held seats, Labour was much more likely: (a) to retain the loyalty of its supporters at the first election in a pair; (b) to win support from those who voted either Conservative or Liberal at the first election, or did not vote at all; and (c) to lose fewer supporters to the Liberals in constituencies where it came second than in those where it came third. The same was true for the Liberals; they performed better where they were second than where Labour was.

Figure 6.16b   Liberal–Labour flows in Conservative-held seats according to second-placed party

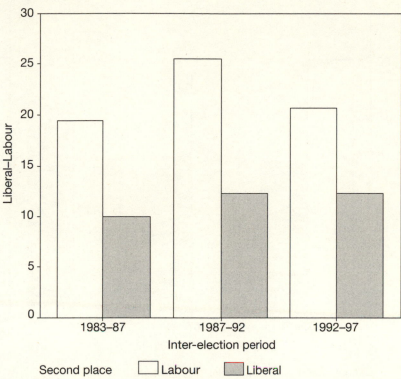

Second place   ☐ Labour   ▨ Liberal

Marginality and the flow-of-the-vote

These conclusions are based on averages over a substantial number of constituencies, however. Were there other differences? One would expect that the more marginal the constituency, i.e. the greater the chances of the second-placed party to overhaul the incumbent, the more tactical voting there would be; the wider the margin, the less the potential for victory and therefore the smaller the stimulus to vote tactically. This was indeed the case, as Figures 6.18–6.20 illustrate for the 1992–97 election period. These show the flows in each Conservative-held constituency separately, according to the margin of Conservative victory in 1992 (the difference between its percentage of the votes cast in 1992 and that of the second-placed party) and which of the two opposing parties came second (seats where a nationalist party candidate came second are excluded). In each case, the smaller the majority, the greater the difference between the constituencies where the two opposition parties came second.

Flows from Liberal to Labour averaged around 20 per cent of 1992 Liberal supporters in seats where Labour came second then and the Conservative

Figure 6.17a   Non-voting–Labour flows in Conservative-held seats according to second-placed party

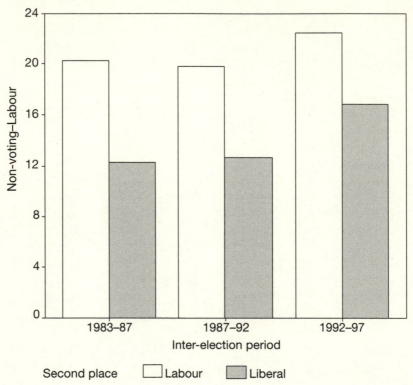

margin of victory was slight (i.e. less than 10 per cent: on the left-hand side of the diagram in Figure 6.18), but less than 10 per cent in seats where the Liberals came second in 1992. As the margin of Conservative victory in 1992 increased, however, so the difference narrowed, as shown by the best-fit regression lines for seats where Labour came second (the solid line) and the Liberals did (the dashed line), converging towards the mean in the Conservatives' safest seats. The greater the potential for Labour to defeat the incumbent, the greater the proportion of Liberal supporters who switched between the two and voted tactically.

Labour loyalty was high between 1992 and 1997, and averaged over 80 per cent across all Conservative-held seats where Labour was second in 1992 (Figure 6.19). Where the Liberals came second, however, Labour loyalty was lower, especially in those constituencies where the Liberals came a close second in 1992 and had a good chance of victory five years later. The smaller the Liberals' chances, however, the larger the Labour loyalty, because the potential benefits from tactical voting were less where the Conservatives had a large majority over the second placed Liberal in 1992. As the best-fit line shows, whereas on average Labour loyalty was just 70 per

Figure 6.17b Non-voting–Liberal flows in Conservative-held seats according to second-placed party

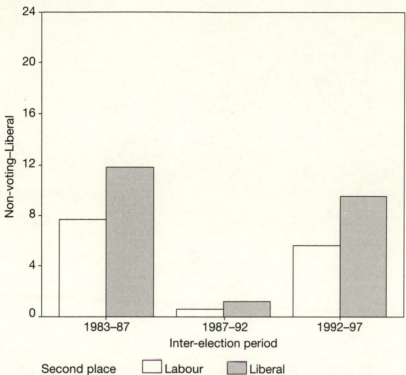

cent in seats where the Liberals came a very close second in 1992, it increased as the margin of the Conservative victory increased, with the two lines meeting on the far right of the diagram, showing no difference in the level of Labour loyalty in the safest Conservative seats, whichever party came second.

Figure 6.20 shows exactly the same pattern for the flow from Conservative to Labour: the smaller the margin of victory for the Conservatives in 1992, the wider the gap between constituencies where Labour and Liberal came second. On average, in the most marginal constituencies some 6 per cent of 1992 Conservative voters shifted their allegiance to Labour where the Liberal came second in 1992, compared to 11 per cent where the Labour candidate came second. As the margin of victory widened, however, so the gap closed, with the best-fit lines converging towards the right of the diagram. Once again, the shifts consistent with tactical voting were greatest where it offered the greatest chances of defeating the incumbent.

Tactical voting was thus an important part of the British electoral scene at the 1987, 1992 and 1997 general elections. The implication is of a sophisticated electorate, aware of the situation in their local constituency and prepared

Figure 6.18 Liberal–Labour flows, 1992–97, in Conservative-held seats according to margin and second-placed party

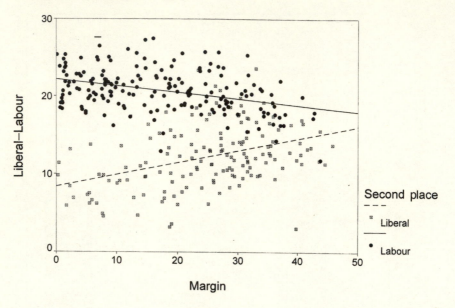

Figure 6.19 Labour loyalty, 1992–97, in Conservative-held seats according to margin and second-placed party

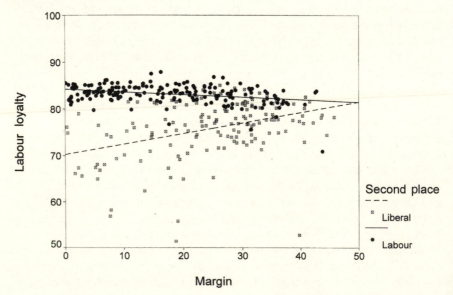

to vote for a party other than their first choice in order to advance the more general cause of removing the incumbent government. But how do members of the electorate become aware of the potential for tactical voting in their constituencies? Some undoubtedly work it out for themselves, being aware of the local electoral situation, and others may learn of the situation either from discussions with family, friends, neighbours and work colleagues or from the local media. But if the parties wish to press the case for tactical voting in a constituency, they need to campaign for it – to inform the electorate of the local situation and to convince them of the desirability of voting tactically there – especially at the 1997 election which was fought in new constituencies, in many of which the local tactical situation was significantly different from that in 1992.[25]

Local campaigning and the flow-of-the-vote

An increasing volume of research in recent years has illustrated the importance of local campaigns at British general elections; in broad terms, it has found that the more intensively a party campaigns in a constituency, the better its performance there. A variety of indicators of campaign intensity has been employed, based on, for example, surveys of party agents and activists.[26] One of the indicators used – which correlates well with all of the others – is the amount that each candidate reports spending on her/his campaign.[27]

Figure 6.20   Conservative–Labour flows, 1992–97, in Conservative-held seats according to margin and second-placed party

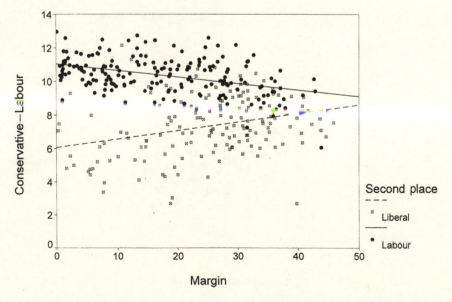

Figure 6.21   Relationship between the relative size of the flows between Labour and Liberal, 1992–97, and the ratio of Labour to Liberal campaign spending, 1997 – in Conservative-held seats

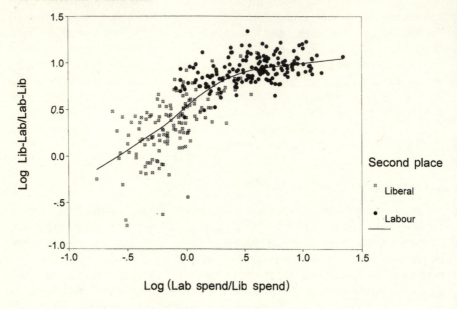

Figure 6.22   Relationship between Liberal loyalty, 1992–97, and the ratio of Labour to Liberal campaign spending, 1997 – in Conservative-held seats

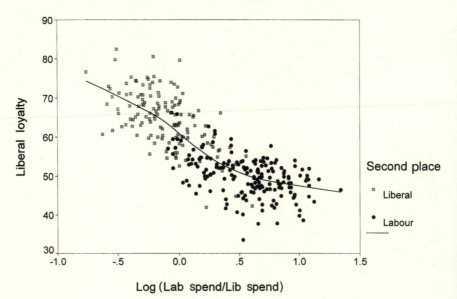

Figure 6.23 Change in Labour percentage of the votes cast in Conservative-held seats, 1992–97, by margin and second-placed party

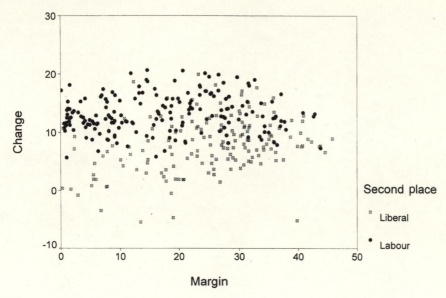

There is a legal maximum set for each constituency, according to whether it is urban or rural and the number of electors there, and studies have shown that the more that is spent relative to that maximum the better the candidate's performance – including success in tactical voting situations.[28] Thus we expect that tactical voting for one party rather than another – the one which campaigns on the message that 'only we can beat the Tories in this constituency' – is more likely to succeed where the party concerned spends a lot on the campaign.

Analyses have shown that this is indeed the case, as illustrated here by two examples from the 1997 general election. Figure 6.21 shows the relationship between the relative amounts spent on the campaign by the Labour and Liberal candidates and the relative size of the flows between the parties, in seats that the Conservatives held. The horizontal axis shows the ratio of Labour to Liberal spending: the larger the positive value, the larger the amount spent by Labour relative to its opponent; the larger the negative value, the larger the amount spent by the Liberal relative to the Labour candidate. The vertical axis shows the ratio of the Liberal–Labour flow according to the constituency flow-of-the-vote matrix and the Labour–Liberal flow: the larger the positive value, the larger the flow from Liberal to Labour relative to the Labour–Liberal flow; the larger the negative value, the larger the flows from Labour to Liberal candidates relative to the flows in the opposite direction.[29]

Figure 6.24   Change in Labour percentage of the votes cast in Conservative-held seats, 1992–97, by margin and winner in 1997

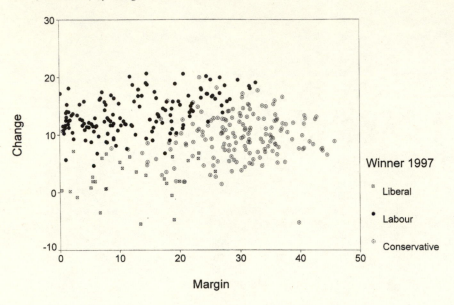

Figure 6.25   Change in Labour percentage of the votes cast in Conservative-held seats, 1987–92, by margin and second-placed party

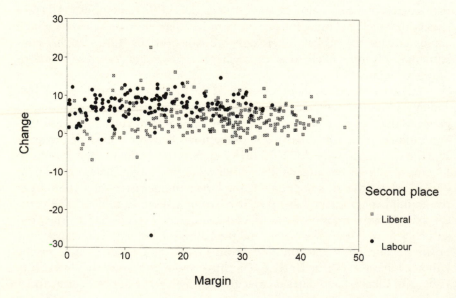

Figure 6.26 Change in Labour percentage of the votes cast in Conservative-held seats, 1987–92, by margin and winner in 1992

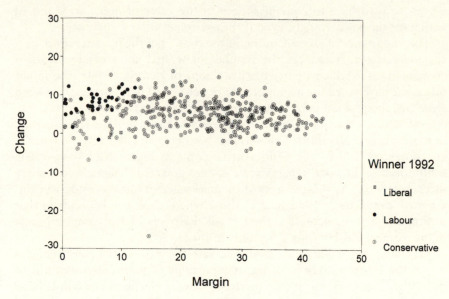

There is a strong relationship in the expected direction: the more that Labour spent relative to the Liberal (the far right on the horizontal axis), the larger the flow from Liberal to Labour relative to the Labour–Liberal flow (the top of the vertical axis). In other words, the more that a party spent relative to its opponent, the better its relative performance at winning over tactical voters. In most cases the party that was in second place spent most – nearly all of the solid dots (indicating that Labour was second in 1992) are for constituencies where the ratio is greater than 0.0 (i.e. Labour spent more than Liberal), but the best-fit line shows that in each case, the more that a party spent where it was second, the better its performance. Intensive campaigning stimulated more tactical voting.

A similar pattern is shown in Figure 6.22, which relates to the pattern of Liberal loyalty between 1992 and 1997 across all constituencies held by the Conservatives. The horizontal axis is the same as in Figure 6.21, and the overall relationship is clear: the more that the Labour candidate spent relative to her/his Liberal opponent, the smaller the percentage of those who voted Liberal in 1992 than did so again in 1997. The best-fit line is steepest on the left-hand side of the diagram: Labour spending was especially effective in reducing the number of Liberal loyalists in constituencies where the Liberals occupied second place in 1992.[30]

Tactical voting was greatest, therefore, in constituencies where the party likely to benefit from it campaigned most intensively – relative to its opponent. People were more likely to vote tactically in a constituency when the parties worked hard to convince them of the value of doing so – and of voting for them accordingly, even if they were not their first choice.

The importance of tactical voting in the context of the infrastructural gerrymander is that it reduces the number of wasted votes per seat lost in constituencies in which a party has little hope of victory; people who might otherwise have voted for it support the better-placed party instead. Between elections, therefore, a party's vote share should increase much more in the constituencies where it occupied second place at the first of the contests than in those where it was third. This was the case between 1992 and 1997 in the constituencies held by the Conservative party, as Figure 6.23 shows. The solid dots and the open squares are clearly segregated. Labour's vote share increased more, on average, in constituencies where it came second to a Conservative candidate in 1992 than in those where the Liberals occupied that position. The mean increase in the Labour share was 13.1 percentage points in the former case, but only 7.8 points in the latter.

Of course, if Labour's vote share increased in most of the constituencies which the Conservatives held, but it won none of them, then its ratio of wasted votes per seat lost would increase between elections, not fall. Labour did win many of those seats, however, as Figure 6.24 shows, and the Liberal Democrats won several more. There is a very clear difference between those two groups of constituencies in the size of the Labour increase. In seats that Labour won, its vote share increased on average by 13.6 percentage points, whereas in those won by the Liberal Democrats it increased by just 2.7 per cent – and in those which the Conservatives retained, Labour's increase averaged 9.6 per cent. Thus in the seats that it lost, Labour lost relatively badly compared to its overall performance, with a consequent effect on its number of wasted votes per seats lost (Figure 1.7) and the operation of the infrastructural gerrymander.

It was the number of Labour victories in 1997 as a result of its overall increase in vote share, plus the tactical voting, that produced this change in the wasted votes ratio, which was a major difference between the situation then and in 1992, when there was also considerable tactical voting alongside a considerable increase in the Labour vote share. Figure 6.25 shows the same general pattern for 1987–92 as Figure 6.23 does for the following inter-electoral period; in most Conservative-held constituencies, Labour's vote share increased more on average where it came second in 1987 than where the Liberal candidate did (the means were 7.2 and 4.2 percentage points, respectively). But neither Labour nor the Liberals won many seats from the Conservatives in 1992 (Figure 6.26). Labour increased its vote share in most of those 329 seats and in the great majority just increased the number of wasted votes per seat lost. Its campaign was geographically much less effective than it was in 1997.

Conclusions

The gerrymander component benefited the Conservatives in the UK's electoral system through most of the period studied here. This is because Labour's vote share was traditionally less effectively distributed geographically; it won seats by larger majorities on average than the Conservatives, thus amassing more surplus votes per seat won; and because the Conservatives tend to win by smaller majorities, Labour obtains more wasted votes per seats lost, on average.

This geographical base to the parties' vote winning has been exacerbated by the infrastructural gerrymander that is implicit in the ways that the Boundary Commissions define constituencies in Great Britain. In areas of Conservative strength, these produce the equivalent of cracked gerrymanders favouring the Conservatives, with Labour winning larger numbers of wasted votes per seat lost as a consequence. In areas of Labour strength, on the other hand, they produce the equivalent of stacked gerrymanders, with Labour amassing large numbers of surplus votes per seat won. In both types of area, therefore, the operation of the infrastructural gerrymander favours the Conservatives, hence the pattern shown in Figure 6.1.

Labour has been unable to influence the stacked gerrymander component to any significant effect over the period, and in 1997 it still amassed more surplus votes per seat won than did the Conservatives (Figure 1.6). But its carefully targeted campaigns in 1992 and, more especially, 1997, allied with a substantial volume of anti-Conservative tactical voting, did allow it to attack the wasted votes per seat lost problem to the extent that – as shown in Figure 1.7 – it had on average fewer votes per seat lost than its opponent, and so turned round that aspect of the infrastructural gerrymander component of the bias measure. This reflected two related aspects of the 1997 result: because of tactical voting, where Labour lost, it tended to lose badly, reducing its number of wasted votes – and the number of 'cracked gerrymander-like' situations; and Labour won a large number of seats from the Conservatives by relatively small margins, increasing its opponent's number of wasted votes per seat lost quite substantially. The infrastructural gerrymander reflects the country's electoral geography, but it can be manipulated by geographically focused campaigns.

Notes

1 The data here refer to the actual election result, and not the estimated result with equal vote shares.
2 For the statistically minded, there is a strong relationship between vote percentage and seats:votes ratio, according to ANOVAs, but none between seats:votes ratio and number of seats – holding vote percentage constant.
3 It is probably the case that some of the Parliamentary Boroughs were treated

separately in the first two reviews, but we have included them in the Counties of which they were a part.

4 One of the reasons why Labour won by large majorities in many parts of cities like Sheffield was the substantial programme of council-house building there in the first three post-war decades. This involved very large estates, both in inner-city areas, where they were part of redevelopment (slum replacement) schemes and in outer suburbs, where large new estates were built. Both types of area provided Labour with very substantial support.

5 In addition, as Labour's support fell nationally in the 1970s and, especially, the 1980s, it also became more concentrated – as indicated by the surplus votes per seat won data in Figure 1.6.

6 Of course, whether it is a permanent shift or merely a feature of that particular election remains to be seen. Others have argued that 1997 may have been a 'critical election' on a number of grounds – though excluding the issue of the translation of votes into seats (Norris and Evans, 1999).

7 Plus new ones, such as Labour's increased appeal to the middle classes in 1997 (see Sanders, 1997).

8 These figures are taken from Rossiter, Johnston and Pattie (1999), which has a full discussion of the Local Inquiries.

9 Bermingham was one of the major actors behind the 1983 case brought by the Labour party against the English Commission's recommendations (see page 124 above).

10 Interestingly, Labour mobilised little grass-roots support for its plans, and it is probable that there was much more backing locally for the Conservative position. But it was not mobilised in time. The Avon Local Inquiry was the first to be held, and clearly illustrates the Conservative party's complacency towards the review. For more details on Westbury-on-Trym, see Schuman (1999).

11 Labour also won both of the seats at the 1997 general election. It won Bristol West, too, as well as Bristol North West, the former as a result of much tactical voting.

12 Colchester was won by the Liberal Democrats at the 1997 general election in a very close three-way contest; Essex North (the constituency virtually encircling Colchester) was won by the Conservatives.

13 In Rossiter, Johnston and Pattie (1999).

14 In both cases, the bias figures assume equal vote shares: the full data are in Johnston, Rossiter and Pattie (1999).

15 For a full discussion of the Fourth Review in Northern Ireland, see Rossiter, Johnston and Pattie (1998).

16 One other tactic, associated with this strategy, was to encourage enrolments in areas where it was possible that an increase in the electoral roll could result in the party being granted an additional seat (or not losing one) – as long as it was likely that Labour would win it.

17 Tactical voting need not be anti-government, therefore. A supporter of party C might decide to vote for party A – the incumbent government – to prevent party B winning power. We focus only on anti-government tactical voting here.

18 See Cox (1997).

19 Except where the incumbent candidate was the Speaker of the House of Commons; normal practice is that the incumbent Speaker stands without a party label and is not opposed by the other main parties.

20 See Crewe and King (1995).
21 See Rallings and Thrasher (1995); the estimates used here are based on the method described in Rossiter, Johnston and Pattie (1997).
22 See, for example, Alvarez and Nagler (2000) and Evans, Curtice and Norris (1998).
23 There were undoubtedly people who voted tactically to prevent Labour retaining seats, especially in the 1980s.
24 The entropy-maximising procedure is described in Johnston and Pattie (2000).
25 During the 1980s many voters became increasingly aware of the potential for tactical voting by the results in constituencies where the second- and third-placed parties 'split the opposition' vote and allowed it to be won by a party lacking majority support. This message was stressed by the Liberal party, which was the major loser in many of those cases, and pressed on the electorate at subsequent elections, while also being used to sustain its case for electoral reform.
26 See, for example, Denver and Hands (1997a) and Whiteley and Seyd (1994).
27 See Pattie *et al.* (1994).
28 See Pattie, Johnston and Fieldhouse (1995) and Johnston *et al.* (1997).
29 These two ratios have been logarithmically transformed to clarify the relationship, which is normal when analysing ratios.
30 The best-fit line shown is a moving average.

7

Reactive malapportionment

There are three components of our bias measure outlined in Chapter 4 whose contribution to the total pattern over the period 1950–97 has yet to be evaluated. As set out there and in Chapter 3, they come about not through the 'classic' processes of malapportionment and gerrymandering, nor even the infrastructural gerrymander discussed in Chapter 6, but because of processes operating within the established constituency template – within which there may be equality of electorates – because of differential patterns of voting behaviour which result in the equivalent of malapportionment. We have termed this reactive malapportionment. Differences between constituencies in the number of electors who abstain, for example, can produce the equivalent of a malapportionment effect if turnout levels are on average much lower in the constituencies won by one party than they are in those held by the other. Similarly, differences between constituencies in the strength of 'third parties' can produce malapportionment-like effects by reducing the number of effective votes needed to win seats in areas where one party is stronger than another – unless the 'third parties' win seats there, which might work against the electoral interests of the stronger of the two main parties.

Abstentions and bias: the geography of turnout

There has been growing concern about the level of turnout at all elections in the United Kingdom (especially Great Britain) in recent years, stimulated in part by the observation that turnout at the 1997 general election, at 71.2 per cent, was at its lowest level since the Second World War. That more than one-quarter of the registered electorate did not vote then is considered evidence of a disillusion with the Parliamentary process that is a harbinger of a crisis of democracy.[1] Turnout has been much lower at other elections, notably those to the European Parliament and to local authorities, which has led to calls both for greater flexibility in voting arrangements and for understanding of why people do not vote.

Figure 7.1 Variations in turnout at general elections in Great Britain, 1950–97

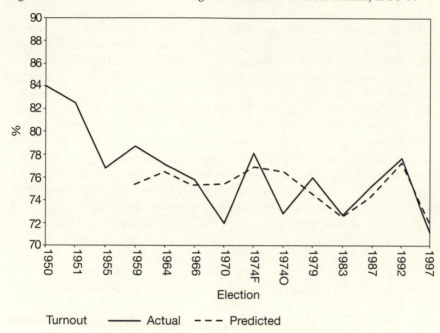

Turnout   —— Actual   - - - Predicted

Although the absolute level of turnout at general elections may indicate a crisis in British democracy, there is less evidence that this has been deepening over recent decades. As the solid line in Figure 7.1 shows, turnout was over 80 per cent at each of the first two elections in our period. It then fell almost continually over the next five elections, reaching a low point of some 72 per cent in 1970. From then on, there was 'trendless fluctuation' between a high of 78.1 in February 1974 (something of a 'crisis' election in itself) and a low of 71.2 in 1997. The latest election did have the lowest turnout, therefore, but not substantially less so than, say, October 1974 and 1983.

Why do people abstain from voting at general elections? Some do so because they are unable to vote on the day, although they wished to – they may be ill, for example, or on holiday or prevented from going to the polling booth for other reasons. (At UK elections, it is necessary for the voter to go to a defined polling booth in the constituency where he or she is registered, and from which he or she may have moved up to 15 months previously, and postal or proxy voting has to be organised well before the election day.) Others fail to vote, however, because they have no stimulus to doing so. They may not believe that their vote matters to the outcome, for example; they may have no commitment to a particular party and its objectives, and may even think that the outcome of the election is irrelevant, because whichever party is in power does not affect what happens to them, and perhaps even to the country; or they may just have no faith in the democratic process.[2]

Figure 7.1 shows the impact of one of these reasons on turnout. If people think that the outcome of the election is a foregone conclusion, that one party is going to win and to win well, then they may well feel that there is little point taking the time and effort to go to the polling booth and vote; whatever they do will have no impact on the outcome. On the other hand, if they think the election is going to be a close thing, and the result either in doubt or likely to be a narrow win for one party, then they may well be much more impelled to vote, especially if they prefer one party to the other among the main contestants. To test whether this is so, we have predicted the turnout at each election since 1959 using opinion poll data from the weeks just before the election. We have shown, as expected, that the greater the difference between the two main parties in the pre-election polls, the lower the turnout. Furthermore, the pattern of our predictions – shown by the dashed line in Figure 7.1 – becomes increasingly close to the actual values from 1979 on. In other words, turnout is generally highest when people think the result is in doubt. The low turnout in 1997 reflects the very widespread belief that Labour was not only going to win, but was going to win well.[3]

Of course, analyses such as these can predict relative variations in the turnout, but not give much indication as to absolute levels. They cannot tell us, for example, why the solid line in Figure 7.1 was not 10 percentage points higher across the graph. Indeed, for some analysts there is a major paradox in the pattern of voting. Given that most people's vote is not going to matter – if they abstain the election result will be no different – then why does anybody vote? Is it rational to spend time collecting information that will help you decide who to vote for, and then going to the polling booth, if you know it does not matter? If not, then why does anybody vote at all? Various answers have been suggested. Some people calculate that if they do not vote, but others do, the result of the election may not be to their liking, so that it is in their interest to vote and ensure that their party wins. Others just see it as their civic duty to vote – it is part of one's obligations as a citizen to take part in the democratic process. Some vote because they are committed to a particular party, and vote in order to sustain it – even if it is likely to lose the election. And some do so because they are convinced that they should by others – notably the political parties who need their support and who campaign for it.

These arguments are all supported by survey data. In 1997, for example, 79 per cent of those interviewed in the British Election Study said that voting is a civic duty and 83 per cent of them voted at that election. By contrast, 20 per cent said that it is only worth voting if you care who wins, and just 51 per cent of them did so at that election. The respondents were also asked – as they are in most voting surveys – if they identified with a particular party, and if so how strongly. Of those who said that they identified very strongly with a party, 88 per cent voted, as did 86 per cent of those who identified fairly strongly with one party and 72 per cent who were not very strong identifiers.

On the other hand, turnout was only 47 per cent among those who did not identify with a party.[4] Finally, turnout was much higher among those who cared who won than among those who did not.

These voting figures relate to the electorate as a whole, however, and tell us very little about variations in turnout across constituencies. That this was very substantial across all 14 elections is shown in Figure 7.2, where the constituencies have been divided into four equal groups or quartiles. Although most of the constituencies cluster tightly around the median value – half of them fall between the first and the third quartiles – the extremes differ substantially from that core, especially the minimum turnout in a constituency at each election. This was never above 60 per cent, fell to its lowest value in 1970 (the only election in the period to have been held in mid-summer, after England's defeat in the semi-final of the soccer World Cup) and in 1997 there was at least one constituency where only approximately half of the electors actually voted.

Why these variations? Our discussion of who votes and who abstains nationally can be applied at the constituency scale in three ways.

1 First, if it is more rational to vote if you think your vote will make a difference, then voters in marginal constituencies – where a relatively small

Figure 7.2 Variations in turnout at general elections in Great Britain, 1950–97, by constituency

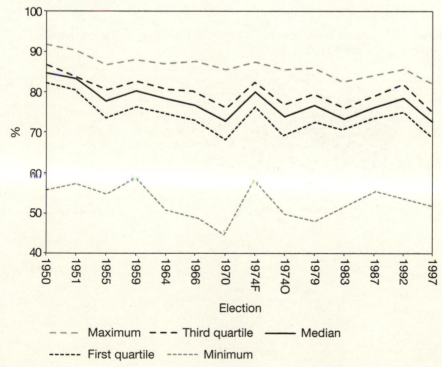

number of votes either way should be enough to swing the contest between the parties – should have a greater incentive to vote than those where the seat seems very safe for one party over the other.

2 Secondly, if people are more likely to vote when they have information about the contest and the participants, then the more that the parties try to get them to turn out – through intensive campaigning – the more likely they are to vote.

3 Thirdly, if people are more likely to vote when they have a stake in the election – they care who wins, and are probably committed to, and maybe identify strongly with, one of the main parties – then if there is a geography of party identification, of support for a party, then this should be reflected in a geography of turnout.

Only the first two of these ideas can be tested directly. We have insufficient information about party identifiers at the constituency scale, but can test the third idea indirectly.

To evaluate the first hypothesis, we have looked at the relationship between the marginality of a constituency at one election and the turnout at the next, expecting there to be a negative relationship – the larger the margin, the smaller the turnout, because the imperative to vote is less where the margin of victory was great last time. Overall, the relationships were weak, as illustrated in Figures 7.3 and 7.4 for the 1966 and 1997 elections.

Figure 7.3   Turnout at the constituency scale in 1966 according to margin of victory in 1964 and winner then

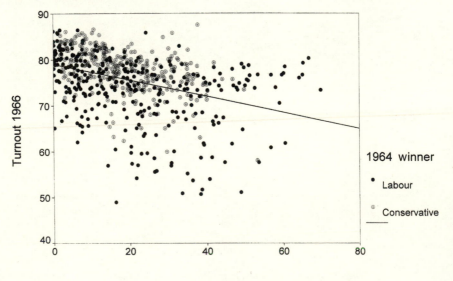

Margin 1964

Figure 7.4 Turnout at the constituency scale in 1997 according to margin of victory in 1992 and winner then

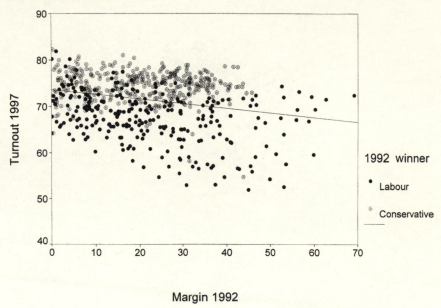

Margin 1992

At both, there was a slight negative relationship, i.e. the best-fit line to the scatter of points sloped downwards to the right, but no more, and it was weaker in 1997 (Figure 7.4) than 1966 (Figure 7.3).[5] In both diagrams, however, there is a clear distinction between seats won by the Conservative party at the previous election and those won by Labour – a distinction to which we return below.[6] Overall, there was little evidence of rational voting behaviour whereby more people turn out in constituencies where their vote is more likely to have an impact (i.e. the most marginal constituencies at the left of the diagrams) and this was the case for all 14 elections.

The second of our three hypotheses suggested that turnout should be higher where the parties campaign hardest. As indicated in Chapter 6, there is considerable evidence from elections over the period studied here that the more intensive a party's campaign in a constituency, the more support it gets. It follows, therefore, that the more intensively all parties campaign, the greater the turnout should be, since all are canvassing support hard. To test this, we related turnout at an election to our indicator of campaign intensity – the amount spent on the campaigns. Looking only at England and the constituencies where all three parties fielded candidates, we summed their total expenditure as a percentage of the allowed maximum. In any constituency, therefore, the amount spent should vary between 0 (no campaigning by any

Figure 7.5   Turnout at the constituency scale in 1966 according to amount spent on the campaign then and winner in 1964

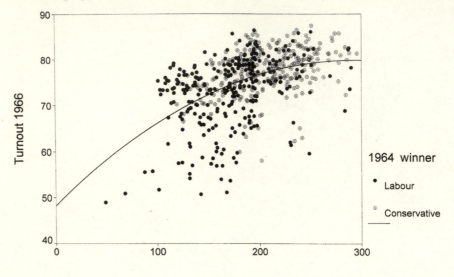

Total campaign expenditure

of the three candidates/parties) and 300 (all three spent the maximum allowed).[7] These show the expected pattern.

Again, we illustrate these findings with the 1966 and 1997 general elections. In 1966, turnout was considerably higher where the parties spent most – especially where the spending index was less than *c*.200 (Figure 7.5). Up to a certain threshold, the more that the parties spent campaigning, the greater the voter response. Above that threshold – where on average each was spending two-thirds or more of its allowed maximum – the variation in turnout was less. Small increases in spending had more impact where relatively little was being spent than where much was being spent – there was a law of diminishing returns. This was even more so in 1997 (Figure 7.6). Above the 200 threshold, the relationship between spending and turnout is almost flat, whereas before that, the more intensive the campaign the more responsive the electorate was.

In Figures 7.5 and 7.6, as in 7.3 and 7.4, we have also distinguished constituencies according to the victor at the previous election (the small number of 'third party' victories are excluded). All four show a very consistent pattern: turnout was on average higher in Conservative-held than in Labour-held seats. This may be linked to our third hypothesis – that different types of voters, living in different types of area, are more likely to vote than are others. There has been considerable work on this in the past, whose results are somewhat paradoxical. At the constituency scale, they tend to show that middle-class, high-income areas have higher turnout levels than

Figure 7.6 Turnout at the constituency scale in 1997 according to amount spent on the campaign then and winner in 1992

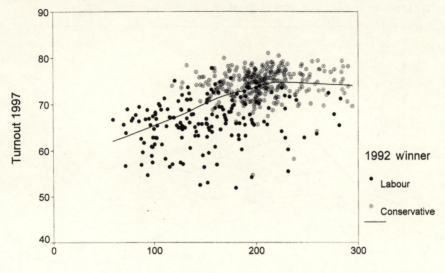

working-class, lower income areas, but survey data find relatively little difference in turnout between class and income groups.[8] Middle-class areas are likely to be Conservative supporting, whereas working-class areas are more likely to return Labour MPs, hence our findings illustrated in Figures 7.3–7.6.

What is the relative importance of these three relationships? To answer that we conducted multivariate statistical analyses in which our focus was on the question 'what proportion of the variation across constituencies can be accounted for by the different influences?'. This involved three stages. At the first, we looked at the relationship with constituency marginality only. At the second, we added which party won the constituency at the previous election. And finally, we also added the total amount of campaign expenditure. These analyses, which could only be conducted for the period 1959–97, are summarised in Figure 7.7.[9] The relative size of the proportion of the variation in turnout at constituency level accounted for over the period for suggests three main findings:

1 Marginality never accounted for more than 20 per cent of the variation (in 1970), and its contribution was very small at the last four contests. If people are voting rationally, this is not as a response to constituency variations in the likely impact of their vote (which may indicate that even in marginal constituencies, people evaluated their chances of affecting the outcome as close to zero).

Figure 7.7 Accounting for variation in turnout across constituencies, 1959–97: proportion of the variation accounted for by marginality, which party won the seat at the previous election and amount spent on constituency campaigns

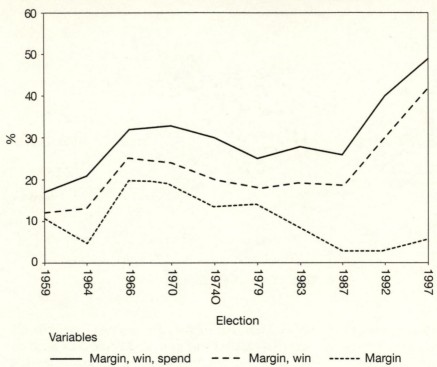

2 There was little difference in turnout between Conservative- and Labour-held seats until the 1980s, but from then on the relative importance of this factor increased substantially, accounting for some 20 per cent of the variation between constituencies in 1983 and 1987, 30 per cent in 1992 and nearly 40 per cent in 1997.[10]

3 The amount of campaign spending had a consistent impact on the outcome, accounting for some 10 per cent of the variation in turnout at most of the elections.

Of these, the second is the most significant finding with regard to the focus of our analyses, electoral bias.

The clear implication to be gained from Figures 7.2–7.7 is that the most important reason for differences between constituencies in their turnout rate was whether they were Conservative or Labour held. This suggests that people living in Labour-held areas were either less concerned about the elections and their results (i.e. were alienated from the political system) or less responsive to the parties' campaigns – or both. Furthermore, the increasing relative importance of this difference over time suggests either that voters in Labour areas have become increasingly disenchanted with the democratic system (and so more likely to believe that it did not matter who won) or that it has been harder for the parties (and especially Labour) to convince them that they should turn out to vote. The first suggestion undoubtedly had some relevance, since Labour areas have suffered most from the economic vicissitudes of recent decades, notably those of the 1980s which produced the so-called north–south divide and considerable working-class alienation in the most affected areas.[11] The second suggestion is in part linked to that, since the 1980s economic changes were linked to other social changes – widely known as 'Thatcherism' – several of which substantially eroded Labour's organisation and mobilising power during the 1980s. The decimation of the coal-mining industry, for example, and the inter-union splits that it stimulated, meant that Labour's ability to turn out large numbers of voters with very little effort in the coalfield constituencies was significantly undermined. In the 1950s and 1960s, for example, many of the highest turnouts – relative to marginality – were in Yorkshire and Welsh mining constituencies such as Hemsworth, Dearne Valley, Rhondda West, Bedwellty, Ebbw Vale, Rhondda East, Bolsover, Aberdare, Don Valley and Pontefract.[12]

Whatever the cause, the period being studied here has seen a significant difference emerge between Labour- and Conservative-held seats in their turnout rates. At first sight, it could be thought that this would have a negative impact on Labour's ability to win seats, but in fact it could be quite the opposite. If turnout is low in Labour areas, then this reduces the number of votes needed for victory there – it means a better seats:votes return and additional votes would not bring more seats. Thus, in terms of bias, low turnout in Labour seats could be to its advantage.

Figures 7.8 and 7.9 show that this was indeed the case. Figure 7.8 shows the average turnout in Conservative- and Labour-held seats at each election, after the calculations to give the two parties equal shares of the votes cast.[13] Over the first four elections, there was little difference between the two – indeed, turnout was slightly higher in the seats that Labour would have won with equal votes shares than in those where the Conservatives would have prevailed in 1950 and 1951. By 1964, however, there was a gap of several percentage points between the two parties, and this remained relatively constant for the rest of the period. The result, as shown in Figure 7.9, was a very small pro-Conservative bias due to abstentions at the first two elections and virtually no bias at all in 1955 and 1959. This then increased to a pro-Labour bias of 17 seats in 1966, which continued for the next three elections. It declined slightly over the three elections won by the Conservatives under Margaret Thatcher, but then increased substantially again in 1992 and 1997 – when it reached its maximum over the full half-century of 24 seats.

Figure 7.8   Variations in average turnout in Conservative- and Labour-held seats, with equal vote shares, 1950–97

Figure 7.9   Bias due to abstentions, 1950–97

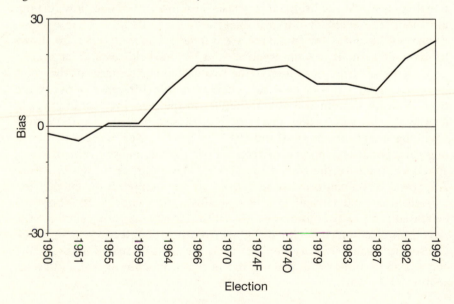

'Third parties' and bias

As noted in Chapters 3 and 4, 'third parties' (i.e. any parties other than the two 'main' parties whose votes and seats shares are being analysed) can have the same impact on seat winning for the main parties as abstentions: the more votes that they get in a constituency, the smaller is the number of effective votes needed for victory there by one of the other two. (With the exception, of course, that 'third parties' can win seats – abstentions cannot; we return to this point below.) Thus if third parties are on average more successful in the seats where one of the main parties is stronger, then they can have an impact on the bias measure. One of the major parties should experience a positive bias if the third parties are relatively successful in the seats that it is strong in, but a negative one otherwise. (When we move votes between the two parties to achieve the equal shares allocation on which the bias measures are based of course the votes for 'third parties' are unchanged; they may, as a consequence, win more or less seats despite their vote being unchanged, as shown in Table 1.3.)

At the beginning of the period being studied here, the two main parties – Conservative and Labour – predominated, winning about 90 per cent of the votes between them at the 1950 election, and over 95 per cent at the next two contests. From then on, there was first a Liberal revival and then an upsurge in support for the two nationalist parties – Plaid Cymru and the SNP. The third parties' big gains came in the two 1974 elections, when they obtained 22.6 and 22.5 per cent of the votes cast in Great Britain between them at the February and October elections, respectively. From then on, the Liberals contested virtually every constituency throughout Great Britain with Plaid Cymru and the SNP contesting every constituency in Wales and Scotland, respectively. Their combined vote share was between 20 and 30 per cent at each of the last four elections of the twentieth century.

This increase in support for the 'third parties' (and for others which received smaller percentages of the votes cast, such as the Green party and in 1997 the Referendum party) will have influenced the bias measure if their support was unequally distributed between the areas of Conservative and Labour strength. Unlike those two parties, the Liberals, their SDP allies in 1983 and 1987 and the Liberal Democrats in 1992 and 1997 have not drawn strong support from particular sectors of society, although some, notably the relatively highly educated, have in general provided slightly more support than others. Their core of support, particularly in the early decades of the period when they contested relatively few seats, tended to be in rural areas where they formed the main anti-Conservative party – as in Wales and in Devon and Cornwall – though they also had pockets of support in some industrial areas, as on the Pennine flanks in Lancashire and Yorkshire.[14] By-election victories saw new pockets of support develop, as in the southern suburbs of Manchester and at Rochdale, and then – in the 1980s when Labour was languishing in

Figure 7.10   The average Liberal vote in Conservative- and Labour-held seats, with equal vote shares, 1950–97

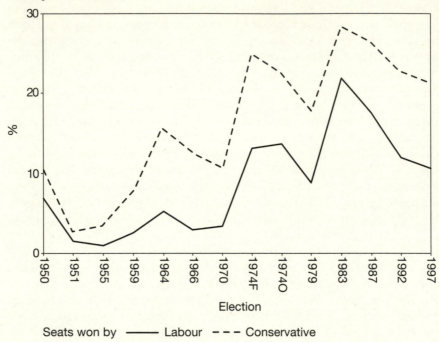

Seats won by ——— Labour   – – – Conservative

the polls – success at local government elections created the foundation for general election assaults, as in southern England (including several suburbs of Greater London), in most cases areas where the Conservatives were the strongest party and Labour's relative weakness became exacerbated.

Across Great Britain as a whole, therefore, the increase in Liberal support from the 1970s on tended to be in Conservative-held rather than Labour-held seats, as shown in Figure 7.10, which gives the average Liberal percentage of the votes cast when those parties had equal shares. From the mid-1950s on, there was a substantial gap in the percentage of Liberal votes between the seats held by the two main parties – as large as 12 percentage points at the February 1974 contest and remaining close to 10 points thereafter. These averages may be somewhat misleading in the early decades, however, because the Liberal party did not contest all constituencies: only 110 in 1955, for example, 216 in 1959, 363 in 1964 and 328 in 1970. Thus a better way of evaluating their potential impact on the two main parties is to look at their average performance in the seats that they contested. The pattern remains the same in general terms (Figure 7.11), although the gap between Conservative- and Labour-held seats is fairly narrow until the 1970s.

Whereas the Liberals' success at vote winning was relatively concentrated in Conservative-held seats, the nationalists in Scotland and Wales performed

Figure 7.11 The average Liberal vote where there was a Liberal candidate in Conservative- and Labour-held seats, with equal vote shares, 1950–97

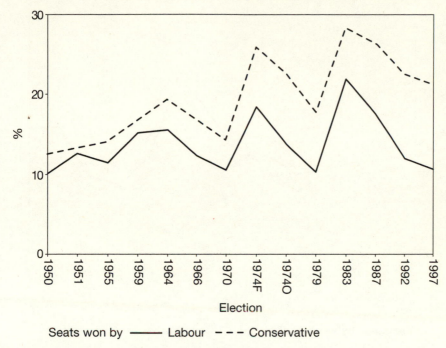

Election

Seats won by ——— Labour – – – Conservative

at about the same level in both types (Figure 7.12). But in the overall British context they are less significant, because they contest a relatively small minority of the seats (112 out of 641 in 1997, for example), whereas the Liberals now contest virtually every one. Thus when we look at their combined effect, we expect the impact of the latter to dominate. This is illustrated in Figure 7.13, which shows the average percentage of all votes cast in Conservative- and Labour-held seats (with equal vote shares) won by the two main parties combined. Throughout the period, the 'third parties' perform best (i.e. Labour and Conservative together get the smallest shares of the votes) in Conservative-held seats. In 1979, for example, the two main parties combined won 88.4 per cent of the votes on average in Labour-held seats, but 80.9 per cent in Conservative-held seats. The gap between the two widened after 1959.

Clearly, then, the Conservative party should have benefited, in terms of seats:votes ratios and the direction of bias, from this concentration of third party support in its areas of relative strength. Figure 7.14 shows that there was indeed a pro-Conservative (i.e. negative) bias due to the pattern of third party support at every one of the 14 elections except 1950, when there was no bias at all. The Conservative party advantage from this bias component was greatest in February 1974, when it was worth 32 seats in the bias measure, and in the 1990s, when it contributed 30 and 36 seats at the two elections, respectively.

Figure 7.12   The average vote for a nationalist party where there was a nationalist candidate in Conservative- and Labour-held seats, with equal vote shares, 1950–97

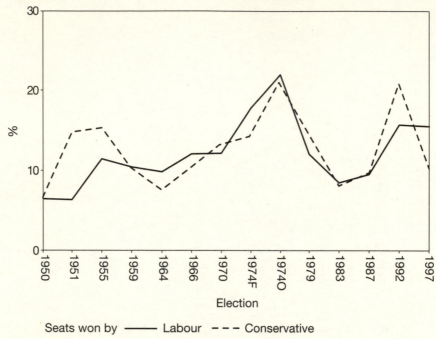

Where third parties have reduced the number of votes needed to win a constituency, this has been to the Conservatives' net advantage throughout the period. But, as already noted, third parties can win seats, unlike abstentions, and if they tend to perform better on average in Conservative-held seats, it is likely that most of the seats that they win will be at that party's expense. Third parties bring substantial advantages where they perform relatively well, but the threat of disadvantages if they do too well – and win! Figure 7.15 shows the number of seats that would have been won by either the Liberals or the nationalist parties from each of the Conservative and Labour parties, which held them after the previous election (if they had equal vote shares).[15] The great majority of these third party victories would have been at the expense of the Conservatives; they would have taken 15 seats from the Conservatives between 1979 and 1983, for example, but only six from Labour. (All but two of the Conservative losses would have been to the Liberals; all six Labour losses would have been to the nationalist parties.) Thus third party victories have clearly operated against the Conservatives' interests since 1979, producing a pro-Labour bias which never exceeded five seats before 1983 (it was just one seat in 1979), but was 12 at that election and 13, 20 and 33, respectively, at the next three (Figure 7.16).

Figure 7.13 The average percentage of all votes cast won by the Conservative and Labour parties combined in Conservative- and Labour-held seats, with equal vote shares, 1950–97

Figure 7.14 Bias due to third party votes, 1950–97

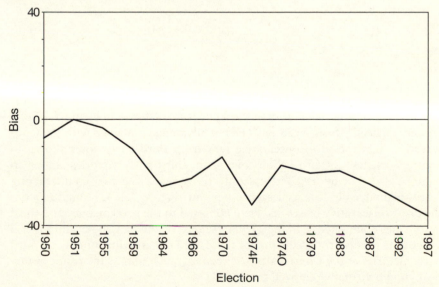

Figure 7.15   Number of Liberal and nationalist victories from Conservative and Labour incumbents, with equal vote shares, 1950–97

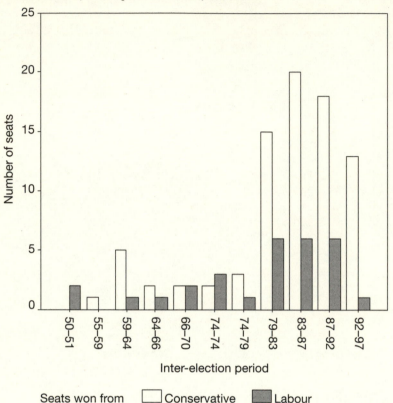

As the third parties increased their ability to win seats, so the Conservative advantage from the pattern of third party votes shown in Figure 7.14 was eroded, especially from 1983 on. The net advantage remained with the Conservatives (i.e. the pro-Conservative bias from third party votes shown in Figure 7.14, less the pro-Labour bias from third party victories shown in Figure 7.16), but by 1997 it was only three seats; the two counteracting forces had virtually balanced each other out (Figure 7.17). From 1959 on, the pro-Conservative biases had been confined to the gerrymander and third party votes components. In the 1990s, tactical voting by Labour and Liberal supporters totally eroded the first of these, and the growing number of third party victories at the Conservatives' expense (much of it as the result of tactical voting) virtually removed the second.

Figure 7.16 Bias due to third party victories, 1950–97

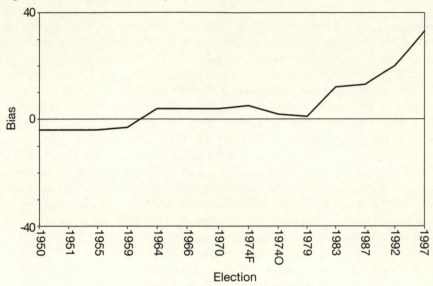

Figure 7.17 Net effect of biases due to third party votes and victories, 1950–97

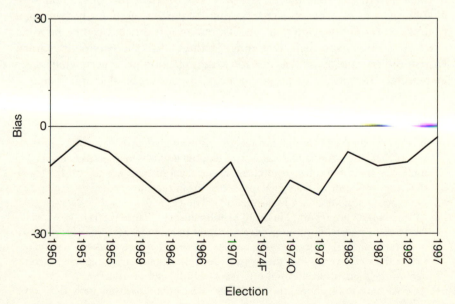

Conclusions

Reactive malapportionment reduces the number of effective votes needed to win in a constituency, because abstentions and votes for third parties both mean that fewer votes are being competed for by the two main parties. In Great Britain, both of these factors came into play after the 1950s, with the growing difference between Conservative- and Labour-held seats in the percentage of abstentions on the one hand and the growth of support for the third parties on the other. Until 1979, these two tended to counteract each other in the pattern of bias. In October 1974, for example, there was a pro-Labour abstentions bias of 17 seats and a pro-Conservative third party votes bias of the same magnitude; Labour's advantage from third party victories was just three seats. From then on, the greater differentiation between the two types of constituency in abstention rates saw Labour's advantage from that source double, and the great number of third party victories removed the Conservatives' advantage from the pattern of third party votes.

In Great Britain, therefore, reactive malapportionment has become increasingly significant as a set of contributors to the electoral bias in recent decades, and this has been almost entirely to Labour's benefit. To a considerable extent this is a serendipitous outcome, but only partly so. By not campaigning hard in its safe seats in 1997, for example, it is almost certain that Labour stimulated higher abstention rates there. Its relatively close ties with the Liberal Democrats then undoubtedly exaggerated their success in Conservative-held as against Labour-held seats; Labour's commitment to devolution for Scotland and Wales undoubtedly retained much of its support in those countries, while the Conservatives, with their pro-Union and anti-devolution stance, lost votes to the nationalist parties there. At the margin, it is almost certainly the case that reactive malapportionment can be manipulated by the parties to their own ends. At the end of the twentieth century, Labour did this and assisted its already bright election prospects, which were increasingly advantaged by just about every aspect of the electoral system.

Notes

1 It is widely believed that non-participation is even greater than the official figures suggest because a substantial number of eligible adults – perhaps as many as 2–3 million – are not enrolled as electors. It is a legal offence not to enrol, but one that is not policed, with very few prosecutions in recent decades.

2 On types of abstainers, see Johnston and Pattie (1997a).

3 These analyses are reported in detail in Johnston and Pattie (2001).

4 All of these figures on turnout refer to actual behaviour. Most surveys overestimate turnout levels (because more people say that they voted when they did not rather than vice versa), but the British Election Studies check reported turnout against the marked-up electoral rolls (see Swaddle and Heath, 1989).

5 As elsewhere in this book, the 1992 data used in comparisons with 1997 refer

to our estimates of the 1992 result if the election had been held in the new constituencies.

6 For the 1997 analysis, the victories in 1992 are estimated, according to the procedures mentioned on page 177 (footnote 21).

7 Similar analyses, with comparable results, have been conducted for Scotland and Wales where there were four candidates and the range of possible spending was 0.0 to 400.0.

8 Constituency variations are analysed by Denver and Hands (1974, 1985, 1997b), survey data by Johnston and Pattie (1997a, 2001), Pattie and Johnston (1998a, 1998b).

9 We could not look at the 1955 election, because we had no estimates of what the 1951 election results would have been if it had been fought in the 1955 constituencies, and so had no marginality measure. Similarly, we had no estimates of the 1970 result in the 1974 constituencies, and so have only been able to analyse the second election in the latter year.

10 The 1983 election was held after the rift between Labour and the SDP, and during a period of considerable conflict within Labour, which undoubtedly stimulated many of its 'core' supporters to abstain.

11 For detailed analyses of the north–south divide and its impact on voting patterns in the 1980s, see Johnston, Pattie and Allsopp (1988).

12 The list is taken from Denver and Hands (1974). The Yorkshire and Wales coalfields were very strongly unionised, as shown by support there for the 1984–85 NUM strike.

13 The shift of votes to produce equal shares for the two main parties does not affect the turnout rate, of course, but is needed in order to evaluat the impact of variations in abstentions across the constituencies on the bias measure.

14 On the Liberals in Wales, see Cox (1970).

15 The lack of data for the first election after the Boundary Commissions' First and Second Periodical Reviews means that there is no information for 1951–55 and 1970–February 1974.

8

Conclusions: electoral reform?

Geography matters – in the operation of electoral systems as in so many other aspects of political, social, economic and cultural life. Where you live can have an important influence on your degree of power within the electoral system, whichever party you support, and the boundaries of the territorial containers within which you are placed – Parliamentary constituencies in this case – strongly affect that power. At one election, you may live in a very marginal constituency where the parties canvass hard to get you to vote (for them); at the next you may live in a very safe seat where it is virtually certain that however you vote will have no impact on the outcome, and the parties virtually ignore you in their campaigns – even though you are the same person living in the same house. It is the constituency boundaries that have been moved, perhaps at one of the party's behest, and in effect impoverished you.

This geography of power is well appreciated; political analysts have for many decades been discussing its impacts and politicians have been seeking to manipulate it – as exemplified by Lord Salisbury's keen interest in the 1867 and 1885 redistributions of Parliamentary constituencies in the UK. One of its impacts is disproportionality. It is extremely rare that parties contesting first-past-the-post (fptp) elections get the same percentage of the seats as they do of the votes. Some, usually though not invariably the largest, get a disproportionately excessive share of the seats whereas others (almost invariably the smallest) get smaller shares of seats than of votes. To some this is manifestly unfair and should be remedied by changing to an electoral system which produces fair outcomes, where fairness is defined as proportional (or near-proportional) representation: 'one person, one vote; one vote, one value'. Others accept the unfairness of the outcome, but argue that it is a price worth paying for other aspects of the electoral system, often expressed as strong government with clear mandates and majorities. These arguments are beyond the scope of this book. Our goal has been to produce further evidence to sustain them, to inform the debate over electoral reform by pointing to aspects of the current UK electoral system that have been under-studied and under-appreciated, and so not rehearsed during the debates. Our concern is with extending our appreciation of the unfairness of the current system by focusing on the associated concept of bias, and its openness to manipulation.[1]

Geography matters in all of this because both the disproportionality and the bias result from the interactions of two sets of geographies – of voters of different persuasions and of constituencies. Graham Gudgin and Peter Taylor have clarified the impact of those interactions on disproportionality, and fully sustained the argument that geography matters as far as the outcome of fptp elections is concerned. In this book, we have done the same for bias. Simple simulated examples have shown that bias is a necessary consequence of the geographical interactions, and detailed empirical studies of 14 general elections in the second half of the twentieth century have shown the extent of that bias, how it has changed over the period and why, and the importance of geography in all of that.

But what are the implications of this argument? Now that we appreciate that the geography of the UK's electoral system produces not only disproportionality but also bias, what can we do about it? This last chapter is not a tract for electoral reform. It merely places our findings in the context of contemporary debates over that issue. First, however, we present a summary of those findings, as a preface to our contribution to the debates.

Bias: how much, why and where?

Disproportionality in election results means that different parties get different returns from the votes that they win, as shown by a very simple measure – the seats:votes ratio. A ratio greater than 1.0 indicates that a party got a larger share of the seats than it did of the votes at the election in question. A ratio below 1.0 indicates that it got a smaller share of the seats than of the votes.

Ratios either substantially larger than or less than 1.0 characterise UK general elections throughout the period being studied, as we showed in Chapter 1, with the two largest parties (Conservative and Labour) both getting ratios greater than 1.0 at the majority of the 14 elections. To that extent both have been advantaged by the system; they got a better return on their votes than the other parties, notably but not only the Liberal party, which got many fewer seats at all of the elections than its vote share would have entitled it to if the UK had had a system of proportional representation.

None of that is new. What is much less well known is that the geographical processes which produced the disproportional outcomes also generated biased results, in which one of the two main parties would have benefited more than the other; the system did not treat the two largest parties equally. At most of the elections studied, the main beneficiary was the Conservative party, whose seats:votes ratio at a given vote share was greater than the Labour party would have achieved with the same share. We have adopted a measure of this bias developed by a New Zealand political scientist in order to get a clear view of its volume. In its raw state, this is a very simple index which merely answers the question 'given the relative geography of support for each party across the map of constituencies, what would the election result have been if each had obtained the same share of the votes cast?'. In other words, our adopted measure does not alter the geography of each party's relative strength across the country – its highs and its lows. All it does is take that equivalent of a relief map and either elevate it slightly by the same amount everywhere, for the party which came second of the two at the election concerned, or, in the case of the victorious party, depress it by the same amount everywhere. The result is two new maps, in which each party has the same relative geography as before but their absolute elevations have been changed so that they have the same vote totals across all constituencies.

This procedure is novel in this application, but far from novel in British electoral study where the concept of 'uniform swing' has long held sway, both in academic analyses and in popular discussions of parties and their prospects – notably during the run-up to elections and in the election-night real-time analyses of constituency-by-constituency results.[2] Uniform swing does not occur everywhere between elections, of course; parties which lose votes between elections tend to do worse in some constituencies than they do in others and vice versa. But it is a useful first approximation and general average that provides substantial insights – as was the case after the 1997 general election when it was realised that if uniform swing were applied across all constituencies so that the Conservative and Labour parties had the same percentages of the votes cast (37), nevertheless Labour would have 82 more seats than its opponent.[3] It would have obtained a much greater return on its votes, with a seats:votes ratio of 1.88, compared to 1.06 for its opponent with the same percentage share of the votes.

Why would Labour have fared so much better at that election than the Conservatives if they had shared the their vote total equally, assuming a uniform swing? The answer lies, as we have illustrated throughout this book, in geography, in the pattern of voting for each party across the 659 constituencies (including 18 which Labour did not contest, in Northern Ireland). The spatial processes generating this unequal – or unfair, or biased – outcome were exactly the same as those involved in producing disproportionality. They were equivalent to the malapportionment and gerrymandering strategies long practised in the United States and elsewhere; despite the establishment of independent Boundary Commissions, election outcomes occurred equivalent to what would have been produced if those abuses had been practised.

We showed why the equivalents of malapportionment and gerrymandering would result in the operation of a UK-like electoral system through the simulated examples deployed in Chapter 2, as a result of a combination of factors, not least of which was differences in the geographies of support for two parties, generating the equivalent of stacked gerrymanders in some areas and cracked gerrymanders in others. Furthermore, we also showed that the equivalent of malapportionment outcomes can be generated by other aspects of the electoral system, such as the performance of 'third parties' and the volume and geography of abstentions – what we termed reactive malapportionment. All three of these – malapportionment, gerrymandering, and reactive malapportionment – occur in the UK and influence the volume of bias, even where none of the outcomes is intentional. Gudgin and Taylor showed in their classic work that disproportionality in election results can be the outcome of either partisan districting (when the constituency boundaries are specifically drawn to produce malapportionment and/or gerrymandering) or non-partisan districting (when the procedure for defining constituencies is handed over to an independent body, but the outcome of its work favours one party over another – because that is, in effect, built in to the system through its geography). As with disproportionality, so with bias; non-partisan procedures for defining the constituencies within which voters are contained for the purposes of conducting elections can result in one party getting a much better return on its votes (a larger seats:votes ratio) than another, even when they have the same share of the votes. This, we found, is readily demonstrated through the concepts of wasted, surplus and effective votes: the more wasted and/or surplus votes that a party gets, the smaller the electoral return in terms of seats (i.e. the smaller its seats:votes ratio); the most favoured party by the geographies of the electoral system is the one that wastes fewest votes in seats that it loses and/or obtains fewest surplus votes in those that it wins.

Our bias measure is a net figure, therefore, the outcome of several processes that might all be operating in the same direction (i.e. favouring the same party), or which may counter each other, to a greater or lesser extent, with some favouring one party and some the other. We thus followed Brookes by identifying six separate components of the geographies that can generate bias – two within the general concept of malapportionment, one related directly to the concept of gerrymandering, and three to what we have termed reactive malapportionment.

The size of each of these bias components has been calculated for each of the 14 elections studied, with the following major findings.

1 *The gross volume of bias increased very substantially over the period*, from the equivalent of some 50 seats at the first three elections (1950, 1951 and 1955) to approaching 200 seats at the 1997 election.
2 *The net bias was greatest at the beginning and end of the period, and close to zero in the middle years*: in the 1950s and the 1990s one party benefited much more than the other; in the 1960s, 1970s and 1980s the benefits to the Conservatives and Labour tended to balance out.
3 *The gross volume of bias towards the Conservative party was approximately the same – some 60 seats – at all 14 elections, whereas Labour*

reaped virtually no benefits from the non-partisan districting process in the 1950s and an increasing volume thereafter.

4 *Over the 14 elections the relative importance of malapportionment-like biases has increased, whereas those associated with gerrymandering have declined.*

5. *Whereas at the early elections in the sequence the net beneficiary of these biases was the Conservative party, by the end – and especially at the 1997 general election – Labour was the beneficiary, to a greater extent that the Conservatives had ever experienced.*

The empirical core of the book (Chapters 5–7) has explored the reasons for these major conclusions through detailed studies of the three sets of bias components, within an appreciation of the non-partisan redistricting processes operated by the Boundary Commissions, set out in Chapter 3.

Malapportionment-like biases have been produced for two reasons. First, Scotland and Wales have guaranteed minimum numbers of seats in the House of Commons which, in combination with other aspects of the procedure, has meant that they are both over-represented (by up to 14 and 8 seats, respectively, in 1999).[4] Because Labour was much stronger than the Conservatives in Wales throughout the period, and had achieved a similar hegemonic status in Scotland by the 1990s, it has benefited from this, to an increasing extent.

Secondly, malapportionment comes about because of population changes after the constituency boundaries have been defined – which we have termed 'creeping malapportionment'. The Commissions have become increasingly successful at achieving electoral equality across all constituencies within their respective countries over the five reviews that they have conducted, but as each set of constituencies ages so electoral inequalities grow, with some experiencing population decline (relative if not absolute) while others grow. From the 1950s on, when the English Commission decided no longer to create smaller constituencies in rural than in urban areas, this 'creeping malapportionment' has increasingly favoured Labour, because it is generally the stronger of the two main parties in the urban areas that experienced population decline over the 50-year period. As the constituencies age, so the average size of those won by Labour has declined whereas the average for Conservative-won seats has grown: increasingly; Labour gets a better return for its votes, because fewer votes are needed on average to win where it is the strongest party. Every time the Boundary Commissions review constituencies, this pro-Labour bias is reduced substantially, so that the longer the period between reviews, the greater the Labour advantage becomes. As we saw in Chapter 5, it is to Labour's advantage to have a long period between reviews, and to fight elections in 'aged constituencies', whereas the Conservatives benefit by having more frequent reviews.

Although we have measured the *gerrymander-like (or efficiency) bias component* by a single measure, we showed in Chapter 5 that it is brought about in three ways. First, and most importantly, there is what we termed an *infra-structural gerrymander*, which results from the interaction of two geographies: the geography of support for the two parties (Labour's is spatially more concentrated than the Conservatives', so that the former has more surplus votes per seat won and more wasted votes per seat lost); and the use of major local government areas as the subnational units to which constituencies are allocated (except in Northern Ireland, where the province is treated as a single unit, no bigger in terms of its entitlement to constituencies than several of the largest English counties). In the areas where Labour is strongest, it tends to win most of the seats by large majorities – the equivalent of a stacked gerrymander; in those where the Conservatives are strongest, however, they tend to win by smaller margins – the equivalent of a cracked gerrymander – and so get a better return for their votes (a better seats:votes ratio). A cracked gerrymander is somewhat more risky than a stacked gerrymander as a partisan strategy, however, as we showed in Chapter 2; this means that when the Conservatives perform badly in the election as a whole, the infrastructural gerrymander could work against them when summed across all of the separate territorial units employed by the Boundary Commissions, as happened in 1997.

Within the infrastructural gerrymander, the parties can influence the bias in two ways. The first is by seeking to manipulate the constituency-definition process in as many of the separate areas as possible, thereby promoting their own interests over their opponents'. As we have seen, the Boundary Commissions are both independent and non-partisan; they take no account of electoral issues and interests when making their recommendations. Furthermore, the Local Inquiries to hear public opinion regarding their recommendations are also non-partisan, and arguments for and against particular configurations can only be presented within the terms set out in their rules regarding electoral equality, fitting within the local government template, disruptions due to change, not breaking community ties and 'special geographical considerations'.[5]

Nevertheless, the parties have become particularly skilled at working within these, at presenting cases for constituency arrangements that will be to their electoral advantage and which are phrased in terms that the Commissions will accept. This has enabled them (especially Labour during the Fourth Periodic Review) to achieve constituency geographies to their advantage, but the overall benefit has been small, certainly no more than ten seats or so.

The second way in which a party can operate within the infrastructural gerrymander is to focus its votes where it can win. Where it has virtually no chance of winning there is little point in campaigning hard to encourage support in a lost cause. But what should its erstwhile supporters do instead? In the 1980s and, especially, the 1990s the answer was 'vote tactically'. All constituencies in England were contested by three national parties then; all constituencies in Scotland and Wales were contested by four. The Conservatives

were in power before each of the elections (1983, 1987, 1992 and 1997).
Each of their opponents (Labour, Liberal, Plaid Cymru and SNP) had many
supporters for whom defeating the Conservatives was a primary goal, and
they were prepared to vote for the candidate in their constituency who was
best placed to achieve that – even if they would not normally support her or
his party. Tactical voting thus became a part of the British electoral landscape.
In England, for example, Labour and Liberal Democrat supporters in Conservative-held seats were canvassed (especially by the Liberal Democrat
party) and encouraged by other interest groups to vote for whichever of the
two had the better chance of defeating the incumbent party. As a result, the
third-placed party's vote tended to fall between elections, whereas that of the
second-placed party increased, and in 1997 much more than at previous elections this resulted in a Conservative defeat. The third-placed party thus
reduced its number of wasted votes per seat lost. This clearly worked to
Labour's benefit in 1997; where it lost, on average, it lost badly relative to
previous elections, thus contributing to the substantial and very significant
shift of the gerrymander component in its favour. At the same time, by winning many more seats from the Conservatives with relatively small majorities
as a result of tactical voting it reduced its average number of surplus votes per
seat won, though it still averaged more than the Conservatives because of the
continued stacked gerrymanders in its heartlands.

Finally, what of *reactive malapportionment*? This has three components.
The first is *abstentions*. As we showed in Chapter 2, the greater the number
of voters in a constituency who abstain, the smaller the number of votes
needed to win there, and so the greater the seats:votes ratio return to the
party strongest in the constituencies where abstention levels are greatest.
Again, over much of the period that we have been studying this has benefited
the Labour party, because turnout has tended to be lower in the urban and
industrial areas of its electoral heartlands. This has become an increasing
benefit over time, in part because of growing voter alienation from the entire
political system in those areas, in part because of the decline in trade union
mobilisation of support (notably on the coalfields) and in part because
Labour has reduced its campaigning activity there: why work hard to capture
more votes in constituencies that you are certainly going to win by a large
margin in any case? Focus your efforts on the marginal constituencies where
more votes can potentially bring electoral benefits. Thus to some extent
Labour has if not encouraged abstention in many places at least not actively
discouraged it. It is almost certainly the case, especially since the 1970s, that
more abstainers would vote Labour than Conservative if they were to go to
the polling booth, but because of where the majority of them live, Labour
would reap very little electoral benefit from that. In terms of Labour winning
seats, they may as well stay at home!

Secondly, there is the twofold impact of *third parties*, an umbrella term in
this case for all parties other than Conservative and Labour. As our theoretical

discussion in Chapter 2 showed, the impact of their vote winning is the same as that of abstentions: they reduce the number of votes needed for victory by one of the other two parties (unless they actually win, which of course abstainers cannot!). And so, if the third parties' vote winning is relatively concentrated in constituencies where one of the two main parties is the stronger, then that party will benefit with a larger seats:votes ratio than its opponent's. As we saw in Chapter 7, this has been the Conservative party, which has been a substantial beneficiary from the relative strength of the third parties (especially the Liberals) in its heartlands – at least until the last four elections in the sequence when third party victories have partially compensated for this – producing a countervailing bias component that favoured Labour.

Geography, then, has not only been the origin of substantial, and increasing, biases in the UK electoral system but in addition the trend in all but one of the bias components has favoured Labour, partly because of changing geographies, partly because of changes in Boundary Commission policy, partly because of the changing local government templates within which the Commissions operate, and partly because of the action of the Labour party itself (plus its tactical voting allies).

Interestingly, perhaps, we have built that case while deploying very few maps, because, except relating to the issue where they were used (in Chapter 6), the actual places are of relatively little consequence. There is, however, one further aspect of the geography of the entire operation which we have not yet addressed explicitly, and which again we can consider without recourse to maps. One much commented-on feature of the results of the general elections of 1983 and 1987 was the geographical polarisation of support for the two main parties – what became known as a 'north–south' divide, with Labour having virtually no MPs in the south of Great Britain outside Greater London and the Conservatives having relatively few in the north.[6] In 1997, this pattern was accentuated in one sense, with the Conservatives winning no seats in either Scotland or Wales and losing most of those which it held in much of the north of England and parts of the Midlands; Labour's successes in the south of England made that much less of a Conservative heartland, however, but the north–south differential remained in place.[7]

The reasons for this north–south divide have been implicit in the previous paragraphs: Labour is the strongest party in the inner cities and the older industrial areas, most of which are in Scotland, Wales and the north of England; the Conservatives are strongest in the suburbs, the smaller towns and the rural areas. But is this spatial variation in electoral support accentuated by the operation of the electoral system, with the northern and urban areas heavily biased towards Labour and the remainder of the country similarly biased towards the Conservatives?

The answer is yes, as demonstrated in Figures 8.1 and 8.2. In the first of these, we have simply divided Great Britain into its urban and rural parts, a coarse split based on the classification that the Boundary Commissions are

Figure 8.1   Electoral biases in urban and rural Britain, 1950–97

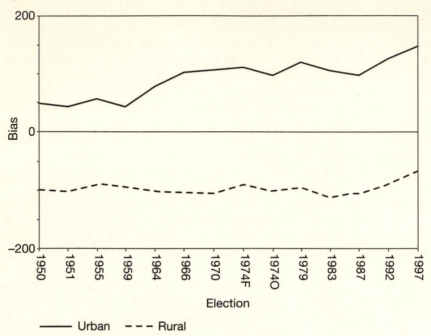

            — Urban   – – – Rural

required to undertake. The legislation restricting the amount that candidates can spend on their constituency campaigns allows greater expenditure per voter in rural than urban areas, on the grounds that candidates have to expend more effort contacting voters in the former, because they are more widely dispersed.[8] We have calculated the net bias separately for these urban and rural areas (the Commissions' terms are Borough and County), and found a very clear divide (Figure 8.1). The urban areas have always had a pro-Labour bias, although it was three times larger at the end of the period than at the beginning. Countering this, the rural areas have always had a pro-Conservative bias, consistently at around 100 seats until 1992 and 1997, when it fell to nearly half of its maximum in 1983.

Rural Britain's Parliamentary representation is substantially biased towards the Conservatives, whereas urban Britain's favours Labour. Extending this, we have further divided Britain into three main geographical regions – North, Midlands and South.[9] Figure 8.2 shows the extremes between 'North urban', whose representation has become increasingly strongly biased to Labour, and 'South rural', increasingly biased to the Conservatives. Between them, both 'North rural' and 'Midlands urban' are pro-Labour, the former increasingly so; the 'Midlands rural' and 'South urban' areas have favoured the Conservatives, although the latter has twice had a small pro-Labour bias, in 1970 and 1997. This geographical divide is what Jenkins

Figure 8.2 Electoral biases and urban–rural division, 1950–97

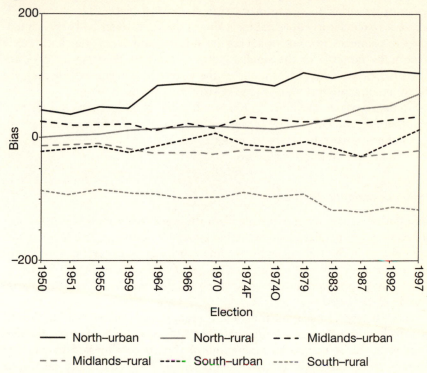

(1998, 8) referred to as 'apartheid in electoral outcome … a new form of Disraeli's two nations'.

The operation of the various biases in the UK has therefore produced both a north–south and an urban–rural divide in Parliamentary representation which is even greater than the comparable divide in electoral support. The 'north' and the 'urban' are Labour strongholds, where its seats:votes ratios have increased over the period studied: the 'south' and the 'rural' are the Conservative heartlands, where the party gets larger percentages of the seats than of the votes. The country's biased electoral system is a product of geography, and in turn produces a geography, so that when the Conservatives are in power this is firmly based in the south and the rural areas, whereas Labour power's foundations are in representatives from the northern and urban areas.

Change within the system

We take it as granted that an electoral system should be not only fair in an aggregate sense, but also fair to all participants. It should neither contain within it elements that are almost certain to produce biased results favouring one party rather than another nor be open to manipulation by political parties in order either to create or to exacerbate such biases. The current UK electoral system clearly does not meet these criteria, as described here: its tendency to produce disproportional results indicates unfairness which generally favours the larger over the smaller parties, while its tendency to produce biases indicates unequal treatment of the two main parties, which they are able to manipulate through a range of strategies and tactics.

Is a better system available? Is fairness feasible or, at least, greater fairness than that currently achieved? In this section, we enquire whether it is possible to alter the current system in order to reduce the bias tendencies; in the next we look at alternative systems.

Removing malapportionment?

Biases in the current system result from three sets of processes – malapportionment, gerrymandering and reactive malapportionment. The first has two components in the UK: malapportionment because of differential treatment of the various countries within the UK, and 'creeping malapportionment' because of population movements which generate inter-constituency variations in electorates.

The first type of malapportionment is readily removed by treating the UK as a single unit with regard to the allocation of seats: no guaranteed number of constituencies (maximum or minimum) should be allocated to any one country, and a single UK electoral quota should be employed to determine each country's entitlement during a review. The ease of doing this was shown with passage of the *Scotland Act 1998* which established the Scottish Parliament following the favourable referendum in September 1997. The clause in the *Parliamentary Constituencies Act 1986* guaranteeing Scotland no fewer than 71 seats (Box 3.7) was repealed and the Boundary Commission for Scotland instructed to use the electoral quota established by the English Commission for its Fifth Periodic Review. This was determined as 69,932 in February 2000; its application to Scotland indicates an allocation of 57.2 seats, which may be increased by one or two seats because of the application of 'special geographical considerations' (Rule 6) in the Highlands and Islands regions. At subsequent reviews, the Scottish Commission will determine its own quota, which will incorporate the 'ratchet effect' described above (p.69), because the extra seats allocated for 'special geographical considerations' will be included in the denominator for the Sixth Review; after perhaps three or four more reviews, Scotland's representation may again be about 72 seats!

This change was introduced because of the devolution of powers to the Scottish Parliament, and a consequential desire to reduce Scotland's influence in the House of Commons.[10] A similar change was not proposed for Wales, however, presumably on the grounds that devolution was transferring many fewer powers there (the issue was not debated in 1998).

There is no need for any country to be guaranteed a number of seats which ensures that it is over-represented in the House of Commons, irrespective of devolution and other policies. The changes introduced by the *Scotland Act 1998* indicate that it is easy to remove this aspect of malapportionment, so that the only difference between the constituent countries of the UK in their levels of representation would be as a result of 'special geographical considerations'. There is a larger issue of what the 'fair' level of representation should be in the House of Commons, given that there has been devolution to three of the four countries (the three smallest). Putting that to one side, however, equal representation of the four countries could be readily and easily achieved.[11]

'Creeping malapportionment' results from population movements between reviews, and produces bias when it favours one party over another – Labour in the UK since the mid-1950s. It is bound to occur, and can only be countered by a combination of more frequent redistributions and a firmer insistence on electoral equality between constituencies. The frequency of redistributions in part depends on attitudes to the frequency of changes although, as we have seen, when they are more frequent the number of constituencies whose boundaries are changed is usually relatively small; it also depends in part on the time taken by a Review.[12] Insistence on electoral equality would mean that criterion being given greater priority. All are feasible, if there is a desire to achieve the outcome. Reviews could be made more frequent and the entire process accelerated, especially if the time-consuming Local Inquiries are abolished (see below). The ability of Parliament to delay a redistribution could also be removed by giving greater power to the Commissions, whose recommendations would be automatically implemented. And equality could be made the primary criterion, while still respecting the local government template. Some creeping malapportionment would still occur, but the bias should be fairly small and of little consequence at all but the closest of elections: the American model of a redistribution every ten years seems a reasonable model.

Ending gerrymandering?

Gerrymandering would be harder to deal with than malapportionment because the infrastructural gerrymander described here is a function, ultimately, of the relative geographical concentration of the two main parties' support. For as long as one party (Labour throughout the period studied here) has more concentrated support than the other, and hence is more subject to stacked gerrymanders and larger numbers of surplus votes per seats won than its opponent, then bias in favour of the Conservatives is likely to occur if Labour's stacked gerrymander is more detrimental to its seats:votes ratio than the Conservatives' cracked gerrymander is to that party. As we showed, Labour was disadvantaged at most of the elections studied by larger numbers of both surplus votes per seat won and wasted votes per seat lost (the latter being a consequence of pro-Conservative cracked gerrymanders in most areas).

The stacked and cracked gerrymanders are probably slightly exaggerated by the importance of the local government map as the template within which constituencies are allocated, notably in England. The number of such units declined after the local government reorganisations of the 1960s and 1970s, but has increased again for two reasons. First, a number of the smaller authorities, notably the London Boroughs, have lost population over recent decades and their entitlement to Parliamentary representation has fallen accordingly. In London, for example, no Borough is now entitled to more than three seats and the majority to only two. The smaller the number of seats, the greater the likelihood that the largest party there will win them all (which may also be associated with malapportionment, since the deviations from the electoral quota are likely to be larger with lots of small areas entitled to two or three seats). The Boundary Commission for England responded to this in the Fourth Review by deciding to pair adjacent London Boroughs in certain circumstances – in the end eight constituencies were created which contained wards from two Boroughs, involving seven Boroughs in all. This policy is being repeated in the Fifth Review.[13]

Secondly, local government reforms in non-metropolitan England in the mid-1990s involved the creation of 52 unitary authorities which, with six exceptions (in Berkshire), are independent and have to be treated separately by the Commission – although it may decide to group either adjacent unitary authorities or a unitary authority with an adjacent county (presumably that from which it was removed) using Rule 5, in the same way that it now groups London Boroughs.[14] Wales now has 22 unitary authorities only but, as indicated in Chapter 3, the eight pre-existing counties have been retained for the allocation of seats by its Boundary Commission. Scotland now also has only unitary authorities; its Commission is likely to work with their boundaries as far as possible – although it is only required to have regard to them – and cross-boundary constituencies will certainly be created.[15]

However, the Commissions allocate constituencies across the local government template, the infrastructural gerrymander will continue to operate so long as the two main parties have different geographies of support. Changing the role of the template will not alter this fundamentally. As we saw in Chapter 6 with regard to Northern Ireland, where the unitary authorities are not mentioned in the legislation and the only constraint is that wards must not be subdivided, nevertheless a partisan outcome is a likely consequence of a Commission's recommendations. Use of single-member constituencies imposed on different geographies of party support is almost certain to produce stacked gerrymander-like situations in some areas and cracked gerrymander-like solutions in others: geography ensures such partisan outcomes however non-partisan the procedure.

We showed in Chapter 6 that the political parties are able to influence the operation of the infrastructural gerrymander through the Local Inquiry process, although the overall impact of this is minor. Nevertheless, we believe that the Inquiries are an unnecessary and time-consuming aspect of the current procedure; they invite a lot of time and effort to be put into gerrymandering exercises, usually for spurious reasons. They should be abandoned. Interested parties should be invited to respond to the Commissions' provisional recommendations in writing only, with a separate panel of Assistant Commissioners evaluating the submissions and making a written report without any further public consultation, on which the Commissions would then act. This would substantially speed up the entire process, with very little loss of public credibility in the outcomes. In addition, 'local ties' (and their breaking) should no longer be included in the rules as an issue to be considered, since this has produced a wide range of spurious arguments by parties and others seeking to promote their electoral interests (in effect, to gerrymander the outcome).

The final way in which the parties can influence the gerrymander bias, as we showed in Chapter 6, is if two or more of them engage in the promotion of tactical voting, whereby their average number of wasted votes per seat lost is reduced. This undoubtedly played a significant part in the switch in the direction and size of the gerrymander bias between the 1992 and 1997 general elections, from pro-Conservative to pro-Labour. There is nothing that can be done within the electoral system to prevent this. With fptp in single-member constituencies, it is a sensible tactic where two or more parties and their supporters perceive the benefits of collaboration (however implicit) to the detriment of a further party. It will clearly only occur where more than two parties are involved and where such collaboration makes political sense; it cannot be prevented within the system.[16]

Stopping reactive malapportionment

The final group of bias components results from malapportionment-like effects of both (a) differential rates of abstention and (b) the differential impact of 'third parties' across constituencies.

The impact of differential abstention rates benefiting one party rather than another could only be ended by a change to the electoral law, making voting compulsory – an issue occasionally discussed in the UK, but no more. Some oppose compulsory voting on principle; for them, to abstain without going to the polling booth and spoiling one's ballot paper is a perfectly acceptable democratic act. Others are resistant on logistic grounds – it would be expensive to police and difficult to enforce unless the current inflexible arrangements that voters are assigned to a single polling booth only (unless either a postal or proxy vote has been arranged in advance) were significantly relaxed, with the likely consequence that it would be several days after the election before all votes were counted and the result known. Without such legislation, if abstention is higher in areas where one party tends to be stronger than another, then some bias is bound to occur. This has benefited Labour in the UK because it tends to suffer more from the stacked gerrymander and have large numbers of surplus votes per seat won; many Labour supporters feel less stimulus to turn out than their Conservative counterparts, therefore, especially if their party implicitly encourages this by not canvassing intensively in the seats it is virtual certain that it will win.

Whereas the impact of abstentions on electoral bias could be removed, that of third parties could not. As we have seen, if they are more successful in constituencies where one of the two main parties tends to be stronger, this will stimulate bias – though towards which party depends on whether they win seats or just reduce the number of votes that the stronger party there needs for victory.

A *new set of rules?*

Is it feasible to implement some of the possible changes just discussed? Box 8.1 gives a set of rules – similar to those currently employed under the *Parliamentary Constituencies Act 1986* (Box 3.7) – which meet the criteria just discussed.[17] Without going through them in great detail they:

1 remove unequal representation between the constituent countries of the UK;
2 make electoral equality the dominant criterion in constituency allocation and definition, with a margin of no more than 10 per cent;
3 employ the current local government structure as the template within which constituencies are defined, requiring the grouping of adjacent units in order to meet the equality criterion;
4 retain the requirement that Commissions take account of inconveniences consequent on change, but only when the other criteria have been met;
5 accelerate the process by eliminating the time-consuming and unnecessary Local Inquiries; and
6 prevent Parliamentary interference with the process (such as delays in implementing recommendations) other than by new legislation.

This will remove some of the biases – notably that between countries – and potentially reduce some others – such as some aspects of the gerrymander. But others again cannot be affected by the process, since they are integral to a multi-party democracy operating the fptp electoral system in single-member constituencies where voting is not compulsory, where the parties have different geographies of support and where tactical voting is sensible in certain circumstances. These new rules will make for more efficient redistributions, but their only real impact will be on levels of malapportionment. Biases will undoubtedly remain, and as the parties become more sophisticated at operating within the system, they may well increase.

Box 8.1 A proposed set of Rules and Procedures for the redistribution of seats using first-past-the-post in single-member constituencies

Rules

1 The target size of the House of Commons shall be x members.

2 The electoral quota for the allocation of seats to England, Scotland, Wales and Northern Ireland shall be the electorate of the United Kingdom on the qualifying date, divided by x. Fractional entitlements should be rounded to the nearest integer.

3 The electoral quota defined in rule 2 shall be used to define constituencies throughout the United Kingdom.

4 Each constituency shall return a single Member of Parliament.

5 The number of electors in each constituency shall be as close to the electoral quota as possible, and no constituency should deviate from it by more than 10 per cent.

6 The basic local government units to be employed in allocating constituencies shall be:

  (a) in England, the Shire Counties, the Metropolitan Counties, the Unitary Authorities and the London Boroughs;

  (b) in Scotland and Wales, the Unitary Authorities; and

  (c) in Northern Ireland, the local government Districts.

7 In defining constituencies, Boundary Commissions may either group or subdivide basic local government units defined in Rule 6 to meet the requirement of Rule 4. The decision whether to group adjacent units shall proceed as follows:

  (a) the Commission shall use the electoral quota to determine the theoretical entitlement to constituencies of each basic local government unit, using its registered electorate on the qualifying date;

  (b) an integer number of constituencies shall be allocated, using the harmonic mean;

  (c) if the average electorate for the constituencies in the basic local government unit deviates from the electoral quota by more than 10 per cent, the Commission will group it with one or more adjacent basic local government units so that their joint theoretical entitlement meets the requirement that the average constituency electorate does not deviate from the electoral quota by more than 10 per cent; and

  (d) only entire basic local government units are to be grouped.

8 No part of a basic local government unit shall be included in a constituency which includes the whole or part of another such unit unless this is necessary to meet the requirement of Rule 5.

9 Local government wards shall not be divided between constituencies.

10 In sparsely-populated areas, the Commission may recommend constituencies having electorates more than 10 per cent below the electoral quota.

11 Boundary Commissions shall take account of the inconveniences attendant on:

  (a) in England, the division between constituencies of Districts within the Metropolitan and Shire Counties;

(b) in Northern Ireland, the division between constituencies of district electoral areas; and

(c) alterations of constituencies.

Definitions:

A For Rule 2, the qualifying date shall be the date on which the Commissions announce that a review has commenced.

B In Shire Counties in England that have elections to both County Council and District Councils, the term local government ward in Rule 9 refers to the areas used for elections to District Councils.

Procedures

1 The Boundary Commissions shall report on reviews of all constituencies within their portion of the United Kingdom no more than ten years after the date of their last report.

2 The Boundary Commissions shall proceed by:

(a) publishing the electoral quota to be used in the review, the theoretical entitlement of each basic local government unit, and any grouping of adjacent units proposed to meet the requirements of rules 5 and 7;

(b) interested parties will be given two months to make representations regarding these proposals, after which the Commission shall publish its final decisions within a further two months;

(c) proposed constituencies will be published for each basic local government unit, or group of adjacent units, and interested parties invited to make representations within two months of publication;

(d) a panel of Assistant Commissioners will review these representations, and make recommendations to the Commission within three months; and

(e) the Commission will announce its final decision within a further three months.

3 The relevant Secretary of State will implement the Commission's final recommendations through an Order in Council within one month of receiving its report.

4 The new constituencies will be used at the next general election following that Order.

Electoral reform

Our conclusion from the previous section, therefore, is that biases are an almost certain consequence of the current UK electoral system, and that only some of their components can be reduced (few can be removed). So what of alternative electoral systems? Can they be less biased – even unbiased?

Electoral reform is a very large subject, with a large number of alternative systems already being operated in the increasing number of countries that have representative democratic systems of government.[18] Reviewing them all, let alone their bias potential, is well outside the brief we have set ourselves here. We concentrate on a small number of systems, all of which have been discussed recently in the UK and some of which are now being operated.

One general point by way of introduction is that all of these systems employ constituencies, territorial divisions of the national territory.[19] Thus geography is doubly implicated in their operation, because those constituencies will be superimposed upon geographies of party support. Furthermore, in the UK context it is clear not only that constituencies are considered fundamental for Parliamentary representation (each MP should represent a defined area), but also that there is strong support for single-member constituencies, sustaining what was defined in the terms of reference for the Jenkins Commission as 'the maintenance of a link between MPs and geographical constituencies'. Our discussion throughout this book has stressed that bias (and disproportionality) are necessary consequences of constituency-based electoral systems, so that the question then becomes whether it is possible to produce systems producing less bias than the current one, while meeting the other element of Jenkins' remit – 'broad proportionality'. We discuss this by grouping alternative systems into three, with variants within each, and concentrating on the last – the hybrids.

Preferential systems

Preferential voting systems involve the electors rank-ordering the candidates in a constituency, in order to produce results in which the elected candidates have the support of more than half of those voting or, at least, those elected are more preferred than those who are not.

Application of this method in single-member constituencies has been promoted in two forms. The first involves the *supplementary vote*, whereby electors are invited to indicate their first and second choice candidates. The first preferences are counted and if a candidate has more than half of the votes cast, he or she is declared elected. If no candidate has more than half of the votes, then all but the two with the largest totals are eliminated, with their second preferences being allocated to the remaining candidates (with those allocated to candidates who have been eliminated being ignored). The remaining candidate with the largest vote total is then declared elected.[20] This system was used to elect the first Mayor of Greater London in May 2000. No candidate got a majority of the first-preference votes cast, and so all but two (Livingstone and Norris) were eliminated; Livingstone then won after second preferences had been allocated, though still with the support of only 45.3 per cent of those who voted (Table 8.1: of the 581,851 whose first preference was for neither Livingstone nor Norris, only 208,253 – some 36 per cent – cast their second preference for either Livingstone or Norris).

The supplementary vote does not ensure that the winner has majority support, therefore. The *alternative vote* (av) does, unless a large number of voters fail to indicate their lower preferences. Electors are invited to rank order all n candidates standing in the constituency from 1 to n, and if no candidate has a majority of the first-preference votes the one with the smallest total is eliminated and her/his second preferences allocated.[21] If still no candidate has a majority of the votes cast, the next lowest is eliminated and her or his second preferences allocated (or third preferences, if the second preferences go to an already-eliminated candidate). This process continues until either one candidate has more than 50 per cent of the votes cast or there are only two left – in which case the candidate with most votes is the winner.

Table 8.1   The result of the election for Mayor of London, May 2000

Candidate	First preferences	Second preferences	Total
Ben-Nathan	9,956		
Clements	5,470		
Dobson	223,884		
Gidoomal	42,060		
Hockney	16,324		
Johnson	38,121		
Kramer	203,452		
Livingstone	667,877	108,550	776,427
Newland	33,569		
Norris	464,434	99,703	564,137
Tanna	9,015		
Total	1,714,162	208,253	1,340,564

Neither of these systems avoids any of the sources of bias identified for fptp – and indeed may exacerbate one of them. The malapportionment biases can be eliminated as outlined above, but the infrastructural gerrymander will remain, along with reactive malapportionment. It is quite possible that the infrastructural gerrymander will be accentuated, because of tactical voting if there are three or more parties involved. (If there are only two, then neither system has any advantage over fptp.) If supporters of particular parties are more likely to give their second and lower preferences to one of the two leading parties rather than the other, then the latter could find that it is defeated in a large number of constituencies – even those where it may have a substantial lead on the first-preference votes. Indeed, this was the main reason for introducing the system in Australia in 1918. The two right-wing parties (Liberal and Country) were able to prevent the single left-wing party (Labor) winning seats where its candidate won most votes, but not a majority, because most of their supporters gave their second preferences to the other right-wing party, thus ensuring that one of them won in all constituencies where there was a right-wing majority.

Patrick Dunleavy and his colleagues have evaluated what the result of the 1997 general election would have been if different electoral systems had been employed, based on surveys conducted with 'mock' ballot papers. They found that, with both methods, the outcome would have been even less proportional than was the case with fptp, as a result of what they term 'the convergence of Labour and Liberal Democrat supporters' second preferences' (Dunleavy *et al.*, 1998, 215: Labour voters were 11 times more likely to give their second preferences to the Liberal Democrats than to the Conservatives, for example, and Liberal Democrat supporters were three times more likely to give their second preferences to Labour than to the Tories).[22]

A final preferential system promoted in the UK by the Liberal Democrats and by the Electoral Reform Society is the *single transferable vote* (stv) in multi-member constituencies – used for elections in the Republic of Ireland, Malta, Tasmania and for the Australian Senate, in local government elections in Northern Ireland since the 1970s, for elections from Northern Ireland to the European Parliament, and for elections to the new Northern Ireland Assembly established in 1999. As with the alternative vote, electors rank order all candidates, but because more than one has to be elected the process of elimination and distribution of preferences is more complicated, involving the allocation of second and lower preferences not only of those candidates eliminated, but also of those elected with more votes than necessary for victory.

As stv was rapidly rejected by the Jenkins Commission – 'STV would be too big a leap from that to which we have become used, and it would be a leap in a confusingly different direction from the other electoral changes which are currently being made in Britain' (p.33: note that the reference is to Britain not the UK) – we will not discuss it in detail here. Suffice it to note that it is open to all of the possible biases that we have identified for fptp, only some of which (those associated with malapportionment) can easily be eliminated. For example, the smaller the number of members to be elected from a constituency, the greater the disproportionality – with smaller parties suffering: that may also stimulate gerrymandering. And tactical voting with regard to the allocation of lower preferences can have a substantial impact on the final outcome.[23]

List systems

List systems are used where proportional representation is the major goal. They involve multi-member constituencies (returning 30 or more members in some cases) in which seats are allocated proportionally to votes, usually to any party whose vote total exceeds a threshold percentage of those cast. The larger the constituency – in terms of the number of members to be elected – the more proportional the outcome.

Because their goal is proportionality, these systems are much less likely to produce biased outcomes since, save at the margin, every vote counts and counts (virtually) equally. Exact proportionality is very unlikely to be achieved, because it is impossible to allocate seats in exact proportion to votes. (One could not give two parties with 45.4 and 33.7 per cent of the votes, respectively, those exact percentages of the seats in a 20-member constituency.) There are bound to be some wasted and surplus votes, but these will be relatively few: the exact number depends on the way in which the final seats are allocated, for which there are many variants.[24]

The benefit of list systems is that, apart from malapportionment (which can readily be remedied), they are unlikely to produce major biases. But Jenkins rejected them for elections to the House of Commons, because they would not incorporate a clear link between an MP and her or his constituency (especially if a national list were used to aim for 'pure proportionality'), producing instead a 'too remote, rigid and party machine-dominated system' (p.18). Nevertheless, a list system was employed for the Great Britain elections to the European Parliament in June 2000, using 11 constituencies and producing the results shown in Table 8.2.[25] The outcome was not very proportional: the Conservative and Labour parties each got c.5 per cent more of the seats than they did of the votes which 'counted' (i.e. for parties that were allocated seats), whereas the Green and UK Independence parties got only about half of their 'entitlement'. The problem for the latter two parties was that in a number of the constituencies the threshold for the allocation of even one seat was too high for them: in the Eastern constituency, for example, the Green party obtained 6.2 per cent of the votes cast, but this was insufficient for it to get any of the eight MEPs who represented that region.[26]

Table 8.2 Results of the 1999 elections to the European Parliament from Great Britain

Party	Votes	%V	%VC	Seats	%S
Conservative	3,578,217	35.8	37.9	36	42.9
Labour	2,803,821	28.0	29.8	29	34.5
Liberal Democrat	1,266,549	12.7	13.4	10	11.9
SNP	268,528	2.7	2.8	2	2.3
Plaid Cymru	185,235	1.9	2.0	2	2.3
Green	625,378	6.3	6.6	2	2.3
UK Indpendence	696,057	7.0	7.4	3	3.6
Other	578,508	5.8		0	0

Key to columns: %V – per cent of all votes; %VC – per cent of votes to parties that were allocated seats; %S – per cent of seats.

Indeed, the Green party obtained at least 5 per cent of the votes cast in all but two of the regions, but gained seats in only two – London and the Southeast, where it got 7.7 and 7.4 per cent, respectively; in the Southwest it got 8.3 per cent of the votes, but no seat. Its vote, like that of the UK Independence party, was too widely spread across the relatively small regions for it to achieve proportional representation, unlike the SNP and PC, which each obtained just under 30 per cent of the votes cast in Scotland and Wales, respectively: the SNP got two of the eight Scottish seats (25 per cent) and PC got two of the five in Wales (40 per cent).

Hybrid systems

Apart from the alternative vote – which commentators in 1999–2000 said may be acceptable to both the Prime Minister and the Liberal Democrats as a compromise between the proportional system (stv) preferred by the latter and the status quo preferred by many in the Labour party – most attention has focused on a particular form of hybrid system. The paradigm for this is the system introduced in West Germany in 1949, known as the *additional member system* (ams: and to some as the *mixed-member proportional system* – mmp). In this, a proportion of those elected are drawn from single-member constituencies where fptp is employed, and the remainder are drawn from multi-member list constituencies with the entire system organised to ensure (near-) proportional representation.

Electors in such a system have two votes. The first is for their constituency representative, and the second for a party in the list vote. Each party's percentage of the second votes is taken as the norm against which proportional representation is determined. Thus if there are 400 seats in the Parliament, with 200 elected from the constituency contests and 200 from the list contests, if a party gets 40 per cent of the votes cast in the list vote, it should get 40 per cent of the Parliamentary seats – 160. If it has won 120 constituency contests, this number is topped up to 160 by allocating 40 seats to the top 40 individuals on its list (excluding those who have won constituency seats, if candidates are allowed to stand for both).

The degree of proportionality achieved depends on a number of factors, such as the threshold percentage that a party has to reach in order to qualify for list seats (in New Zealand, it is either 5 per cent of the votes cast in the list vote or one constituency victory), the size of the list constituencies, and the number of list seats as against constituency seats. In Germany, the 16 Länder are used as the list constituencies (with half of the seats allocated to each of the types of contest), whereas in New Zealand – which adopted the system in 1993 and used it for general elections in 1996 and 1999 – the entire country is used for a single list contest (returning 55 MPs in 1996, compared to 65 from the single-member constituencies). The outcome in both countries tends to be close to proportional, as shown in Table 8.3 for

Table 8.3   Results of the three mmp elections

Party	%CV	%LV	ConstS	ListS	TotS	%S	%S– %LV
New Zealand 1996							
National	33.9	33.8	30	14	44	36.7	2.9
Labour	31.1	28.2	26	11	37	30.8	2.6
New Zealand First	13.5	13.3	6	11	17	14.2	0.9
Alliance	11.3	10.1	1	12	13	10.8	0.7
ACT	3.7	6.1	1	7	8	6.7	0.6
United	2.1	0.9	1	0	1	0.8	–0.1
Christian Coalition	1.5	4.3	0	0	0	0	–4.3
Others	2.9	3.2	0	0	0	0	–3.2
Total							15.3
Index							7.65
Scotland 1999							
Conservative	15.5	15.4	0	18	18	14.0	–1.4
Labour	38.8	33.6	53	3	56	43.4	9.8
Liberal Democrat	14.2	12.4	12	5	17	13.2	0.8
SNP	28.7	27.3	7	28	35	27.1	–0.2
Others	2.7	11.2	1	2	3	2.3	–8.9
Total							21.1
Index							10.55
Wales 1999							
Conservative	15.8	16.5	1	8	9	15.0	–1.5
Labour	37.6	35.4	27	1	28	46.7	11.3
Liberal Democrat	13.5	12.5	3	3	6	10.0	–2.5
Plaid Cymru	28.4	30.5	9	8	17	28.3	–2.2
Others	4.7	5.1	0	0	0	0	–5.1
Total							22.6
Index							11.3

Key to columns: %CV – percentage of the votes cast in the constituencies; %LV – percentage of the votes cast on the party lists; ConstS – number of constituency seats won; ListS – number of list seats won; TotS – total number of seats won; %S – percentage of total number of seats won; %S – %LV – difference between the percentage of the total number of seats won and percentage of the list votes.

The Totals for the differences between %S and %LV are calculated irrespective of sign.

New Zealand's 1996 general election, when the index of disproportionality between the percentage of the list votes and percentage of the seats was 7.65 (see p.2): the only party that was substantially under-represented was the Christian Coalition which, with 4.3 per cent of the list votes and no constituency seats failed to cross the threshold for representation; the greatest over-representation was for the largest party – National – which obtained 33.8 per cent of the list votes, but 36.7 per cent of the seats.

This hybrid system was adopted for the elections to the Scottish Parliament and Welsh Assembly in 1999, although with relatively larger proportions of those elected being drawn from the constituency contests and small list contest constituencies. In Scotland, for example, 73 MSPs were elected from single-member constituencies via fptp and a further 56 from eight regions, each returning seven MSPs chosen to reflect the list vote there and with the constituency MSPs from that region excluded: in Wales, 40 AMs were elected from single-member constituencies plus five each from four regions (Table 8.3). The indices of disproportionality were larger than in New Zealand because of this use of smaller 'top-up regions': 10.55 in Scotland and 11.3 in Wales (in each case, the largest party – Labour – was over-represented).[27]

The Jenkins Commission recommended an ams system for elections to the House of Commons, because it offered 'broad proportionality', 'an extension of voter choice' and 'the maintenance of a link between MPs and geographical constituencies' – key terms in the Commission's remit. (The other was 'the need for stable government', which was taken to mean a high probability that one party would win a majority of MPs.) It differed from the systems already in place in Germany, New Zealand, Scotland and Wales in three main respects, however: in the ratio of constituency to list MPs; the size of the 'top-up' regions; and the use of the alternative vote in the constituency contests.[28]

In determining the relative proportion of constituency and 'top-up' MPs, the Commission had to balance the various criteria set out in its terms of reference: basically, the more 'top-up' members, the greater the proportionality but also the greater the possibility that no party would gain a majority of MPs. It decided to give priority to constituency links and 'firm government', with a recommendation that the number of 'top-up seats' be no more than 15–20 per cent of MPs; it gave examples using 17.5 per cent 'top-up seats'

Table 8.4 The estimated number of MPs per party, at the 1992 and 1997 general elections in the UK, using the Jenkins' Commission recommendations

Party	1992		1997	
	fptp	ams	fptp	ams
Conservative	336	316	165	168
Labour	271	240	419	368
Liberal Democrat	20	74	46	89
SNP/PC	7	11	10	15
Northern Ireland	17	18	18	18

Key to electoral systems: fptp – first-past-the-post; ams – alternative member system.
Source: Jenkins (1998, 46).

(i.e. 115 of the current complement of 659) to estimate the results of the 1992 and 1997 elections (Table 8.4) for which it calculated indices of disproportionality of 9.0 and 13.2, respectively.

The 1997 scheme was set out in some detail; it used the eight and five 'top-up regions' established for the Scottish Parliament and Welsh Assembly elections respectively, plus a further 65 in England (42 in the Shire Counties – of which only Essex, Hampshire, Kent and Lancashire were divided; 16 in the Metropolitan Counties; and 7 in Greater London) and two in Northern Ireland. Of these 80 regions, 36 would return 2 'top-up' MPs each and the other 44 would each return just one. In effect, the infrastructural gerrymander described in Chapter 6 would continue to operate in each of those 80, and be slightly ameliorated by allocating the one or two 'top-up' seats to the smaller parties. This would somewhat reduce the 'electoral apartheid' identified by Jenkins (see above, p.207), with parties winning one or two extra seats in areas where normally they would win none (the Conservatives in the 'north', and Labour in the 'south', for example).

The small 'top up' regions would mean that the relatively small number of list MPs would represent relatively small areas, even if they were not single-member constituencies: the 'traditional' UK system would only be slightly tampered with to move it towards proportionality. It would still be open to malapportionment and gerrymandering biases, however, which would be somewhat ameliorated by the 'top up' mechanism. (Malapportionment would be an issue at both scales, with the potential for 'creeping malapportionment' in both the fptp constituencies, as now, and the 'top up' regions.)

A final aspect of the proposals increases the possibility of gerrymander biases, however – the recommendation (opposed by one of the Commission's members) that the alternative vote be used in the single-member constituencies. It was argued (p.38) that this would be beneficial because:

1 there would be many fewer wasted votes and a larger proportion of the electorate would influence the constituency outcome, which it was hoped would encourage turnout and participation; and
2 it would encourage candidates to appeal to a wider spectrum of the electorate than their 'hard-core faithful' in order to win seats – leading to a 'more inclusive' style of politics and less inter-party bitterness, since each party would be wanting to attract second preferences from its opponents' supporters.

But where there are several parties on one 'ideological wing' of the country's politics and fewer on the other wing – as is currently the case in Great Britain (Labour, the Liberal Democrats, Plaid Cymru and the SNP are all left-of-centre, with only the Conservatives on the right) – this will encourage tactical voting, and the consequent bias. Table 8.4 illustrates this with estimates of the Liberal Democrats' likely performance in 1992 and 1997 under the proposed ams system compared to its actual performance under fptp. Furthermore, in the parts of the country where a party does not expect to win constituency seats, it is likely to focus its efforts on the list seats only, reasoning that there is little to be gained from investing heavily in an intensive campaign for candidates fighting constituency seats.[29]

Rules for defining constituencies under ams/mmp

The details of various proposals for electoral reform in the UK are largely outside the basic subject matter of this book, as are debates about how voting behaviour would change should they be implemented.[30] Our major concern is whether the new systems are likely to produce biased election results, in the way that the current one does, and whether any of the bias components can be avoided.

The ams/mmp system recommended by Jenkins is based on constituencies – some 580 fptp constituencies and 80 list regions (or 'top-up' constituencies), with the former nesting into the latter. Malapportionment and gerrymandering are thus potentially important issues. The former can be tackled through the rules for defining constituencies operated by the Boundary Commissions. Our proposed set of rules to be used if fptp is retained (Box 8.1) is modified in Box 8.2 to cover the two sets of constituencies required under the Jenkins proposals.[31] These incorporate the rules for single-member constituencies set out in Box 8.1, and the additional rules have the multi-member constituencies as groups of five to ten of the

---

Box 8.2 A proposed set of Rules and Procedures for the redistribution of seats using both single- and multi-member constituencies

Rules
1 The target size of the House of Commons shall be x members.
2 Of those x members, y shall be elected from single-member constituencies and z shall be elected from multi-member constituencies.
3 The electoral quota for the allocation of single member constituencies to England, Scotland, Wales and Northern Ireland shall be the electorate of the United Kingdom on the qualifying date, divided by y. Fractional entitlements should be rounded to the nearest integer.
4 The electoral quota for the allocation of multi-member constituencies to England, Scotland, Wales and Northern Ireland shall be the electorate of the United Kingdom on the qualifying date, divided by z. Fractional entitlements should be rounded to the nearest integer.
5 The electoral quotas defined in rules 3 and 4 shall be used to define constituencies throughout the United Kingdom.
6 The number of electors in each single-member constituency shall be as close to the electoral quota established in rule 3 as possible, and no constituency should deviate from it by more than 10 per cent.

7 The basic local government units to be employed in allocating single-member constituencies shall be:
   (a) in England, the Shire Counties, the Metropolitan Counties, the Unitary Authorities and the London Boroughs;
   (b) in Scotland and Wales, the Unitary Authorities; and
   (c) in Northern Ireland, the local government Districts.

8 In defining single-member constituencies, Boundary Commissions may either group or subdivide basic local government units defined in rule 7 to meet the requirement of rule 6. The decision whether to group adjacent units shall proceed as follows:
   (a) the Commission shall use the electoral quota to determine the theoretical entitlement to constituencies of each basic local government unit, using its registered electorate on the qualifying date;
   (b) an integer number of constituencies shall be allocated, using the harmonic mean;
   (c) if the average electorate for the constituencies in the basic local government unit deviates from the electoral quota by more than 10 per cent, the Commission will group it with one or more adjacent basic local government units so that their joint theoretical entitlement meets the requirement that the average constituency electorate does not deviate from the electoral quota by more than 10 per cent; and
   (d) only entire basic local government units are to be grouped.

9 No part of a basic local government unit shall be included in a single-member constituency which includes the whole or part of another such unit unless this is necessary to meet the requirement of rule 6.

10 Local government wards shall not be divided between single-member constituencies.

11 In sparsely-populated areas, a Commission may recommend constituencies having electorates more than 10 per cent below the electoral quota.

12 Boundary Commissions shall take account of the inconveniences attendant on:
   (a) in England, the division between constituencies of Districts within the Metropolitan and Shire Counties;
   (b) in Northern Ireland, the division between constituencies of district electoral areas; and
   (c) alterations of constituencies.

13 Each multi-member constituency shall consist of no less than five and no more than ten single-member constituencies.

14 Each multi-member constituency shall return no more than u and no less than v members.

15 No multi-member constituency shall contain single-member constituencies in more than one of England, Northern Ireland, Scotland and Wales.

16 In defining multi-member constituencies, Boundary Commissions shall take account of:
   (a) in England, the boundaries of Shire Counties, Metropolitan Counties, Unitary Authorities and London Boroughs;
   (b) in Scotland and Wales, the boundaries of Unitary Authorities; and
   (c) in Northern Ireland, the boundaries of local government Districts.

Definitions:

A For Rule 2, the qualifying date shall be the date on which the Commissions announce that a review has commenced.

B In Shire Counties in England that have elections to both County Council and District Councils, the term local government ward in Rule 10 refers to the areas used for elections to District Councils.

Procedures

1 The Boundary Commissions shall report on reviews of all constituencies within their portion of the United Kingdom no more than ten years after the date of their last report.

2 The Boundary Commissions shall proceed by:

(a) publishing the electoral quota to be used in the review; the theoretical entitlement of each basic local government unit, any grouping of adjacent units proposed to meet the requirements of rules 6 and 8, and its proposed multi-member constituencies under rule 16;

(b) interested parties will be given two months to make representations regarding these proposals, after which the Commission shall publish its final decisions within a further two months;

(c) proposed constituencies will be published for each basic local government unit, or group of adjacent units, and interested parties invited to make representations within two months of publication;

(d) a panel of Assistant Commissioners will review these representations, and make recommendations to the Commission within three months; and

(e) the Commission will announce its final decision within a further three months.

3 The relevant Secretary of State will implement the Commission's final recommendations through an Order in Council within one month of receiving its report.

4 The new constituencies will be used at the next general election following that Order.

single-member units, with the boundaries of the basic local government units taken into account.

Conclusions

Geography not only matters; it is here to stay. For as long as the UK's electoral system is based on either or both of single-member constituencies and small multi-member constituencies, disproportionality and bias are likely electoral outcomes because support for parties is not the same across the country. Furthermore, increasingly sophisticated appreciation of that situation by one or more of the political parties will probably see the disproportionality and bias increase.

Nor can most of the effects of geography be removed. We have shown here that bias results from three groups of components – akin to malapportionment, gerrymandering, and reactive malapportionment. The first can be handled: malapportionment between countries can be removed and 'creeping malapportionment' controlled by frequent reviews of constituencies and a firmer insistence on electoral equality as the basis for redistricting. But that is all. Bias resulting from non-partisan gerrymandering is a necessary consequence of the interaction between the two geographies of constituencies and party support, and can be exacerbated by tactical voting. And reactive malapportionment is also bound to occur for so long as abstention and/or support for third parties is unevenly distributed across the constituencies. Changing the rules cannot affect these. The system for redistributing constituencies can be more efficient and effective, as our proposed rules indicate, but cannot have a significant impact on non-partisan (i.e. unintentional) gerrymanders.

Changing the electoral system may, of course, remove both malapportionment and gerrymandering. But the proposals to change the electoral system currently being discussed in the UK will hardly affect gerrymandering at all, even if malapportionment is handled in the way that we propose here. The Jenkins proposals for a variant of ams/mmp – what he terms av+ – will only slightly ameliorate the gerrymander effect at best, and may exacerbate it because use of the alternative vote encourages tactical voting. Retaining a system with single-member constituencies only, but using the alternative vote instead of fptp (which appears to be the only 'reform' currently acceptable), will almost certainly leave the gerrymander and reactive malapportionment biases intact.

Geography reigns – supreme!

Notes

1 Fairness in the operation of electoral systems extends well beyond the issues raised here and, as we have shown elsewhere (Johnston, 1998, 1999; Johnston and Pattie, 1997b), even achieving fairness with regard to disproportionality and bias may not be enough to ensure fairness on other dimensions. It is much easier to achieve 'one person, one vote' than 'one vote, one value'.

2 The most sustained work on 'uniform swing' is in the classic seminal work by Butler and Stokes (1974).

3 See Norris (1997).

4 Using the 1999 electorate data and the quota applied by the Boundary Commission for England at the start of its Fifth Periodic Review (69,982), Scotland would be entitled to 57.2 seats, Wales to 32.0 and Northern Ireland 17.2. Scotland may get perhaps two more because of special geographical circumstances and Wales one. The consequence of the changes in Scotland will undoubtedly be a reduction in the benefit to Labour from this bias component.

5 In the volume produced to describe its work at the outset of the Fifth Periodic Review, the Boundary Commission for England (2000, 2) again makes the very

clear statement that: 'The Commission are an independent, non-political and totally impartial body. They emphasise very strongly that the results of previous elections do not and should not enter their considerations when they are deciding their recommendations. Nor do the Commission consider the effects of their recommendations on future voting patterns'.

6 On the north–south divide, see Johnston, Pattie and Allsopp (1988).

7 See Johnston *et al.* (1998).

8 On British campaign spending law, see Johnston and Pattie (1993).

9 This was done using the country's Standard Regions. 'North' combines Yorkshire and Humberside, Northwest, Northeast, Scotland and Wales; 'Midlands' comprises the East and West Midland regions; and the 'South' incorporates Greater London, the Southeast and Southwest regions, and East Anglia.

10 Scottish MPs may still have a great influence there, however, depending on the balance of parties in the UK as a whole.

11 Interestingly, it may be that the provisions of the *Scotland Act 1998* do not come into operation until *c.*2009. A general election is very likely in 2001 and the Commissions will not complete their Fifth Periodic Reviews until 2005. A further election may have been held by then, so the first election using the new constituencies and with Scotland's reduced representation may not occur until that Parliament has completed a four- to five-year term.

12 Interestingly, the Local Government Commission for England, which is responsible for redrawing ward boundaries, takes projected electorates over a five-year period into account, although it has a firmer requirement to achieve electoral equality.

13 The provisional recommendations for London were published in early 2001.

14 Of those unitary authorities, 12 will probably be allocated just one seat, 23 will get two, nine will get three and one each will get four and five: Rutland, with less than 26,000 voters, will undoubtedly be merged with Leicestershire.

15 Of those 32 authorities, as many as 17 have an entitlement to only one seat.

16 On tactical versus 'sincere' voting in various electoral systems, see Dummett (1997).

17 They were first published, in virtually this form, in Johnston, Pattie and Rossiter (1998a).

18 For a comprehensive listing – albeit dated as soon as it was produced – see IDEA (1997).

19 Non-constituency-based systems, whereby the country is not divided and the legislature is elected from a national list, are operated – notably in Israel and the Netherlands. They are not considered here, as their introduction for the UK House of Commons is extremely unlikely.

20 The French employ a variant of the supplementary vote – the double ballot. If no candidate wins a majority of the votes cast in a constituency in the first ballot, a second ballot is held (usually two weeks later) when candidates who obtained less than a set percentage of the votes cast (usually ten) in the first ballot are eliminated and others may withdraw. The second ballot is then between the leading candidates only, which involves many electors voting for their second-choice candidate/party.

21 This system is used for elections to the lower house of the Australian Parliament and for elections to the lower houses of several State Parliaments there.

22 In 1992, because there was much less 'convergence', AV/SV would have produced a more proportional result than first-past-the-post.

23 See Paddison (1976) and Johnston, Pattie and Rossiter (1998b). Dunleavy *et al.* (1998) found that *stv* would not have produced a proportional result in 1997, using five-member constituencies: Labour would have won 53 per cent of the seats with 44 per cent of the votes.

24 In a ten-member constituency, where party A gets 62 votes, for example, party B gets 22, party C gets 13 and party D 3, A, B and C will get 6, 3 and 2 seats, respectively, but which will get the tenth seat?

25 The original establishment of the directly elected European Parliament in the late 1970s required all member states to employ the same, proportional, system, but this was resisted by the UK government until 1999, except for Northern Ireland, where *stv* has been used since 1979. There was considerable debate when the system was being established over the exact mechanism for allocating MEPs to regions, and over the exact form of the voting procedure – whether electors were required to vote for a party's list of candidates, in the order given or could change that order. On the 1999 elections, see Butler and Westlake (2000).

26 The UK Independence party got a seat there with 8.9 per cent of the votes.

27 Dunleavy *et al.* (1998) found that mmp produced the most proportional outcome in their 1997 experiments – with half of the seats contested in constituencies and half through a list system.

28 See Margetts and Dunleavy (1999) and Dunleavy and Margetts (1999) for evaluations of the Jenkins proposals.

29 The Commission claimed that the extent of tactical voting could be exaggerated, since it is currently a minority activity (indulged in by no more than one-tenth of the electorate: many more may be prepared to, of course, if the opportunity arose in their constituency!) and that for it to increase substantially required greater party cohesion and 'obedience' than was likely.

30 One issue of interest, however, concerns constituency campaigning. We saw in Chapters 6 and 7 that the intensity of campaigning in a constituency can influence both turnout and voter choice (including tactical voting there). How much parties are allowed to spend is thus an issue that should be addressed, but it was largely ignored by a recent report on political party funding (Neill, 1998), largely because the conventional wisdom is that campaign intensity has no impact on the outcome. Our analyses strongly dispute this, however (as do results of our studies of the impact of campaign spending on results in alternative-vote-based electoral systems: Johnston and Forrest, 2000), and if every vote counts in a new system, parties will want to spend more canvassing for them.

31 These are derived from Johnston, Pattie and Rossiter (1998c).

Appendix: the formulae for calculating the bias components

The algebraic derivation of the formula used for decomposing the bias is detailed fully in Brookes (1959) and Johnston (1977). We do not repeat that here, therefore, and only set out the final formulae, following Mortimore's (1992) suggestions. In addition, we have made one entirely cosmetic modification which makes the metric even more transparent. Brookes expresses the bias as the number of seats that would have to change hands between the two parties to achieve equality, whereas we express it as the difference in the number of seats won between the two parties: Brookes' measure is therefore exactly one-half of ours.

Let:

x = the number of seats won by party A with a certain percentage of the votes cast;

y = the number of seats won by party B with the same percentage of the votes cast;

b = the number of seats in which party A has more votes than party B, when A has the percentage of votes used in calculating x;

f = the number of seats in which party B has more votes than party A, when B has the percentage of votes used in calculating y;

P = the average number of votes cast for parties A and B in seats where A has more votes than B, when A has the percentage of votes used in calculating x;

Q = the average number of votes cast for parties A and B in seats where B has more votes than A, when B has the percentage of votes used in calculating y;

J = the average national electorate in seats where A has more votes than B, when A has the percentage of votes used in calculating x;

K = the average national electorate in seats where B has more votes than A, when B has the percentage of votes used in calculating y;

R = the average registered electorate in seats where A has more votes than B, when A has the percentage of votes used in calculating x;

S = the average registered electorate in seats where B has more votes than A, when B has the percentage of votes used in calculating y;

C = the average number of abstentions in seats where A has more votes than B, when A has the percentage of votes used in calculating x;

D   = the average number of abstentions in seats where B has more votes than A, when B has the percentage of votes used in calculating y;

U   = the average number of minor party votes in seats where A has more votes than B, when A has the percentage of votes used in calculating x;

V   = the average number of minor party votes in seats where B has more votes than A, when B has the percentage of votes used in calculating y;

G   = the gerrymander effect;

NEQ = the national quotas component of the malapportionment effect;

CSV = the electorate component of the malapportionment effect;

A   = the abstentions component of the reactive malapportionment effect;

TPV = the third party votes component of the reactive malapportionment effect; and

TPW = the third party victories component of the reactive malapportionment effect;

$$G = [\{f(Pb/Qf\text{-}1)\} - \{b(Qf/Pb\text{-}1)\}]/2$$

$$NEQ = [\{f(K/J\text{-}1)\} - \{b(J/K\text{-}1)\}]/2$$

$$CSV = [\{f(S/R\text{-}1)\} - \{b(R/S\text{-}1)\}]/2$$

$$A = [f\{(R/(R\text{-}C))\ \{(C/R)\text{-}(D/S)\}\} - b\{(S/(S\text{-}D))\ \{(D/S)\text{-}(C/R)\}\}]/2$$

$$TPV = [f\{(R/(R\text{-}U))\ \{(U/R)\text{-}(V/S)\}\} - b\{(S/(S\text{-}V))\ \{(V/S)\text{-}(U/R)\}\}]/2$$

$$TPW = (x - b) - (y - f)$$

These formulae omit the interactions among the various components.

Full proofs are given in Brookes' papers (1959, 1960)

References

Alvarez, R. M. and Nagler, J. (2000) A new approach to modelling strategic voting in multiparty elections, *British Journal of Political Science*, 30, 57–76.

Blackburn, R. (1995) *The Electoral System in Britain*. London, Macmillan.

Boundary Commission for England (1947) *Initial Report of the Boundary Commission for England*. Cmd 720, London, HMSO.

Boundary Commission for England (1954) *First Periodical Report*. Cmd 9311, London, HMSO.

Boundary Commission for England (1995) *Fourth Periodic Report*, Cm 433-i, London, HMSO.

Boundary Commission for England (2000) *The Review of Parliamentary Constituencies in England*. London, Boundary Commission for England.

Brookes, R. H. (1958) Legislative representation and party vote in New Zealand: reflections on the March analysis, *Public Opinion Quarterly*, 22, 288–91.

Brookes, R. H. (1959) Electoral distortion in New Zealand, *Australian Journal of Politics and History*, 5, 218–33.

Brookes, R. H. (1960) The analysis of distorted representation in two-party, single-member elections, *Political Science*, 12, 158–67.

Brown, G. (1972) *In My Way*. London, Penguin Books.

Butler, D. (1963) *The Electoral System in Britain since 1918*. Oxford, The Clarendon Press.

Butler, D. and McLean, I. (1996) The redrawing of Parliamentary boundaries in Britain, in I. McLean and D. Butler, editors, *Fixing the Boundaries: defining and Redefining Single-Member Electoral Districts*. Aldershot, Dartmouth, 1–38.

Butler, D. and Stokes, D. (1974) *Political Change in Britain: The Evolution of Electoral Choice*. London, Macmillan.

Butler, D. and Westlake, M. (2000) *British Politics and European Elections, 1999*. London, Macmillan.

Callaghan, J. (1987) *Time and Chance*. London, Collins.

Champion, A. G. (1994) Population change and migration in Britain since 1981: evidence for continuing deconcentration, *Environment and Planning A*, 26, 1501–20.

Coleman, D. and Salt, J. (1992) *The British Population: Patterns, Trends and Processes*. Oxford, Oxford University Press.

Cox, G. W. (1997) *Making Votes Count: Strategic Coordination in the World's Electoral Systems*. Cambridge, Cambridge University Press.

Cox, K. R. (1970) Geography, social contexts and voting behavior in Wales, 1861–1951, in E. Allardt and S. Rokkan, editors, *Mass Politics*. New York, The Free Press, 117–59.

Crewe, I. and King, A. (1995) *SDP: The Birth, Life and Death of the Social Democratic Party*. Oxford, Oxford University Press.

Crossman, R. H. S. (1978) *The Diaries of a Cabinet Minister: Volume Three: Secretary of State for Social Services 1968–1970*. London, Hamish Hamilton and Jonathan Cape.

Denver, D. and Hands, G. (1974) Marginality and turnout in British general elections, *British Journal of Political Science*, 4, 17–35.

Denver, D. and Hands, G. (1985) Marginality and turnout in general elections in the 1970s, *British Journal of Political Science*, 15, 381–8.

Denver, D. and Hands, G. (1997a) *Modern Constituency Electioneering: the 1992 General Election*. London, Frank Cass.

Denver, D. and Hands, G. (1997b) Turnout, in P. Norris and N. Gavin, editors, *Britain Votes 1997*. Oxford, Oxford University Press, 212–24.

Dixon, R. G. Jr. (1968) *Democratic Representation: Reapportionment in Law and Practice*. New York, Oxford University Press.

Dummett, M. (1997) *Electoral Reform*. Oxford, Oxford University Press.

Dunleavy, P. and Margetts, H. (1997) The electoral system, in P. Norris and N. Gavin, editors, *Britain Votes 1997*. Oxford, Oxford University Press, 225–41.

Dunleavy, P. and Margetts, H. (1999) Mixed electoral systems in Britain and the Jenkins Commission on electoral reform, *British Journal of Politics and International Relations*, 1, 12–38.

Dunleavy, P., Margetts, H., Duffy, B. and Weir, S. (1998) Remodelling the 1997 general election: how Britain would have voted under alternative electoral systems, in D. Denver, J. Fisher, P. Cowley and C. Pattie, editors, *British Elections and Parties Review*, 8. London, Frank Cass, 208–29.

Evans, G., Curtice, J. and Norris, P. (1998) New Labour, new tactical voting? The causes and consequences of tactical voting in the 1997 general election, in D. Denver, J. Fisher, P. Cowley and C. Pattie, editors, *British Elections and Parties Review*, 8. London, Frank Cass, 65–79.

French, F.-J. (1978) Submission to *Mr. Speaker's Conference on Electoral Law*. 70–iii, Session 1977–78, 2, London, HMSO, 25–36.

Government Reply (1988) *Redistribution of Seats*. Cm 308, London, HMSO.

Grofman, B. (1998) *Race and Redistricting in the 1990s*. New York, Agathon Press.

Gudgin, G. and Taylor, P. J. (1979) *Seats, Votes and the Spatial Organisation of Elections*. London, Pion.

Hart, J. (1992) *Proportional Representation: Critics of the British Electoral System 1820–1945*. Oxford, The Clarendon Press.

Heffer, S. (1998) *Like the Roman: The Life of Enoch Powell*. London, Phoenix.

Home Affairs Committee (1986–87) *Redistribution of Seats*. London, HMSO.

IDEA (1997) *The International IDEA Handbook of Electoral System Design*. Stockholm Institute for Democracy and Electoral Assistance.

Jenkins, Lord (1998) *The Report of the Independent Commission on the Voting System*. Cm 4090–I. London, HMSO.

Johnston, R. J. (1976) Parliamentary seat redistribution: more opinions on the theme. *Area*, 8, 30–4.

Johnston, R. J. (1977) Spatial structure, plurality systems and electoral bias, *The Canadian Geographer*, 20, 310–28.

Johnston, R. J. (1978) *Multivariate Statistical Analysis in Geography: A Primer on the General Linear Model*. London, Longman.

Johnston, R. J. (1979) *Political, Electoral and Spatial Systems*. Oxford, Oxford University Press.

Johnston, R. J. (1998) Proportional representation and a 'fair electoral system' for the United Kingdom, *Journal of Legislative Studies*, 4, 128–48.

Johnston, R. J. (1999) Geography, fairness and liberal democracy, in J. D. Proctor and D. M. Smith, editors, *Geography and Ethics: Journeys in a Moral Terrain*. London, Routledge, 44–58.

Johnston, R. J. and Forrest, J. (2000) Constituency election campaigning under the alternative vote: the New South Wales legislative Assembly election, 1995, *Area*, 32, 107–18.

Johnston, R. J. and Pattie, C. J. (1993) Great Britain: twentieth century parties operating under nineteenth century regulations, in A. B. Gunlicks, editor, *Campaign and Party Finance in North America and Western Europe*. Boulder, Westview Press, 123–54.

Johnston, R. J. and Pattie, C. J. (1997a) Towards an understanding of turnout at general elections: voluntary and involuntary abstentions in 1992. *Parliamentary Affairs*, 50, 280–91.

Johnston, R. J. and Pattie, C. J. (1997b) Electoral reform without constitutional reform: questions raised by the proposed referendum on proportional representation in the United Kingdom, *The Political Quarterly*, 68, 379–87.

Johnston, R. J., Pattie, C. J., Dorling, D. F. L., Rossiter, D. J., Tunstall, H. and MacAllister, I. D. (1998) New Labour landslide – same old electoral geography? In D. Denver, J. Fisher, P. Cowley and C. Pattie, editors, *British Elections and Parties Review*, 8. London, Frank Cass, 35–64.

Johnston, R. J. and Pattie, C. J. (2000) Ecological inference and entropy-maximizing: an alternative estimating procedure for split-ticket voting, *Political Analysis*, 8, 333–45.

Johnston, R. J. and Pattie, C. J. (2001) Is there a crisis of democracy in Great Britain? turnout at general elections reconsidered, in K. Dowding, J. Hughes and H. Margetts, editors, *The Challenges to Democracy*. London, Macmillan.

Johnston, R. J., Pattie, C. J. and Allsopp, J. G. (1988) *A Nation Dividing? Britain's Changing Electoral Map, 1979–1987*. London, Longman.

Johnston, R. J., Pattie, C. J. and Fieldhouse, E. A. (1994) The geography of voting and representation: regions and the declining importance of the cube law, in A. Heath, R. Jowell and J. Curtice, editors, *Labour's Last Chance? The 1992 Election and Beyond*. Aldershot, Dartmouth, 255–74.

Johnston, R. J., Pattie, C. J., MacAllister I., Rossiter, D. J., Dorling, D. F. L. and Tunstall, H. (1997) Spatial variations in voter choice: modelling tactical voting at the 1997 general election in Great Britain, *Geographical and Environmental Modelling*, 1, 153–79.

Johnston, R. J., Pattie, C. J. and Rossiter, D. J. (1998a) Electoral reform: establishing principles for constituency definition, *Renewal*, 6 (1), 42–54.

Johnston, R. J., Pattie, C. J. and Rossiter, D. J. (1998b) Can we ever get rid of geography? Observations on the possible use of stv in United Kingdom General Elections, *Representation*, 35, 63–9.

Johnston, R. J., Pattie, C. J. and Rossiter, D. J. (1998c) Electoral reform: establishing principles for proportional representation, *Renewal*, 6 (3), 72–83.

Johnston, R. J., Rhind, D. W., Openshaw, S. and Rossiter, D. J. (1984) Spatial scientists and representational democracy: the role of information-processing technology in the design of parliamentary and other constituencies, *Environment and Planning C: Government and Policy*, 2, 57–66.

Johnston, R. J. and Rossiter, D. J. (1981) Shape and the definition of Parliamentary constituencies, *Urban Studies*, 18, 219–33.

Johnston, R. J. and Rossiter, D. J. (1982) Constituency building, political representation and electoral bias in urban England, in D. T. Herbert and R. J. Johnston, editors, *Geography and the Urban Environment: Volume V*. Chichester, John Wiley, 113–54.

Johnston, R. J., Rossiter, D. J. and Pattie, C. J. (1999) Integrating and decomposing the sources of partisan bias: Brookes' method and the impact of redistricting in Great Britain, *Electoral Studies*, 18, 367–78.

Kousser, J. M. (1999) *Colorblind Injustice: Minority Voting Rights and the Undoing of the Second Reconstruction*. Chapel Hill, University of North Carolina Press.

Lijphart, A. (1994) *Electoral Systems and Party Systems: A Study of Twenty-seven Democracies 1945–1990*. Oxford, The Clarendon Press.

Linton, M. and Southcott, M. (1998) *Making Votes Count: The Case for Electoral Reform*. London, Profile Books.

Loosemore, J. and Hanby, V. J. (1971) The theoretical limits of maximum distortion: some analytic expressions for electoral systems, *British Journal of Political Science*, 1, 467–77.

McLean, I. (1995) Are Scotland and Wales over-represented in the House of Commons? *The Political Quarterly*, 66, 250–68.

Margetts, H. and Dunleavy, P. (1999) Reforming the Westminster electoral system: evaluating the Jenkins Commission proposals, in J. Fisher, P. Cowley, D. Denver and A. Russell, editors, *British Elections and Parties Review 9*. London, Frank Cass, 46–71.

Marquand, D. (1997) *Ramsay MacDonald*. London, Richard Cohen Books.

Morgan, K. O. (1997) *Callaghan: A Life*. Oxford, Oxford University Press.

Morrill, R. L. (1973) Ideal and reality in reapportionment, *Annals of the Association of American Geographers*, 63, 463–77.

Mortimore, R. (1992) *The Constituency Structure and the Boundary Commissions: the Rules for the Redistribution of Seats and their effect on the British Electoral System, 1950–1987*. D.Phil. thesis, University of Oxford.

Neill, Lord (1998) *Standards in Public Life: The Funding of Political Parties in the United Kingdom*. Cm 4057–I, London, HMSO.

Norris, P. (1997) Anatomy of a Labour landslide, in P. Norris and N. Gavin, editors, *Britain Votes 1997*. Oxford, Oxford University Press, 1–24.

Norris, P. and Evans, G., editors (1999) *Critical Elections: British Parties and Voters in Long-Term Perspective*. London, Sage Publications.

Paddison, R. (1976) Spatial bias and redistricting in proportional representation electoral systems: a case-study of the Republic of Ireland, *Tijdschrift voor Economische en Sociale Geografie*, 657, 230–40.

Parliamentary Boundary Commission for England (1981) *The Review of Parliamentary Constituencies*. London, Boundary Commission for England.

Pattie, C. J. and Johnston, R. J. (1998a) Voter turnout and constituency marginality: geography and rational choice, *Area*, 30, 38–48.

Pattie, C. J. and Johnston, R. J. (1998b) Voter turnout at the British general election of 1992: rational choice, social standing or political efficacy? *European Journal of Political Research*, 33, 263–83.

Pattie, C. J., Johnston, R. J. and Fieldhouse, E. A. (1995) Winning the local vote: the effectiveness of constituency campaign spending in Great Britain, 1983–1992, *American Political Science Review*, 89, 969–86.

Pattie, C. J., Whiteley, P., Johnston, R. J. and Seyd, P. (1994) Measuring local political effects: Labour Party constituency campaigning at the 1987 general election. *Political Studies* 42, 469–79.

Plant, R. (1999) Proportional representation, in R. Blackburn and R. Plant, editors, *Constitutional Reform: The Labour Government's Constitutional Reform Agenda*. London, Longman, 66–81.

Rae, D. W. Jr. (1971) *The Political Consequences of Electoral Laws* (second edition). New Haven, Yale University Press.

Rallings, C. and Thrasher, M. (1995) *Media Guide to the New Parliamentary Constituencies*. Plymouth, Local Government Chronicle Elections Centre for BBC/ITN/PANews/SkyNews.

Rawlings, H. F. (1988) *Law and the Electoral Process*. London, Sweet and Maxwell.

Roberts, A. (1999) *Salisbury: Victorian Titan*. London, Weidenfeld & Nicolson.

Rossiter, D. J. and Johnston, R. J. (1981) Program GROUP: the identification of all possible solutions to a constituency delimitation problem, *Environment and Planning A*, 13, 231–8.

Rossiter, D. J. and Johnston, R. J. (1983) The definition of Parliamentary constituencies in Great Britain: a computer-based information system, *Journal of the Operational Research Society*, 34, 1079–84.

Rossiter, D. J., Johnston, R. J. and Pattie, C. J. (1997) Estimating the partisan impact of redistricting in Great Britain, *British Journal of Political Science*, 27, 319–31.

Rossiter, D. J., Johnston, R. J. and Pattie, C. J. (1998) The partisan impacts of non-partisan redistricting: Northern Ireland 1993–1995, *Transactions, Institute of British Geographers*, NS24, 455–80.

Rossiter, D. J., Johnston, R. J. and Pattie, C. J. (1999) *The Boundary Commissions: Redrawing the UK's Map of Parliamentary Constituencies*. Manchester, Manchester University Press.

Sanders, D. (1997) The new electoral battleground, in A. King, editor, *New Labour Triumphs: Britain at the Polls*. Chatham, Chatham House, 209–48.

Schuman, A. W. (1999) *Boundary Changes, Local Political Activism and the Importance of the Electoral Ward: an Electoral Geography of Bristol 1996–1999*. PhD Thesis, University of Bristol.

Shepherd, R. (1997) *Enoch Powell: A Biography*. London, Pimlico.

Swaddle, K. and Heath, A. (1989) Official and reported turnout in the British general election of 1989, *British Journal of Political Science*, 19, 537–51.

Taagepera, R. and Shugart, M. S. (1989) *Seats and Votes: the Effects and Determinants of Electoral Systems*. New Haven CT, Yale University Press.

Taylor, P. J. (1973) Some implications of the spatial organization of elections, *Transactions, Institute of British Geographers*, 60, 121–36.

Taylor, P. J. and Johnston, R. J. (1979) *Geography of Elections*. London, Penguin Books.

Vivian Committee (1942) *Report of the Committee on Electoral Machinery*. Cmd 6408, London, HMSO.

Waller, R. J. (1983) The 1983 Boundary Commission: policies and effects. *Electoral Studies*, 2, 195–206.

Whiteley, P. and Seyd, P. (1994) Local party campaigning and voting behavior in Britain. *Journal of Politics*, 56, 242–51.

Wilson, H. (1974) *The Labour Government 1964–1970: A Personal Record*. London, Penguin Books.

Worcester, R. M. and Mortimore, R. (1999) *Explaining Labour's Landslide*. London, Politico's.

Index